REMARKABLE
Homes of NW3

REMARKABLE Homes of NW3

Hampstead · Belsize Park · Primrose Hill

For Emma + Andrew
Best Wishes

David S Percy

David S Percy

KIRE
KEEPING IT REAL ESTATE

REMARKABLE
Homes of NW3

Copyright © David S Percy 2024

The right of David S Percy to be identified as the author of this work has been asserted by him in accordance with the Copyright, Designs and Patents Act of 1998.

All rights reserved. No part of this publication can be reproduced, stored in a retrieval system, or transmitted in any form or by any means, electronic, mechanical, recording, or otherwise, without the prior permission from the publisher.

All present day photographs David S Percy
except where otherwise stated.

Archive images Public Domain or Creative Commons licences
except where indicated.

Cover illustration by Seb Willett from an
orginal photograph by the author

KIRE Publishing
Penthouse
Akenside Court
London NW3 5QT
www.kire.life

ISBN 978-1-7384334-0-7

British Library Cataloguing-in-Publication Data
A catalogue record of this book is available from the British Library

Printed and bound by SRP Ltd Exeter UK

In memory of Christopher Wade and F Peter Woodford.

In time it may be realised that a beautiful suburb such as Hampstead, with its glorious Heath and charming old-world surroundings, is an asset not only to its own inhabitants but to London itself. If these suburbs must be built over then let the architects and builders work together and make the consequent bricks and mortar as much at home with their surroundings as possible.

– CHB Quennell, July 1906

Contents

Preface and Sponsorship — ix

Foreword — x

Introduction — xi

The Remarkable Homes — 1

Bibliography — 299

Index — 300

Acknowledgements — 304

Map of the NW3 Area — 305

About the Author — 306

What is the Bay of Naples, with its bitter, relentless gentian blue overhead, and its sun-scorched, dusty and grassless ground beneath, compared to this view from Hampstead Heath? Where else can you find such satisfying beauty?

– Phil Robinson *The Contemporary Review,* 1894

Preface and Sponsorship

KIRE co-founder Michael McHale

Growing up on Eton Avenue in Belsize Park since birth, I naturally developed an interest in architecture. Even as a five-year-old, I remember asking my mother what the monsters were on some of the houses on Eton Avenue that I passed on my way to Hereward House School. I was told of gargoyles and gryphons, which set my young imagination racing and seeded my love for these beautiful creations, sparking my long-term interest in our neighbourhood.

These beautiful, artistic sculptures not only please the eye and stimulate emotions, they also adorn buildings where memories have been created for decades. These buildings nurture their families, keeping them safe and warm. Most importantly, they are places where stories are read, and made. They are places for laughter, sadness, experiences and growth.

The idea for this book emerged naturally over afternoon tea with my neighbour and friend, local historian and resident David S Percy as we discussed our mutual passion for the area's exceptional history, architecture and inhabitants. Wouldn't it be great to delve into, document and preserve the rich history of some of the remarkable properties in our corner of London for future generations while also recognising their beauty and charm?

I also envisioned the project aligning with KIRE's mission to enhance the lives of our community, fostering a sense of happiness and fulfilment by creating a reason to bring neighbours with mutual interests together, creating a network we aspire to cultivate in our role as "community creators". Even though my talents are focused on selling beautiful homes, I couldn't refuse the opportunity to provide financial support for this historically significant project.

Throughout 2022-23, we had the pleasure of visiting various properties in Hampstead and the surrounding areas. Each of the owners had fascinating stories to tell. Every story is unique, and every home distinctive in its own way. None of the homes were specially set-dressed or otherwise staged – they were photographed just as we found them during our visits. We are indeed thankful for, and proud of David's hard work, which has resulted in a captivating book that is as riveting for its vibrant photography as it is for the stories and history captured and uncovered. All of these properties are notable in different ways – truly remarkable homes built by remarkable people.

I, Michael McHale and my co-founder Samuel Patterson at KIRE take great pleasure in sponsoring this project, a celebration of the remarkable homes and their owners living within our local area of NW3.

While the publication of this book has been made possible through the generous sponsorship of KIRE this project is also supported by

The Heath & Hampstead Society

The Belsize Society

Belsize Conservation Area Advisory Committee

KIRE
KEEPING IT REAL ESTATE

Foreword
Tom Conti

I first came to Hampstead in the early 1960s, having been offered a mattress on the floor of a flat belonging to Robin Hall, a fine Scottish folk singer of the time. This place was opposite what used to be the Photocraft shop on Heath Street. I fell in love with the village and surrounding streets and dreamed of one day living here. It took about twenty five years.

In the late sixties Kara and I married and I brought her to see Hampstead. There had been a heavy snowfall, and driving along West Heath Road at night, the trees, sagging from the weight of snow were a wonderful sight. In 1985, my luck having changed considerably, due to the talents of, among others, Frederic Raphael, Christopher Hampton, Neil Simon, and Julius Epstein, we acquired The Wabe in Redington Road. A dream home, partly Scottish Baronial in style and partly Arts and Crafts, and sitting on about three quarters of an acre of garden. The house hosted many greats during its lifetime, Bernard Shaw, Isadora Duncan, through to Rod Steiger, Georg Solti, David Bowie, Arthur Miller and many more. Our close friends Gordon Jackson and Rona Anderson, Pauline Collins and John Alderton also lived on Redington Road.

It is impossible to walk around the older parts of Hampstead without seeing something extraordinary never before noticed. This most welcome local history project features a wonderful variety of properties and an array of differing architectural styles. A borough of London for over a thousand years, how could it not be magical?

Tom Conti, 2023

Tom Conti is a theatre, film, & television actor and novelist. His latest films are *Paddington 2* (2017) as Judge Gerald Biggleswade, and *Oppenheimer* (2023) as Albert Einstein.

Tom Conti

Introduction
Setting the Scene

For generations, people have documented their homes in various ways, capturing their uniqueness and beauty. The tradition of sharing one's living space has evolved from sketches and oil paintings to photographs. In the late 19th century, it became customary to send postcards featuring images of one's street, allowing others to catch a glimpse of their homes. The collection of images in this book, focusing on London's NW3, serves as a contemporary equivalent to those postcards.

Within this vibrant area, filled with stunning architecture, we delve into the stories of some truly remarkable homes. We explore their origins, tracing back to the visionaries – landowners, architects and builders – who integrated their structures into the countryside. Along the way, we encounter the individuals who have briefly resided in these houses, leaving an indelible mark on history. Our journey takes us through a range of residences, both large and small, and whenever possible, we connect with the present owners who now serve as custodians of this selection of properties. Starting from the southern reaches of the Elsworthy area, our coverage extends to the highest point in Hampstead.

To help navigate, each house is accompanied by a corresponding letter on the street map (see page 305).

The borough has been home to distinctive residences since the early 1700s. Back then, a trip to the hilltop village in the northern heights of London would only pass a handful of isolated properties. For the following century and a half, the area remained largely unchanged, with vast expanses of grassland dotted sporadically by scattered dwellings.

In former times the most direct approach to Hampstead from London by road was, as now, by way of Tottenham Court Road, Hampstead Road, Chalk Farm, and Haverstock Hill. It was along this route that the old eighteenth and early nineteenth-century coaches ran, bringing visitors to the relaxations of the Wells, of Belsize, or of the Heath. It was by this way that the horse-omnibuses which only ceased to run within recent years accomplished their strenuous journeyings up Hampstead Hill.

– Novelist Sir Max Pemberton (1863-1950)
The Annals of Hampstead, 1911

Venturing beyond London in the past was an entirely different experience. In those days, travel relied on horse-drawn coaches, and as a result, roadside inns played a crucial role in serving the needs of locals, as well as those travelling to and from the City or heading northward. To truly transport ourselves into that era, let us envision a diary entry that chronicles a coach journey heading to Hampstead in the mid-1820s.

A Journey to Hampstead Village
May 15, 1826, at eight o'clock in the morning

With Jack, our coachman, firmly grasping the reins, our early morning journey commences from the Blue Posts, Tottenham Court Road. Accompanied by my father, who has paid 1s 6d for each inside seat, this marks an exhilarating beginning to my first day of working alongside him. As we navigate through the turnpike, the cacophony of clattering wheels on the paved streets transforms into a grinding sound, accompanied by a jolting,

Tottenham Court Turnpike, Church of St James, Hampstead Road, *W H Prior*.

swaying motion. Despite the coach being suspended by leather straps, the journey northward remains a lively, undulating affair. I'm told that adverse weather conditions transform the wheel tracks into muddy troughs, brimming with dirty water that sloshes and splatters in every direction. Although the road is flanked by deep ditches designed to drain the fields, when travelling through these low lying areas it is not uncommon for the encroachment of these waters into the carriage! My father attributes this inconvenience to a lack of proper knowledge of drainage. Fortunately for us, the sun shines on this late spring day, the sky is blue, and the winds are light.

As we depart the City, we also leave behind its diverse concoction of smells. The dirt, dust and grime fall away, and we welcome the fresher air. Almost immediately, we find ourselves in open country. Pretty meadows abound, with nature's natural beauty of flowers, butterflies and bees on full display. Just the odd cottage is visible amid the expansive surroundings. But then the road deteriorates, and the ride becomes noticeably bumpier and rougher.

The *Load of Hay*, c.1820, Camden Local Studies and Archives Centre.

Sir Richard Steele's Cottage, published c.1878, later hand colour.

Belsize House in 1800, *W H Prior*, later hand colour.

Halfway House, *Old Mother Red Cap c.1746, W H Prior.*

View towards Hampstead, watercolour *J White*, late 1800s, *British Museum.*

The coachman cries out, "Halfway House gentlemen," jerking his whip to the right hand, but we are not stopping. Instead, we are continuing onwards, passing the occasional dwelling. We soon come upon the Chalcots area [Chalk Farm], *where field after field of grass and pasture are given over to hay production for London's many horses.*

We now begin our climb up Haverstock Hill. After travelling three miles or thereabouts, we pass a few houses known as Moll King's Row on our right, and reach the Load of Hay tavern, where travellers can pause for refreshment in the tea garden. Horses can be changed here. And when needed, an additional strong horse called the 'Cock' (since he leads the team) assists in pulling heavy carriages up the increasingly steep hill. The tavern [previously known as the Coach and Horses] *also offers a much-needed respite for the long-distance London-bound stagecoaches.*

When I ask, Father has nothing to say about the origins of Moll King's Row, but he tells me a little of the history of the other houses as we pass them by: Steele's Cottage is to our left. Then Upper Chalk House Lane [England's Lane] *is a little further on, and just off the road on the right is a handsome old house originating in the mid-1700s* [Crown Lodge]. *We are now in the subordinate Manor of Belsize. Set in the estate's extensive grounds and surrounded by beautiful gardens is the truly grand Belsize House, accessed from Haverstock Hill by its broad carriageway lined with Elms* [today's Belsize Avenue].

Further up the hill, we come to The George tavern on the right, owned by a brewery founded in the 15th century. The hostelry was originally called The Great Tree, as this is where the famous Hollow Elm once stood on Hampstead Green.

xii

Visitors could access the 33-foot-high viewing platform by climbing its internal ladder of 42 rungs. Continuing onwards, we pass the open space of The Green. This is the fashionable Pond Street area – the haunt of poets and painters, and home to doctors.

Next on the left is the very ancient, picturesque Belsize Lane, bordered by hedgerows and overhung by tall trees. We now start the climb up Red Lion Hill – so named after the tavern of that name [known today as Rosslyn Hill]. Set back to the left is Rosslyn House, once the home of the Earl of Rosslyn.

Onwards and upwards we go, and off to our right is Downshire Hill, considered the most elegant place to live hereabouts. Father says 'tis likely named after the politician Wills Hill, the first Marquis of Downshire. The Red Lion tavern is now on the left, and the Old Kitchen House is on our right. We then glimpse Vane House [home of Sir Harry Vane, beheaded June 14, 1662] as we pass it on the left.

We finally arrive in Hampstead village [later Hampstead town]. Our coach pulls to a stop as Jack cries out, "The Bird in Hand, gentlemen." Our journey is over at this tavern [on what is now Hampstead High Street]. Jack sets us down, and with a change of horses if needed, the coach is ready for the return journey down to London. I learn that this is the terminus for over 35 journeys each day to and from the City and the West End.

We shall return later, but for now, we must work. Father is an architect commissioned to design a house, and we have come here to inspect the lie of the land. ■

The George tavern, Haverstock Hill, 1856, *archive*.

Rosslyn House, engraving published 1878, *W H Prior*.

Vane House, once home of Sir Henry Vane, 1813, *William Davidson*.

View towards St John's Wood from Hampstead Churchyard, 1822.

The *Bird-in-Hand* as it was in 1908, *archive*.

I have known Hampstead for thirty-five years and never for a day has my affection for 'the village' abated. Builders come and go but Hampstead remains. About her, there breathes a spirit of majesty and of isolation which remains wonderful in the story of the greater city. She wins the love of her children and retains it through the years. We return to her as to the precincts of a home. Our affection survives even the brutalities of modernity and its tentacles outstretched. May she flourish even as the city that was set upon the hill.

– Sir Max Pemberton (1863-1950)
The Annals of Hampstead, 1911

Hampstead… is full of quaint beauty and surprising charm. But behind the Hampstead [of today] is the Hampstead which has been. Some houses and buildings still standing have memories of famous and interesting persons; and sites are known, where the buildings have disappeared, on which scenes of human life, action, and creation were transacted.

– Robert F Horton, 1912

Elsworthy Road

Running alongside Primrose Hill, Elsworthy Road was initially laid out across ground formerly belonging to the Eton and Middlesex Cricket Club. Dating from 1890, most of the houses at the western end of Elsworthy Road, nestled behind mature trees and hedges, were built by William Willett Jr, and designed by Amos Faulkner. Significantly, built by 1904, No.33 is one of the few exceptions, having been designed by J J Stevenson, a Queen Anne revival style specialist, working with his early business partner Henry 'Harry' Redfern.

The current owners of No.33, Georgina and Bernard have lived here since 1995. An artistic family, Georgina is a freelance interior designer previously having worked in the Liberty's interior contracts department, then Blanchard of Sloane Street, going on to design and manufacture bed linen for her own Sleeping Company shops in Fulham Road and Wigmore Street. Now Georgina is concentrating on making furniture, sculpture and mixed media pieces, and has exhibited at the Royal Academy Summer Exhibition. "I find it very satisfying to get involved hands-on with the making process, as does my husband," Georgina says. Bernard is an artist specialising in large abstract works and has exhibited in London and Aldeburgh. Their son James is a songwriter and international performer for a successful electronics duo with an Ivor Novello songwriting award, while their daughter Holly is following in the creative tradition.

"We have two children and lots of siblings," says Georgina. "We moved here from a sweet house on Clifton Hill in St John's Wood when we found this house. Georgina explains some of the building's history. "Winston Churchill's specialist physician lived here at No.33, so it is likely that Churchill visited the house." Coming to the more recent past, she continues, "And David Cohen, who owned the house before us, was also a doctor; he had his GP's surgery on the top floor where his consulting rooms were also located. There were actually two consulting rooms; so it might have been a joint practice."

After moving in, the property underwent a significant refurbishment programme which took a year. "The only thing we changed at the front was to replace the porch and the front door," explains Georgina. "However, internally, we redid everything, from

No.33 Elsworthy Road with its original porch over 75 years ago before the tree reached maturity. The alteration to the front left of the house, providing a garage, was made between 1947 and 1995, *archive*.

2

the plumbing to the electrics, and we even installed an industrial-sized boiler! In total, there are now 6 bedrooms, but these days some have other purposes such as a study and two light-filled studios." Although Georgina is responsible for the interior design, an architect friend helped them with the internal remodelling. "There was quite a lot of restructuring," Georgina continues. "Where there is now a larder/pantry, there was originally a lift to all floors. We also changed the original layout of the dining room by taking down a wall. And we added beautiful wooden panelling to the walls in the main bedroom."

The house today is beautifully finished with many clever interior design features and details, such as creating a satisfying view through to the garden from the entrance hall. "I loved the striking lime green hallway shown in the fabulous sales brochure, which I still have, and in a way, I wish we had kept that colour!" says Georgina. In 2020, the couple redid their sitting room. "It's now mid-century modern, more like it was years ago, and very different to the country house look we had previously." So what do they enjoy most about their home? "Living here," Georgina replies, "it does feel like we are living in the country, right in the middle of London. We truly appreciate the local architecture and love the coffee culture, yet we can walk through greenery to Baker Street and the West End."

The elegant round archway to the staircase.

The light-filled Conservatory.

This house also has historical significance, as do some of its neighbours. The very first emergency phone call in the world leading to an arrest was made from No.33 Elsworthy Road on 7 July 1937 by Mrs Stanley Beard. At 4.30 am her husband heard a sound and saw an intruder outside the house. Mr Beard chased the man on foot while his wife dialled 999. "My wife dialled 999 as soon as she heard the noise, and the reply was instantaneous," said Mr Beard, an architect. Shortly afterwards police radio patrol cars raced to the spot and a man in his 20s was subsequently arrested and charged with an attempted break-in. The UK was the first nation to establish a universal emergency telephone number in 1937. But astonishingly, it would be another 31 years before the US instigated such a prompt response service, when AT&T introduced the 911 system in 1968.

Part of the beautiful garden with Primrose Hill beyond.

View from the entrance hall through the living room to the garden.

Remarkable Homes of NW3

No.35 Elsworthy Road featured elegant reception rooms with high ceilings and a host of original features, built c.1904 by William Willett Jr. For his layout of 'Elsworthy Village' Willett is regarded as the pioneer of the garden suburb concept.

Next door, No.35 Elsworthy Road, was home from the early 1930s to the formidable family of Alice and Harold Hemming. Moving abroad during the war, the family returned to their Elsworthy Road home in 1945. Their eldest child, Louisa Service OBE JP, the first wife of architectural historian Alastair Service (see page 169), would come to occupy the house for over 80 years. The explorer Dr John Hemming, CMG, FSA, FRSL, FRGS, is her younger brother. Louisa's mother at that time was a journalist.

Actors Dame Gladys Cooper and Philip Merivale reportedly occupied No.35 during their 1938-39 British theatre season, performing in London and touring the Midlands.

Sir Georg Solti's house, No.51 Elsworthy Road.

No.48 Elsworthy Road, recalling Edward and Mrs Simpson.

Sigmund Freud (1856-1939) lived at No.39 Elsworthy Road when he first came to Britain in 1938. The conductor Sir Georg Solti (1912-1997), lived for many years at No.51.

Notably, in the early 1930s, No.48 Elsworthy Road was home to Viscount Furness and his second wife, Thelma. She introduced the future Edward VIII to her friend, Mrs Wallis Simpson. At the time of the abdication, thanks to her own acquaintance with Mrs Simpson, Louisa's mother, Alice Hemming, was granted an exclusive interview with Wallis Simpson, that was syndicated worldwide. ∎

No.7 Elsworthy Road was the Vicarage for St Mary's Primrose Hill from 1907 until 1984.

Lower Merton Rise

An absolutely enchanting property stands at the end of Lower Merton Rise. Designed by Amos Faulkner in 1911, No.1 was built to serve the original house on the corner of Wadham Gardens and Lower Merton Rise. Françoise Findlay, who owns the home and has lived here since 1952, explains the background. "This was once the coach house and stables belonging to an adjacent property with a wonderful name – *Sibertswold*." Apart from Françoise's home originally being a coach house and stables, the building is exceptional for other reasons. Willett-built was a byword for quality, lovely features and ornate details. "By 1890 the Willetts didn't want domestics living in their developments, so the houses were built without basements and without service quarters," says Françoise. "The servants were housed separately in two sets of mews to the north, where the horses and carriages were also kept." The coach house was the exception to this rule, as it was constructed within the grounds of the *Sibertswold* property but around the corner. "*Sibertswold* is now known as No.19 Wadham Gardens," Françoise continues. "Back in 1947, it was owned by Mr and Mrs Eldon, a Romanian couple, and they converted the stables, divided up the garden, retaining the entire corner area for No.19, and then sold off the conversion."

Remarkable Homes of NW3

Original drawing of the coach house and stables by the architect Amos Faulkner.

The relocated carriage doors still in full working order.

Sibertswold, No.19 Wadham Gardens.

"Interestingly, their daughter, Rita, married Richard Pankhurst (son of Sylvia, grandson of Emmeline, best remembered for organising the UK suffragette movement, see also p191), and they lived mostly in Ethiopia until his death. Their daughter, Dr Helen Pankhurst, lives locally."

The majority of the houses in Wadham Gardens were also designed by Amos Faulkner for William Willett, as part of the pioneering garden suburb he developed on the site of the Eton and Marylebone Cricket Club. Willett developed an eclectic style with gables and porches of Dutch and Queen Anne influence, and irregular fenestration with small panes, white glazing bars and mostly no symmetry. The houses were expensive, for an elite clientele.

This story encompasses a group of three properties. As with many of these grand houses, No.19 Wadham Gardens is today divided up into apartments. One day in May 1984, a planning application was submitted by the new owner of No.19. It proposed the construction of five houses on this corner garden plot, attached to the main house by a glass infill, along with a swimming pool and changing rooms. A total of 16 poplars would have to be felled around the perimeter of the site to accommodate this proposal.

A mighty tussle then ensued between the developer(s) and the locals affected by the destruction and loss of this corner plot. Organised by Françoise, over 40 local objections to the scheme resulted in the proposal being reduced to three 4-bedroom houses by November 1985. Françoise continued to manage the local objections campaign, and a further petition was lodged in January 1986. The inspector refused appeals made by the developer to these objections in July 1987. As a result, the plan was again revised, becoming a single, 2-storey, six-bedroom house with an attic by December 1987. Even so, it was not a perfect fit with its location and in October 1988, Françoise delivered a Notice of Motion for an order squashing the decision of the Secretary of State on a planning appeal. The argument was that "the inspector failed to have regard to the desirability of preserving and enhancing the Conservation Area's character or appearance."

Finally in 1990, when the single house was built on the corner garden plot, its style echoed the other William Willett buildings along Wadham Gardens and, as Françoise remarks, "people are surprised to learn that the house is not an original." The new house, now No.21 Wadham Gardens, is described on the following pages. ■

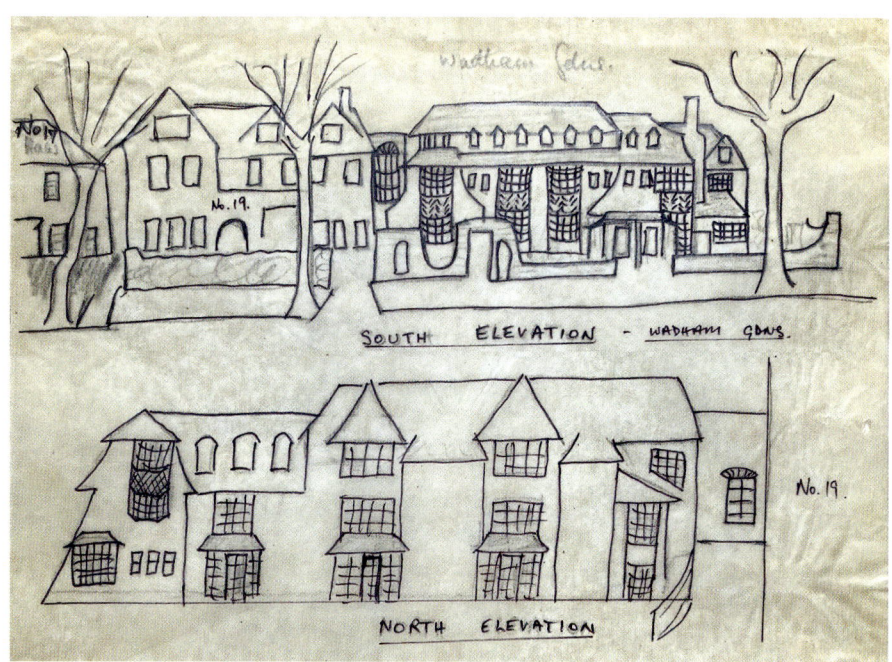

Drawing of the original 1984 Wadham Gardens scheme.

Initially, No.19 used all the land as its garden, with the stables and coach house confined to its north-eastern corner. The stable conversion was then fenced off from the main property. After the 1980s corner plot planning battle was resolved, No.21 was allocated its own garden, here outlined in red.

The corner of Wadham Gardens before the development, *photo, Françoise Findlay*.

Wadham Gardens

View through the main hall towards the living room.

Alan Steinfeld, a barrister, and Josi, an opera singer, lecturer, opera and theatre critic, are the proud owners of this beautiful house, having bought No.21 Wadham Gardens upon its completion. "We understand the history of this corner plot and the two adjacent houses," says Josi.

Back in 1991, when the couple were house searching, an attractive well-produced brochure for the new corner house caught her eye. Josi immediately requested a viewing and loved it on sight. "I went to South Hampstead High School and have always lived in North West London. At the time Wadham Gardens was rather run down," she notes, "but this was a new build, so we bought it, moving in during 1991."

Today, the gently-curved Wadham Gardens is somewhat quieter than the neighbouring section of Elsworthy Road, as it benefits from less passing traffic. Amos Faulkner designed virtually all the houses on this tree-lined road at the turn of C20 with designs inspired by Arts and Crafts principles. Professor of modern history FML Thompson describes these spacious Willett-built houses as incorporating the free-flowing use of "gables and porches of Dutch or Queen Anne influence, tile-hung gable-ends, bay windows, and comparatively low elevations."

Emulating some of these details, No.21 Wadham Gardens also benefits from being a corner plot, so the house enjoys plenty of light throughout the day due to its triple-aspect location. "The light that flows through the large high window in the hallway and down the staircase is just wonderful," says Josi.

Josi at her grand piano.

And what is especially important for Josi is having enough space in the living room for her grand piano. "But as I don't like dark walls we had the living room redecorated in lighter shades," she adds. The couple also changed the floors from the original wood and installed under-floor heating beneath the tiles. Then, after receiving the go-ahead from the Camden planners, they added a large rectangular orangery to the eastern side of the house. "We very much enjoy all the architectural detailing, such as the doors, and especially the south-facing balcony," Josi continues. "It's a place we had never properly used until the Covid lockdown of March 2020." As Alan had to work from home, he enjoyed spending time on the balcony reading the newspaper during his breaks. "And when sitting out there, he discovered how wonderfully protected it feels," adds Josi.

Daylight floods into the picture-lined staircase.

The house is set back from the road behind double hedging, making its south-facing balcony feel secluded.

Remarkable Homes of NW3

The triple-aspect orangery.

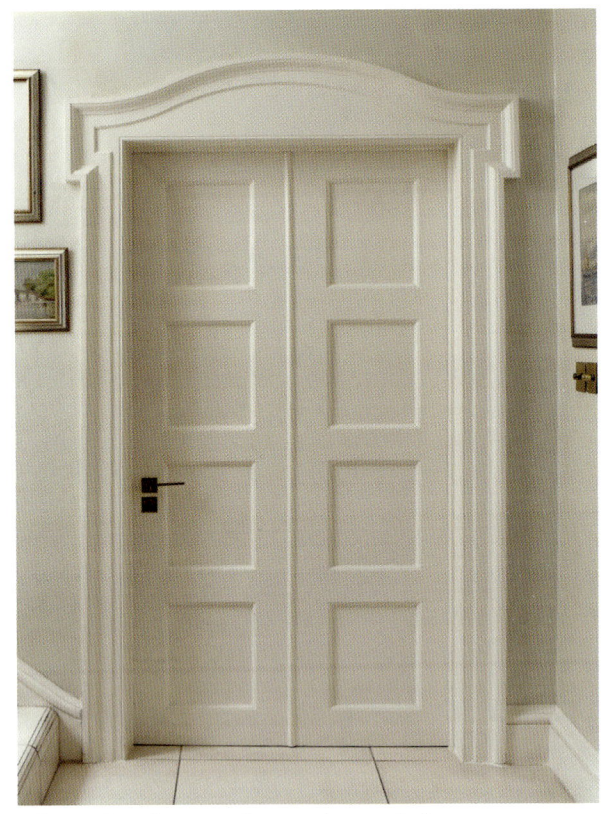

A door with its decorative frame in the main hall.

"I just love this house in every way; it's extremely well thought out," Josi enthuses. True harmony in the style of William Willett. "But although we have many interior walls we are still hard-pressed to find enough space for all my grandfather's paintings." These most certainly add colour and provide varied adornment to all the wall surfaces throughout their charming home. ∎

William Willett & Son, later called Willett Building Services, was founded by William Willett Sr (b 1837), later joined by his son, the young William Willett. Responsible for many luxury building developments in NW3, the Willetts were speculative builders working with their in-house architects Harry Measures and Amos Faulkner.

The Willetts extended Elsworthy Road, forming an elongated oval with the new Wadham Gardens, which they then linked to Avenue Road. Built from 1895 on land originally owned by Eton College and laid out on the former site of the Eton and Middlesex Cricket Ground, this became a highly desirable area due to its proximity to Primrose Hill. By building these houses behind privet hedges rather than garden walls, the Willetts' Wadham Garden development could lay claim to being an early, if not the very first, propagator of the Garden Suburb concept.

William Willett Jr (1856-1915) is recognised for promoting the concept of Daylight Saving Time in the UK. It was finally passed into law in 1916, unfortunately a year too late for Willett himself to see the result of his efforts.

Hardanger, Wadham Gardens

Wadham Gardens was the Willett company's final 'take' in the district. The road was built up between 1895 and 1904, and the Wadham Gardens houses "adopt a more suburban 'Old English' style," records architectural historian Professor Andrew Saint. "These richly detailed houses are every bit as good as anything built at Hampstead Garden Suburb, which they actually antedate by a few years."

Named by William Willett as *Hardanger,* the house as it stands today has a fascinating history. A rainwater hopper on No.4 Wadham Gardens, inscribed with the date of 1897, sets this house as one of the earliest of this nine-year development.

The very first owners were the Arrobus family. Montague Arrobus was a quill manufacturer and ostrich feather merchant. At that time, just 1lb of ostrich feathers was worth £500. The garden was laid out in the shape of the Prince of Wales's feathers, a compliment to the master of the house. Montague's son Sydney Arrobus (1901-1990) studied at Heatherley's School of Fine Art and specialised in street scenes. He sketched an illustration of his old family home in 1987.

Illustration by Sydney Arrobus, 1987, *image courtesy Françoise Findlay.*

No.4 Wadham Gardens *c.*2005, *photo, Knight Frank.*

Originally, the entire building was leased from the Eton College Estate. Around 2004, after acquiring this property along with several other leases from the estate, a ground rent investor sold off the studio house as a separate property. By then, the house had already been transformed into two flats – a conversion likely carried out during the 1950s by Marian Harrison, the second owner after the Arrobus family. Marian resided here for 44 years and, around 1980, added a garage on the right side (where the second segmented arch was situated).

The present owners procured the freehold of No.4 Wadham Gardens from Marian Harrison in 2005 with the intention of reverting it to a singular dwelling. They resided here in its existing state for two years, then commenced an extensive restoration project that significantly surpassed their initial projections. Unfolding over a span of three years, the project encompassed a substantial basement-level addition, culminating in their return to the property in 2010.

Some four years later, the studio house came on the market, prompting the new owners of No.4 to purchase it. They proceeded to renovate the studio, preparing it for potential tenancy. But they later decided to amalgamate the studio with the principal residence, envisioning a unified family home. After securing the necessary planning permissions which included expanding the basement throughout the entire building, they completed their ambitious project in 2017.

From the outset the owners had wanted to return the house to a one-family home. For example, the fireplaces had been blocked off, and the chimney stacks were unstable, "We have retained the stacks," says the owner, "and we also reinstated the broken and missing Champion chimney pots." Many of the original fireplaces have been reinstated, most of which are now functioning.

"Our consistent aim was to retain the originality of the house," says the owner. Although interesting architecturally, the house "was a battleship grey colour with pale blue windows, looking very sad and tired," the owner recalls. "All the render was in a poor state, there were numerous cracks and blown bubbles such that it had to be completely removed and replaced, so we had the exterior completely stripped." The only part of the house with exposed brick was the ground floor. "We were insistent that we should retain the original appearance of the front of the property. Therefore, the structure and façade remain as it was originally."

The stucco has been repainted white and will require repainting every five to seven years. "It's not a straightforward job – it's a major scaffolding task, especially erecting around the chimneys – it takes time due to its boomerang shape. Everything was carefully thought through to ensure the house appeared aesthetically balanced. The roof needed major work. Fortunately, it was possible to retain many of the original tiles. Actually, the tiles are of varying sizes," adds the owner. "They are larger at the bottom above the gutters and smaller as they progress upwards. There were many broken and missing tiles. We were adamant that the front utilised all the old tiles, and the roofers did their best to source similar tiles for the back, which proved somewhat difficult."

The owners reinstalled the sash windows on the ground floor and first floor. While the top floor windows at the rear, which are too short for sashes, now have opening casement windows. This window upgrade allows more light into the rooms. While improving its overall appearance, the building is now more balanced, especially at the rear.

Inevitably, this lengthy rebuilding project was not without its problems. Nevertheless, the works are now virtually complete, and the house is finally beginning to feel like home to these worthy custodians of such a remarkable property.

The owners often see people stopping outside to admire the house and to take pictures – a most rewarding outcome as they know that it was a concession for William Willett Jr to construct a building in an Arts and Crafts style. With its finely stippled finish to the stucco, this remarkable house is now regarded as one of the best examples of the Arts and Crafts movement. ∎

A *Hardanger* fireplace and a corner of the original billiards room, *archive.*

The original grand dining room *c.*1900, *archive, Willett Building Services.* Note the ceiling plasterwork and ornate cornice, a Willett feature of the houses in the area.

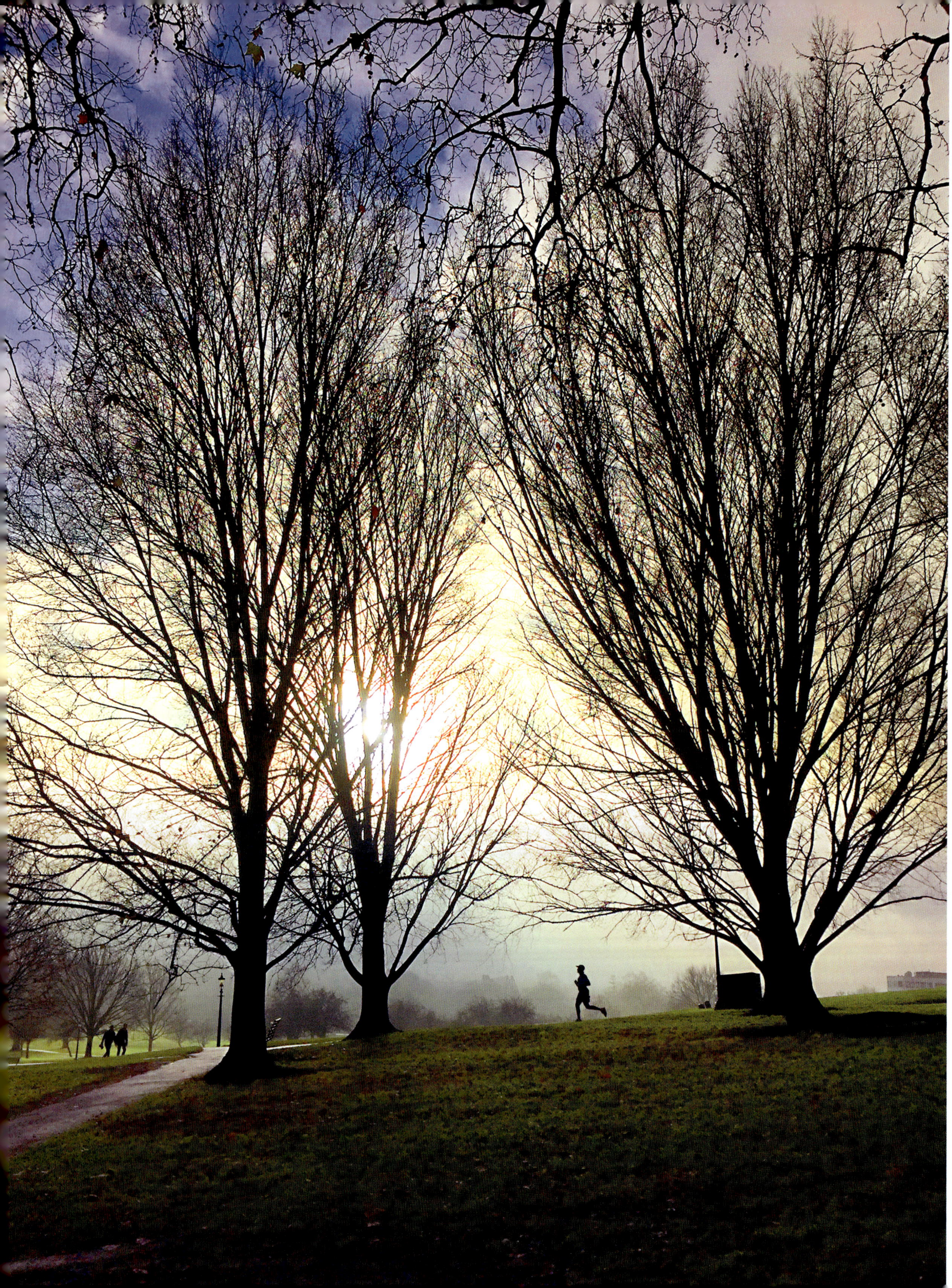

Ainger Road

George Pownall, John Shaw's successor as the Eton Estate surveyor, proposed the construction of new roads in the area in 1868. Ainger Road was built up from 1869, and by 1879, a total of 38 houses plus stables were built. Initially called Windsor Road, it was renamed in 1882 after Arthur Campbell Ainger MVO (1841-1919) the Eton school master and lyricist of the College song *Carmen Etonense*. The year of his birth, Sir Thomas Maryon Wilson had presented his father, the Rev Thomas Ainger (1799-1863), with the perpetual curacy of Hampstead Parish Church.

No.52 Ainger Road is a white-painted stucco and yellow brick house on this quiet thoroughfare that runs from King Henry's Road to Primrose Hill. The view from the street belies the homely and interesting interior.

"We relocated to Ainger Road in 2019," says Maria Novoa, currently engaged in the study of positive psychology and happiness with Tal Ben-Shahar. Originally hailing from Santiago, Chile, Maria and her husband Mario, who works in finance, have traversed different parts of the world. "After spending a period in New York, we ventured to the UK, settling in the Parkhill Road area, Belsize Park," Maria continues. "Subsequently, we returned to New York briefly before finally establishing our roots here."

The couple have lived in the Belsize neighbourhood for the past nine years. They especially enjoy the proximity to Primrose Hill, with Mario harbouring a particular fondness for Chalcot Square. Consequently, when it came time to move, they naturally gravitated towards this area, narrowing their choices down to two or three potential houses. "With the imminent arrival of our third child," explains Mario, "we were determined to find the perfect home." So for about two years they diligently scoured online listings, wasting no time to view any properties that piqued their interest.

One day in 2018, Maria sent Mario the description of this house that she thought would be perfect. The pictures weren't particularly impressive, but Maria immediately realised how she could make it work. "When we saw this place, we instantly fell in love with the garden — it's quite large for the Primrose Hill area," explains Maria. "At some point in the past the garden was extended lengthwise and part of it is now wider than originally," adds Mario.

The house had been split into two flats and very little work had been done on the lower ground floor. The previous owners had decorated the house to their very unconventional taste. The internal walls were painted throughout in dark colours and Retrouvius, an architectural reclamation and design company, had installed reclaimed fireplaces, unusual bathroom fittings and woodblock flooring. Then the previous owners got divorced, and so it was on the market. "Originally the front door opened into one large space and that wasn't suitable for us, so we installed a short separating wall to provide more privacy. Having said that, many of the unique elements of this house appealed to us, it felt authentic," explains Maria. "We realised that when decorated in our own style it could become more interesting than if we had started ourselves from scratch."

No.52 Ainger Road.

The lower ground floor kitchen/dining area with direct garden access.

> Maria and Mario renovated the entire lower ground floor and made a number of changes to the upper ground floor. "We lived here for three months alongside the builders while the works were underway," says Maria. "I particularly enjoy the house layout, especially as the kitchen and the garden are on one level," Maria adds. "There's a playroom for the three girls downstairs, while the ground-floor living room is used mainly for friends and entertaining. We love living and being together – it's a real family home."

The couple used some of the reclaimed wood block flooring to re-tread the stairs leading down to the lower ground level, where the floor is polished concrete throughout, resulting in a very practical surface. "The floor goes very well with the kitchen's overall design and functionality that benefits greatly from the ceiling light transfer," says Maria. Part of the lower ground floor is given over to a playroom for the children with a glass wall and doors. "We also introduced the large windows leading to the terraced garden," explains Mario.

How was the house furnished? "Some of the furniture was brought with us, which is part of our family history," Maria recalls. "For example, we purchased the big living room sofa in New York. The Chesterfield leather sofa is actually a sofabed, so we have an extra bed for family members visiting from Chile.

"We have a very good friend who has lived all her life in this neighbourhood," says Maria. "She used to play with the children living in this house decades ago and has commented on how much this house has changed inside."

Surrounded by an abundance of trees, the most prominent green areas in the vicinity are Chalcot Square and the triangular area bordered by King Henry's Road, Oppidans Road, and Ainger Road. Positioned at the centre of this verdant triangle, the house has the advantage of being surrounded by majestic tall trees and a lush, leafy outlook. "It's one of the reasons, if not the main reason, for buying this house is that it feels like a nature sanctuary," notes Maria. "Primrose Hill is a very friendly neighbourhood and it's great for families," she adds. "Our neighbours come from a variety of backgrounds and are of many different nationalities." ■

The rear elevation of No.52 Ainger Road from the terraced garden.

Eton Villas

Eton Villas forms an attractive enclave on one side of a triangular and picturesque open space. This development of early and mid-Victorian semi-detached villas, dating from about 1849, "Reflects the more refined taste of the Eton Estate Surveyor John Shaw Jr" (1803-1870), as noted by architectural historian Nikolaus Pevsner. Bisected by Eton Road, these listed houses on Eton Villas exude elegance with their restrained classical detailing and steps up to their porches. Unsurprisingly, this beautiful area has been a magnet for individuals associated with the arts, especially Nos. 6, 9 and 18, on the north side of Eton Road.

No.1 graces the southern end of Eton Villas. Listed Grade II, this early Victorian gable-fronted semi-detached villa is faced in white stucco. Much like its paired counterparts in the vicinity, this residence showcases windows admired for their impeccable proportions. The design of the ground floor window surrounds bears a striking resemblance to a portion of the Choragic monument of Thrasyllos in Athens.

No.1 Eton Villas looking towards St Saviour's from the junction of Provost Road and Eton College Road.

No.1 Eton Villas window.    Athenian detail, Thrasyllos.

No.1 Eton Villas was the home of Sir John Summerson for more than forty years until his death in 1992. Renowned as the director of Sir John Soane's Museum from 1945 to 1984, Sir John Summerson was a distinguished architectural historian. Gavin Stamp, a prominent architectural conservationist, effectively captures Summerson's legacy: "Sir John Summerson, who extensively explored Georgian architecture and beyond, stood as the epitome of eloquence and elegance among British architectural historians."

The front door and porch of No.1 with the blue plaque commemorating Sir John Summerson on the adjacent wall.

Full of charm and character, No.9 with its shallow shared gables, is another rustic Italian-style villa once home to the highly talented artist and decorator Alfred Stevens (1817-1875). His major work was the 1858 commission for the monument to the Duke of Wellington inside St Paul's Cathedral. A project that would take the rest of his life, but it did not deter him from undertaking several other projects, including the design for the mosaics of the four prophets featured in the dome of St Paul's (see next page).

No.9 Eton Villas, home to Alfred Stevens from 1859 until his death in 1875.

The trim front hedge marks the garden of No.18 Eton Villas.

No.18 Eton Villas front garden.

Jocelyne's comfortable ground floor sitting room as once enjoyed by Annigoni.

Jocelyne's grandson uses his grandfather's library whenever he is in residence.

The Wellington Monument in St Paul's by Alfred Stevens.

Located north of Eton Road and also designed by the Eton College architect John Shaw, No.18, at the upper end of Eton Villas is one of several equally charming but smaller semi-detached properties. From 1958 to 1960 it was home to Pietro Annigoni, the Italian painter renowned for his portraiture of the young HM Queen Elizabeth II.

The painter was followed by the broadcaster Jocelyne Tobin and her husband. Julian Tobin was a well-respected borough councillor who served the Adelaide ward for 30 years from 1968. And Tobin Close, just off Fellows Road, is named after him (see next page). Jocelyne Tobin has been involved in broadcasting for all her professional life.

Jocelyne Tobin.

Born in Dunstan Road, Golders Green, Jocelyne Tobin attended South Hampstead High School and then worked for 15 years at the BBC, becoming a studio manager at BBC Bush House. A member of the Voice of the Listener & Viewer's (VLV) Membership and Operations Committee, Jocelyne helped Chris Bell set up the VLV Awards for Excellence in Broadcasting in 1991 and then organised these awards for several years of that decade. Until 2004, she was a director of VLV Ltd and a Trustee of the Voice of the Listener Trust. Locally, Jocelyne was a Trustee at The Hampstead Wells and Campden Trust from 2002 to 2013.

The couple moved into No.18 in the latter half of 1960. "After we had been here a year or so, we were offered the freehold," recalls Jocelyne, now 94 years of age. "We paid something in the region of £5,000." Between their professional commitments, the couple carried out a fair amount of work on the house, including laying an outside patio. Jocelyne really appreciates the large windows and the many period features, including the original fireplaces. The family has thoroughly enjoyed living in this lovely home. "Over the years we have had a few tenants, but not any longer," says Jocelyne. "Now I just have my carer housekeeper, but my grandchildren often stay here too." ∎

Tobin Close

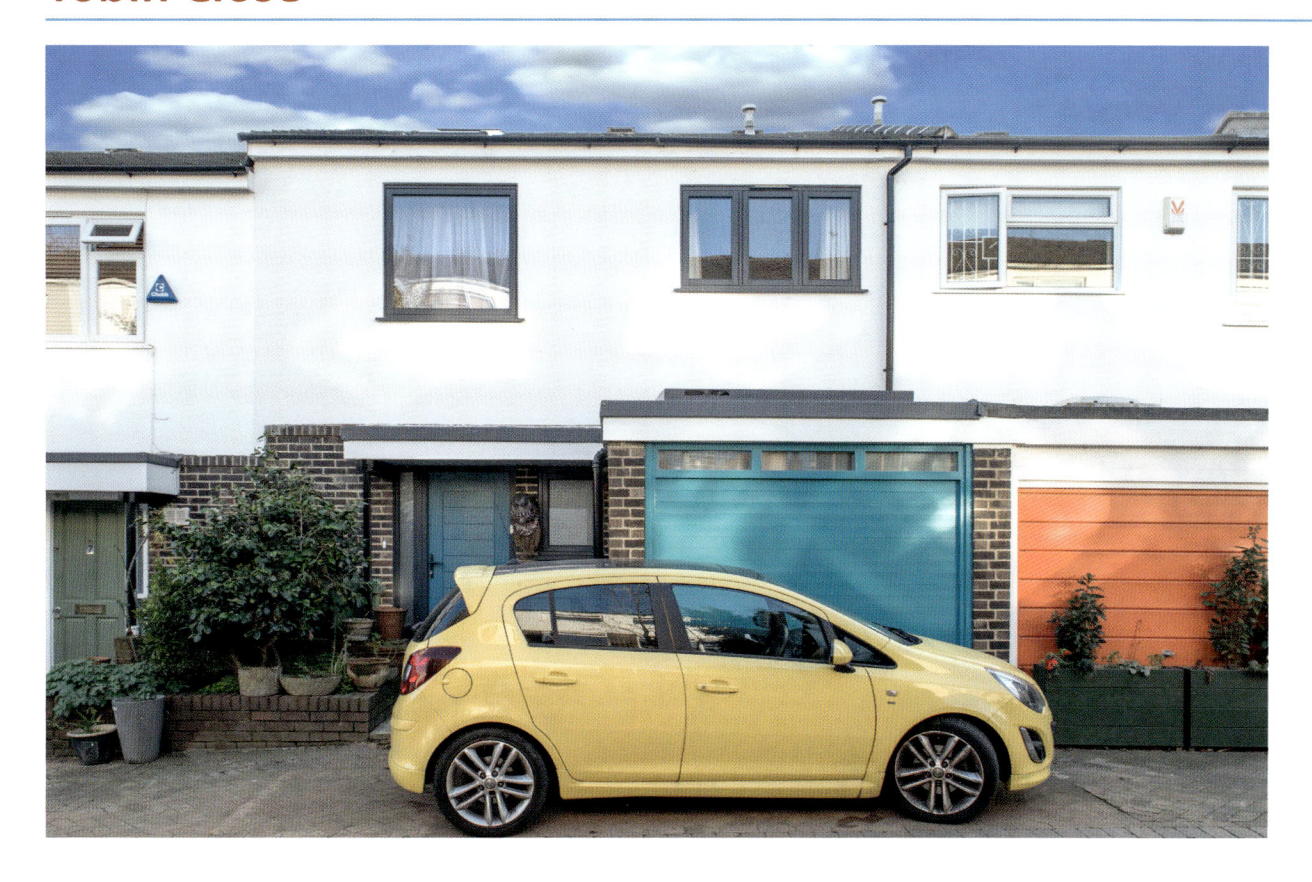

A seemingly typical 1970s-style terraced house unexpectedly holds enchanting surprises within. Located near Primrose Hill Road on the Chalcot Estate, Tobin Close is named after the long-serving local councillor Julian Tobin (see previous page) who represented the Adelaide ward for 30 years from 1968.

Lesley Isaacson, who has been practising and teaching yoga for over 30 years, lived with her husband in a family home in Ruislip. Following her husband's death, Lesley needed to downsize. "I already knew Belsize Park," she says. "But while house hunting in this area, I came to realise that my priorities were to have personal outside space and my own front door, as opposed to living in a flat in a converted Victorian house." That realisation led to this exciting redevelopment of what was pretty much an unchanged '70s interior at the time of purchase. Today, Lesley's distinctive colour choices carry through from exterior to interior in contrasting depths of colour. The front door colour is recalled in a paler version within the open-plan kitchen area.

Lesley moved in during December 2020. And after living here for a while, she found the most challenging thing to get used to wasn't the smaller size of the house and garden but the potential of being overlooked. "It's very different to backing onto woods in Ruislip!" she says. But she had already seen the possibility of improving her outlook. "I hadn't even purchased the place when I realised there was a strip of land two meters wide beyond the rear garden. No man's land, as it were.." "I researched the owner," Lesley continues, "and together with my neighbours on either side we purchased the land and extended our gardens by a good two metres."

When it came to the house interior, Lesley wisely took her time to evaluate the interior space before enacting any changes. "For the first 12 months it was like camping out in my own home. Then, after selecting Dean Willars as architect, we started again on a total redesign. The bathroom, for example, was really old-fashioned, dating back well over 40 years; it was dreadful," she recalls.

The work commenced in earnest in February 2022 when Lesley moved out, and the interior was gutted. Although the conversion was a joint project with her architect, it was still a massive undertaking. "In early July 2022, when I moved back in, the wonderful builders, DCS Universal, were a long way from finishing up," Lesley recalls. Then, echoing the common sentiment of those who have undertaken the radical overhaul of a house, "I underestimated how onerous it would all be; I had no idea what I was letting myself into," she confesses.

"It was the architect's idea to open the entrance area right up to the roof, creating a triple-height space that accommodates the newly-located and hand-built staircase. The main bedroom also extends up into the roof space. The architect created a light-filled house, which met my brief perfectly, the sunny light of South Africa in NW3!"

Remarkable Homes of NW3

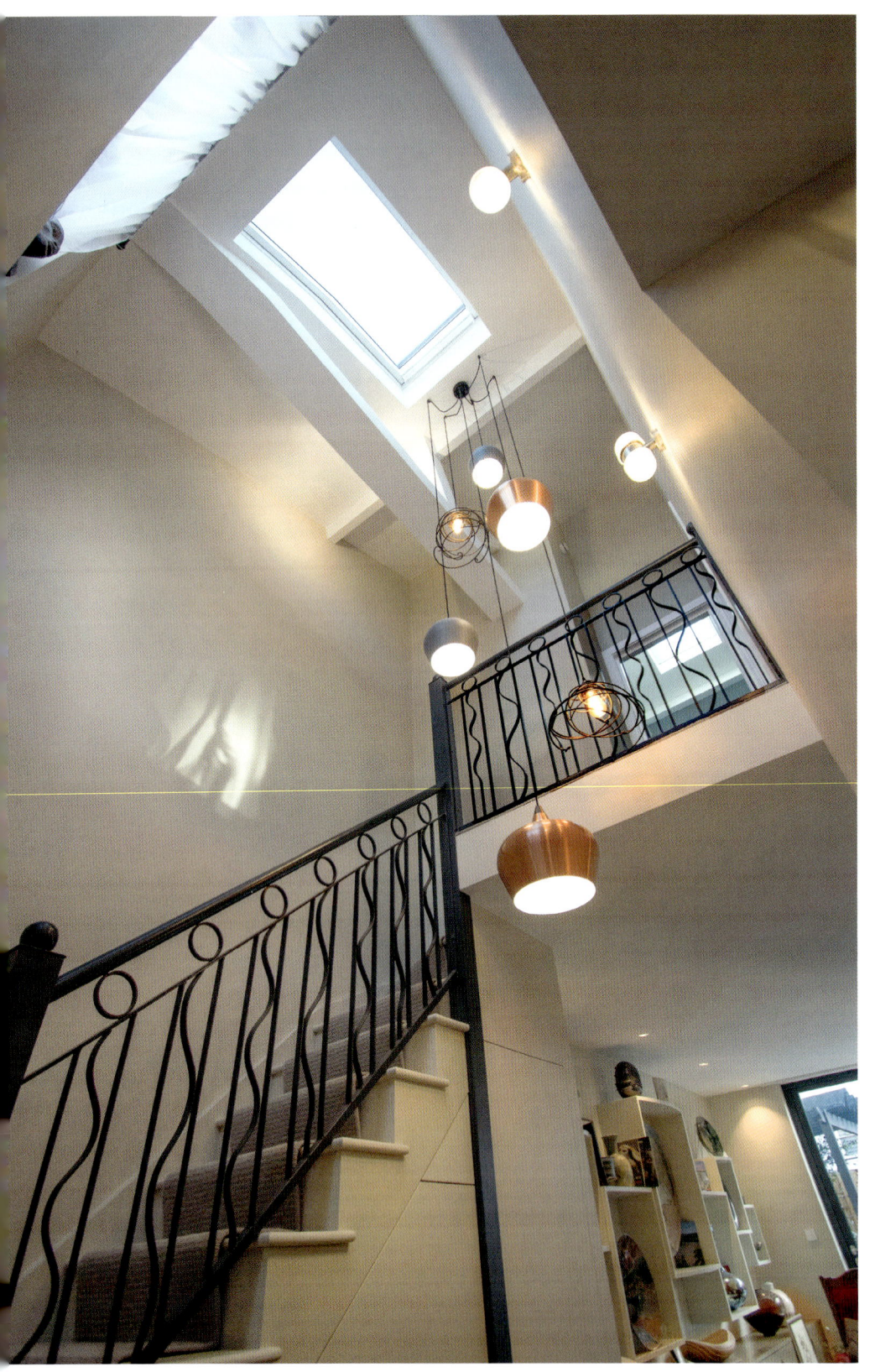

The area inside the front door was opened to the roof, creating an impressive triple-height entrance full of light and airiness. The living area of the open-plan ground floor is just visible.

The metalwork in the house arises from Lesley's attention to her surroundings. "I slipped a note through the door of a neighbour who had some striking metalwork at the front of their house asking for the name of the company they had used," Lesley continues. "The owner introduced me to the craftsman responsible, and he manufactured the metalwork and black nest light fittings for the staircase to our combined design."

Within the open plan ground floor the curved wooden coffee table offsets the angularity of the white display and grey storage units on the left, while the mix of contemporary and traditional furniture nicely balances the old with the new. The bifold doors extend the room and draw the eye out into the garden. "I wanted to create a seamless transition between interior and exterior spaces, through the use of wall-to-wall folding doors, with the interior flooring and patio slabs following the same line," she explains.

Lesley had in mind a particular design for the kitchen and Tomas Kitchen Living in Hampstead Garden Suburb specialised in the curves Lesley wanted for the isle unit. Curves are a theme that run throughout the house and garden, even extending to the wooden sleepers around the patio.

The discrete lines of the kitchen units quietly balance the opposite display wall of the living room. Detailing under all the countertops subtly recalls the colour of the storage units, and the curved lines of the specially designed island unit complement those of the coffee table and the many artworks.

Lesley has always had a connection to Belsize Park. "An aunt of mine used to live in Elsworthy Road, my son lives in Maida Vale, and my daughter owns a flat in Hampstead. I enjoy the surrounding neighbourhood, I'm so near Primrose Hill and it's just a short bike ride to Regents Park or Kenwood Ladies Ponds for a bracing dip." ∎

Bifold doors extend the open plan ground floor into the garden, creating an organised framing of the view.

The main bedroom extends upwards into the roof space.

Curves are a theme that run throughout the house and garden.

Remarkable Homes of NW3

Eton Road

Part of the original 1850 plan for the Eton College Estate. It was only after 1865 that Eton College changed the name of the road running alongside St Saviour's from Church Road to Eton Road. The shorter north-south stretch of Provost Road is today the southern stretch of Eton Villas.

Although the name of this road is linked to the famous public school, Eton College, the architectural historian Sir John Summerson notes that the Provost and Fellows "took little interest in their fields at Chalcots until in the 1840s when they were persuaded that they were sitting on what was, if not exactly a gold mine, property of more value as building land than for grazing cattle." At which point these worthies woke up and "the surveyor John Shaw was instructed to make a plan for the new development."

This part of the Eton College Estate would surround the focal point of St Saviour's. This church, built by the Lucas Brothers after a design by Edward Barry (son of Sir Charles), later architect of the Royal Opera House, Covent Garden, had itself been at the centre of an earlier scheme set out by H E Kendall. It's highly probable that the original houses in Eton Road were developed by Samuel Cuming, the builder who constructed over 100 houses in the Chalcots area. As historian F M L Thompson notes, Samuel Cuming was "a godsend to the Eton estate." And it is on record that Cuming continued building on the estate until his death in 1870.

Eton Road has had its share of famous residents; the prominent psychiatrist R D Laing lived at No.2 Eton Road for many years. He is remembered as the author of *The Divided Self*, published in 1960, and for the many controversies he caused personally and professionally. Influenced by Timothy Leary, he notably experimented with using LSD as a tool in his professional arsenal.

The frontages to Nos. 7 to 16 on the north-western side of Eton Road are particularly well preserved. These are substantial semi-detached Italianate villas on four floors. And it is No.14 that is the focus of our attention.

Built in yellow stock brick, visible on the upper floors, and faced in stucco at the lower ground and ground floor level. The villas feature round-headed windows on the first three floors, and Doric columns support the projecting porch.

Intriguingly, in the 1980s, No.14 Eton Road was occupied by Bananarama, the biggest girl group in the world at the time with hits such as *Cruel Summer* and *Venus*. However, as the current owner, Robert Leeming, explains: "Even before the days of Bananarama, there was a group of musicians who had a music studio in the garden, and they were probably responsible for its construction. And so, for decades, music was being recorded in the large studio at the rear of our house."

Is that why the Leeming family came to Eton Road? "No, but that Bananarama connection was a plus!" says Robert. "Initially, we were looking for a place within walking distance of Primrose Hill and England's Lane, somewhere between Eton Road and Steele's Road." And so Robert and Frances soon found this beautiful property at No.14. "We purchased the house from Jane Barclay when she moved to South Hill Park Gardens," says Robert.

Bold, round-headed bay windows on the lower and ground floor level.

The paired villas of Nos.14 &16 Eton Road with the well-preserved acorn caps to the gate posts of No.14.

An early poster featuring the original 1981 Bananarama trio of Sara Dallin, Keren Woodward and Siobhan Fahey. Between 1982 and 1987 the group had nine hit singles. Five months after the September 1987 release of the *WOW!* album, Siobhan left the group to form Shakespears Sister.

In fact, Jane Barclay had acquired the property from the Banarama founding member Siobhan Fahey. "Siobhan used the studio building in the garden as her music studio," says Jane, "but when I bought the house she had moved to L.A." At that time it was a collection of flats and bedsits, so Jane immediately set about returning the house to a single residence. "I completely gutted it," Jane continues. "I removed the entire second floor, raised the ceiling, and added an extra floor at the top, so at one point all that remained were the outer walls, the staircase, and nothing above the first floor."

The old studio has been replaced with the present-day garden room – the white-painted stucco building beyond the garden room is the side of the distinctive No.2 Fellows Road (see p.25).

Some of the original character has been retained, including the cornices around the 14ft high ceilings, working shutters and the grand fireplaces.

"We moved in during 2015," says Frances. "After removing the large music studio, over an 18-month period we renovated the upper ground floor and created a large playroom on the lower ground floor." The couple replaced the studio footprint with their garden room when they redid the garden. They also added the side entrance to the house accessing the lower ground floor directly. "It's our everyday 'back door', but the smart front door does get used sometimes!" Robert adds smiling. Their home is beautifully light, and they love the proportions of the house.

The couple particularly enjoy not being overlooked either from the front or the rear, and delight in their magnificent vistas of London. "As you go higher up the house," says Robert, "you see more and more of the view across the London skyline."

Robert and Frances have created a comfortable family home – although Robert has one more restoration project in mind. "All I really want is a blue plaque to celebrate Bananarama living and recording here," Robert says jokingly.

Sweeping vews from the attic terrace extend across to the City and West End.

Seaford Lodge, Fellows Road

This large detached house, visible beyond the rear garden of No.14 Eton Road, was constructed following the implementation of the 1850 Eton College Estate plan (see p22). This exquisite residence once served as home to the philanthropist and pioneer in the field of industrial life assurance, Sir Henry Harben (1823-1911), who also became Hampstead's first mayor in 1900. It now belongs to a professional couple.

One of the current owners was formerly director of collections at the Tate which he left in 2002. Since then, he has worked from home as an independent curator. The other owner is a homeopath and she also works from home. "When we purchased the house we were informed that it had been built for his family by the builder who developed Steele's Road," says the owner, "and that's why our garden, which is the full width of the house, appears to have taken up part of the gardens belonging to those on Steele's Road."

At some point, *Seaford Lodge*, having passed into the Plunkett family, was turned into a rooming house. Inherited by Caroline Plunkett in the late 1980s, she changed its function again. It became a guesthouse when permission was refused to convert it into to a hotel. "The building was remodelled at that point, and some of the original features removed," explains the owner. "But by 1992, the enterprise went into liquidation, and the house was repossessed by The Mortgage Corporation."

The present owners had previously visited the house while Caroline Plunkett was still living there, asking if they could look at some rooms. "A developer had secured a contract to buy it from The Mortgage Corporation, and the

Seaford Lodge, No.2 Fellows Road, with its distinctive round-headed windows and cast iron window guards dated *c.*1849.

View across all the neighbouring gardens from an upper floor.

> house was offered to us by him off market," recalls the owner. "Although it was clearly far too big for us – it's a huge building – we realised that if we turned the lower ground floor into two flats, we could live in the rest of the house. So we entered into discussions with the developer and managed to buy it." Caroline Plunkett moved out at the end of 1993, leaving the property empty. "At that time, my wife was living in South Hill Park, and I still had a flat on Fitzjohn's Avenue. We sold both, bought the house in January 1994 and moved in during March."

Caroline Plunkett had split the building into 15 or 16 bedrooms plus bathrooms. What is now the kitchen was once a bedroom, a bathroom, a separate loo and a reception area. Fortunately, the rather grand living room had avoided division.

"We completed the demolitions before we moved in. We then set up a temporary kitchen and camped in a bedroom upstairs while the works were completed. We did it slowly, over some two years. Then in 2004 one of the flats came back into our possession and became a study." In 2017, rather than downsizing after their two grown-up children had moved out, they opted to transform the house into their perfect home reinstating the rooms to their original Victorian dimensions.

The couple love living here. "We are within easy reach of Primrose Hill and the Heath – the transport connections from here are great from Chalk Farm and Swiss Cottage. There are cinemas and theatres

Original cornicing in the living room.

making it a cultural hub," they note. "The abundance of natural light in the house is absolutely wonderful. The living room is north facing with tall windows that extend almost to the ceiling. With generous ceiling heights, it's spacious but with thick walls it's relatively easy to keep warm while remaining cool in the summer." By 2019, the interior was completely redone, and the lower ground floor was extended slightly at the back. They then set about removing all the failing exterior stucco. The need to re-render provided the opportunity for necessary structural repair work, including around the chimney stacks which were restored to their original appearance. The large rear garden also benefitted from a complete redesign.

The owners shed some light on the origins of the studio at No.14 Eton Road. "The artist and printmaker David T Smith (1930-1999) used to live there, constructing the original studio. Subsequently, it became a recording studio, most famously used by Siobhan Fahey of Bananarama. When Jane Barclay bought and modernised the house, she knocked down the studio and rebuilt it before eventually selling the property to the present owners. They, in turn, demolished Jane's studio and built a garden room. Hence, both that house and the studio have undergone several iterations."

Both owners continue to enjoy working from home. "We spend a lot of time in the kitchen, which was relocated from its initial position on the lower ground floor to the raised ground floor," they explain. Apart from the excellent layout of the kitchen, the key feature is the very unusual front window which brings considerable character to the room – the afternoon sun flooding the space with light.

Numerous original features have survived, including cornice work in the hallway and in the full-width living room, the latter of which originally had a fireplace at each end, and still retains one of these in situ. ∎

The kitchen with its magnificent window.

Provost Road

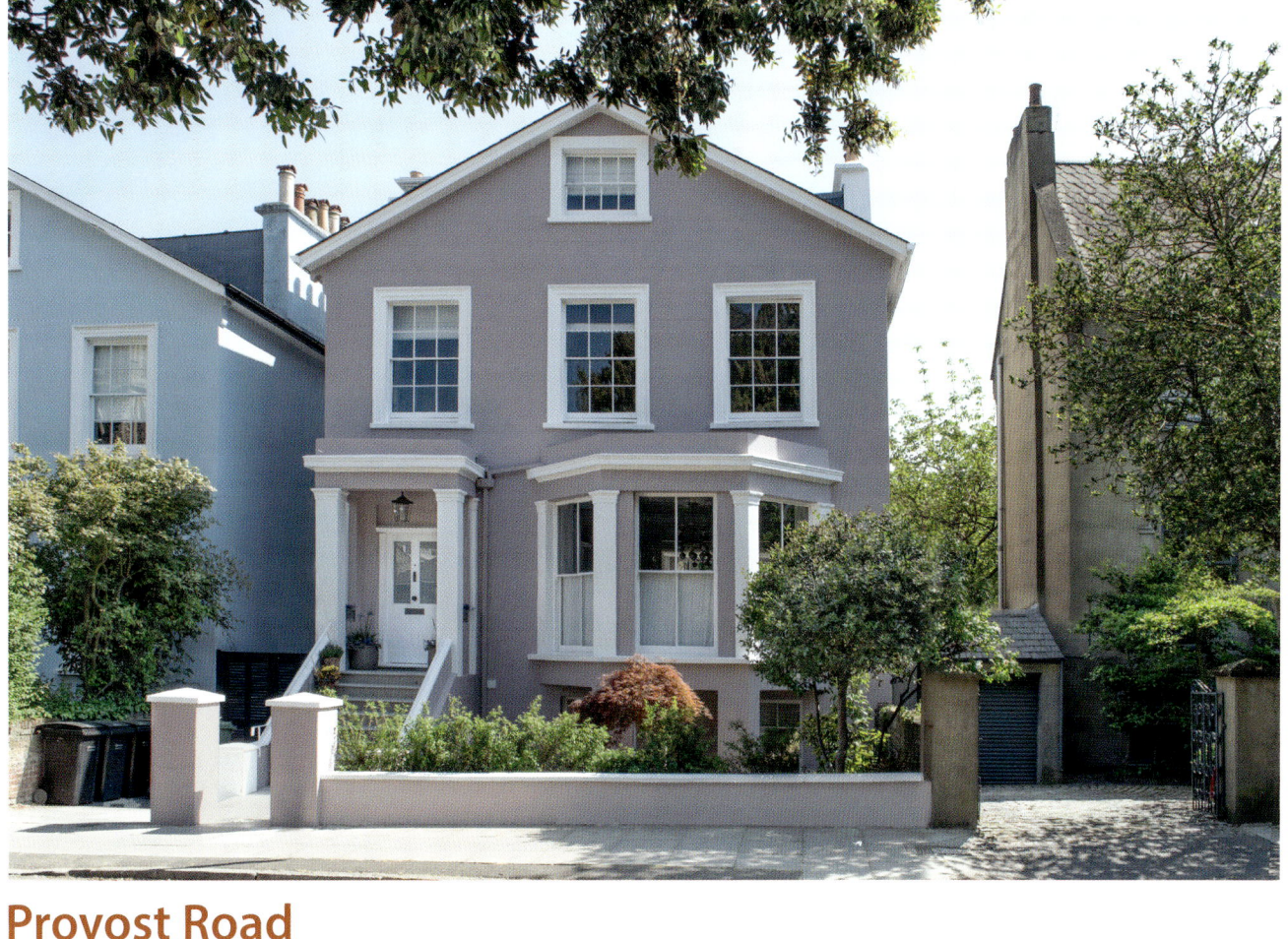

Here, in Provost Road, we find a group of rather good-looking detached and semi-detached pairs of villas, some with shared gables, finished in a lovely medley of pastel colours. "Reflecting", as Pevsner says, "the more refined taste of the Eton Estate surveyor, John Shaw Jr."

These houses, built in a rustic Italian style, are in the school of John Nash, according to Sir John Summerson, and probably inspired by the Nash villas in Regents Park. They were constructed by Samuel Cuming in the mid-1840s. Indeed, John Shaw was said to be "very much pleased" with the overall development. St Saviour's Church, the centrepiece of the estate is located virtually opposite.

Looking fabulous in the spring sunshine, the Grade II detached No.19 Provost Road is home to Chris and George, who have been together for 15 years. Chris Thelen is from the US but was raised in Bedford. George Delius is from south west London. Chris has always loved the Camden area where he has lived since 2010. "We previously had a three-bedroom terraced house on Harmood Street, NW1," he says. Chris is a travel specialist who sold his travel management company in 2015. And as a result, he was able to purchase this home which is unique on the road, as it is the only one with a bay window. "After selling my travel company I was advised to buy a house as an investment, so we did just that," says Chris. They looked around for the right place for about a year, and then Chris found this house online.

The existing exterior colour was not to their taste and it had at some point had been divided into two flats. But as Chris recalls, "everything else looked most promising and when we first arrived for a viewing, we both fell in love with the place. So we went ahead and bought it in May 2015 from the previous owners who had lived here for 25 years."

"For the first five or six years we rented out the property," Chris explains. "When it was time for us to move in the tenant was really sad to leave as he liked it so much. We decided to live here for twelve months or so while we thought about what we could do with the house." As little to nothing had been done to the place for some two decades, Chris and George were considering not only structural restorations but also an updating of the essential services together with a total interior redesign.

"We found an up-and-coming young architectural firm, Will Gamble Architects, who specialise in Grade II-listed buildings," says George. "And fortunately, there were very few obstructions when it came to obtaining planning permission for the changes." With all the works completed to their satisfaction they were able to move back in February 2023.

The expansive living and entertaining areas. A fabulous space extending across the ground floor to the 'Martini Lounge' beyond.

The superb seating in the 'Martini lounge' bay window invites garden views over the grass roof of the lower ground floor extension.

Extensive use of Douglas fir in the lower ground floor extension links to the garden in a scheme inspired by Modernist ideals.

The multifunctional living space along the lower ground floor accommodates different uses – working, entertaining and relaxing.

The doorway from the hall into the front living room was enlarged to form a double opening. "We recreated the original cornices, and installed them in most of the rooms. We also reproduced the ceiling roses in the living areas as well," says George.

Major changes ensued downstairs on the lower ground level, which now has a beautifully polished concrete floor. This lower ground floor is superbly well designed. The garden end of the room occupies part of the newly-built extension, and it has a grass lawn roof. Thanks to the creative inspiration of the architect, further into the extension, there is a marvellous multi-purpose open space. The wall panelling is nothing short of ingenious.

The panelling in the kitchen dining space can be manoeuvred by pulling it out on tracks from its parked position. This opens up the possibility of creating a more formal meeting room/boardroom. Capable of hosting up to 24 people, the space is complete with a screen and presentation wall. And when not needed it can all disappear back again into the 'open-aspect' position. "I have run businesses for a long time, and we still regularly entertain as many as 40 or 50 people," Chris explains. He now owns another travel company that operates in the UK, Ireland and the US. Coincidentally it's called Eton Travel Management — a most appropriate name. Especially so, as the company does business with Eton College.

"When it comes to entertaining, the dining table can accommodate up to 20 people. And we can also cut the kitchen off if we want to when we are holding meetings," Chris says.

Upstairs, the primary bedroom was reworked in order to create a walk-in closet and a larger bathroom. The room has a close up view of St Saviour's Church. "And we reconfigured the very top floor with a second primary bedroom," says Chris. Two other bedrooms have been converted into separate studies for George and for Chris. George is a graphic designer and at the far end of the redesigned garden that also features a pond, he has a large garden office clad externally in natural cork – which looks superb. Various artworks around the house include those by George.

Although much of the upgraded interior is very contemporary, it works superbly well with the traditional aspects of this charming house. It is all beautifully done, resulting in a modern, comfortable, warm feel throughout this remarkable home. ■

St Saviour's from the primary bedroom window.

The view from the terrace to the Douglas fir glazed extension with its green roof.

The garden studio clad with weather-proof cork. The studio wall opposite the house is partially clad in mirror, reflecting back the lower terrace.

Steele's Cottage detail, c.1829, *Edward Finden*.

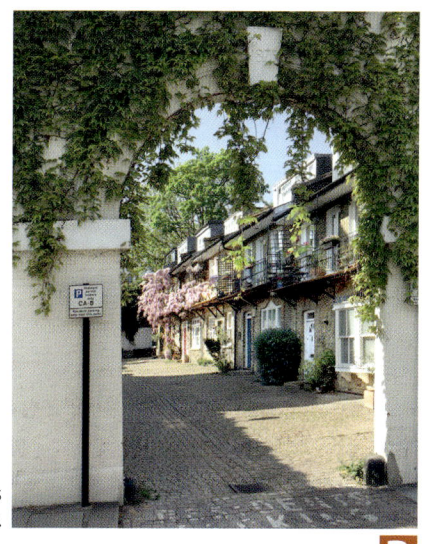

Steele's Mews North today.

Linton Studio, Steele's Road

A picturesque cottage once stood on Haverstock Hill opposite the famous *Load of Hay Tavern*. This abode was once the home of Sir Richard Steele, co-founder and editor of *The Spectator* – first published in 1711. The demolition of Steele's Cottage in 1867 made way for the Steele's Road development.

Some splendid houses are to be found on Steele's Road, blatantly individualistic in plan and eclectic in detail. "If you are looking for uniqueness in architecture, the north side of Steele's Road is the place to look; there are no houses anywhere in England like these," says architectural historian Professor Andrew Saint. "Wonderfully robust, heavy, and massive, and in terms of style, they start at one end rather Gothic, and by the time you get to the Haverstock Hill end, they are much more fully Queen Anne."

No.35 Steele's Road, designed by Batterbury & Huxley, was built in 1875 for Sir James D Linton, painter and twice President of the Royal Institute of Painters in Watercolours. Artists love north light, so the studios were located at the back and were not visible from the street. But unusually, in this case, the artist's window faces east.

Home to Gary Miles and Kate, the Linton Studio is extraordinary. "My friend Mike found it for me – at the time, he said: 'You've really got to look at this semi-detached house; it's unique.' Although it was divided up in a rather weird way, there were odd walls all over the place, I immediately realised I could do something wonderful with the interior." Gary went ahead and closed on the deal in July 2018. "The best part is that I found my wife Kate through the house!" says Gary with a big smile. "I was living as a bachelor previously, and some people said this house is too big for me, but before I knew it, my Goddaughter and then another friend had joined my daughter and myself – and then I met Kate."

Listed Grade II, No.35 Steele's Road in red brick with a large, tiled mansard roof and dormers.

Linton's Studio house viewed from the large garden.

The Linton Studio entrance, No.35 Steele's Road.

A delightful view to the garden.

Visible brickwork is part of the original back of the house.

The double-height studio with its magnificent east-facing window.

Gary had already found a builder, an architect and a project manager, but he still wanted help to achieve a holistic feel for the house. "I wanted to make the house itself comfortable and artistic," he continues. "I interviewed several designers, but none hit the mark. Then I met Kate, who is both an artist and a professional in conservation. When Kate arrived, she immediately started talking about how the space could be arranged and how best to make it beautiful and comfortable. She has an amazing sense of aesthetics that has made this house unique."

Gary did as Kate suggested. They got on really well together, and she moved in with Gary during the Covid era. "We pared back a lot of the ideas, less became more, and living in the house during the reconstruction enabled us to see how we should best shape the place for it to work for the both of us. It has all worked out beautifully, so now I've got a family, we're expanding into the house nicely."

Although this is a listed building, the rear part, from the external wall towards the garden, was added at some point over 40 years ago. "Therefore, as this section is so recent, we were able to make the internal changes we wanted. We removed some walls and opened up the whole area. We added a new door from the kitchen accessing directly to the garden, and these changes have altered the whole dynamic of the house," adds Gary. "Overall, the construction works took 18 months to complete."

So what's the most wonderful thing about living in this house? "Apart from the updated interior, I'd say the garden and all the garden spaces," says Kate. One of the previous owners was a professional gardener; she installed all the infrastructure of the garden. "But when I arrived, it had become a jungly mess," adds Gary. "I cleaned it up; although a lot of work still needs to be done, the foundation is so easy to work with. Several sheds, including a sauna, are at the foot of the garden. I can disappear to work and sit outside undercover – even in the rain. It's all back there at the end of the garden."

A key feature of the house is Linton's superb east-facing studio window. The evolution of this home is a truly romantic story. "It's wonderful that Kate is an artist, and that this is an artist's house," says Gary. ▪

Steele's Road has been home to many actors and musicians in recent years. No. 9 was previously home to Noel Gallagher and later David Walliams.

Also on the north side Steele's Road, the elaborate Grade II-listed No.31 was designed by JM Brydon, architect of Chelsea Town Hall, built in 1874. Brydon lived here briefly. The singer and pianist Leslie Hutchinson also lived here, as did Sir Derek Jacobi.

England's Lane c.1895 with landau – one of the oldest thoroughfares in the area renamed when the farm was leased to James England in 1776.

No.16 Chalcot Gardens – once home to illustrator Arthur Rackham.

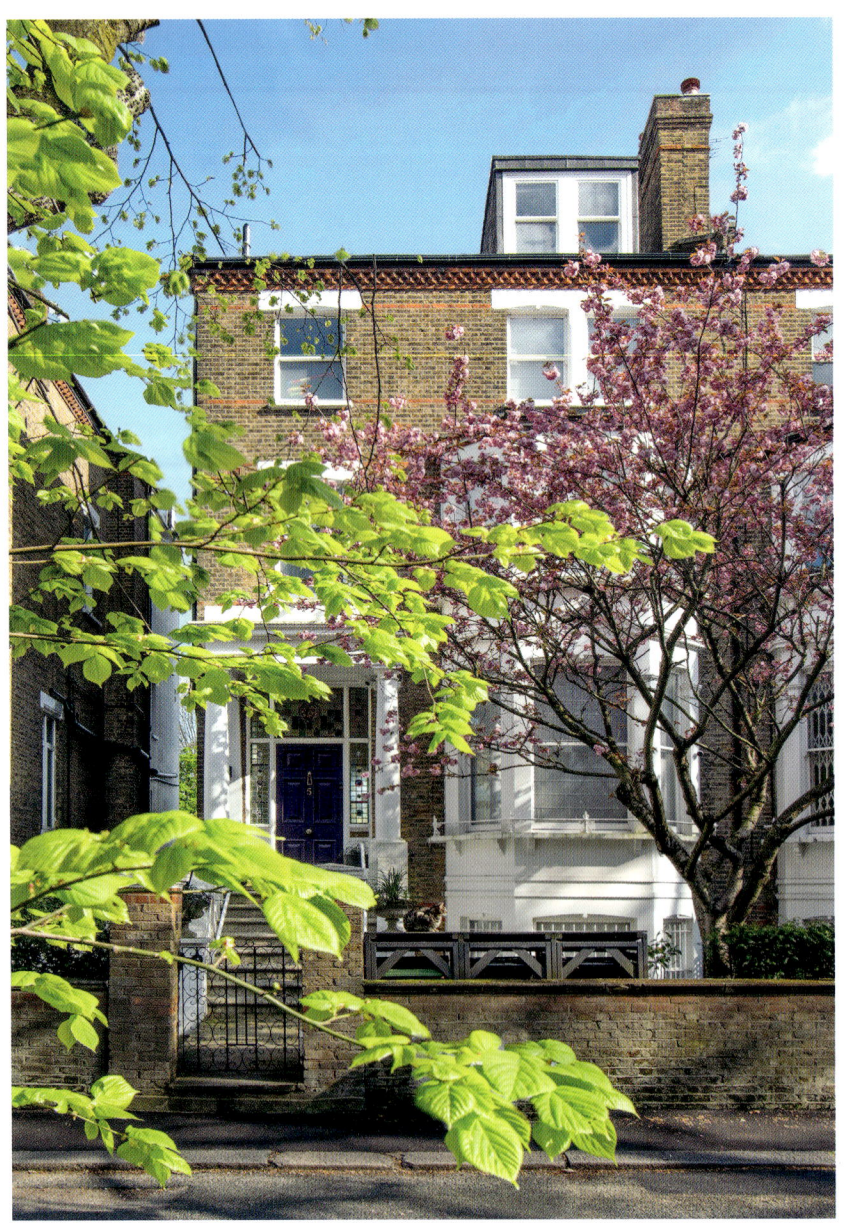

Chalcot Gardens

Running along the south side of England's Lane, a long brick wall bounds a row of beautiful mature trees bordering the road known as Chalcot Gardens. Here we find some distinctive artists' studio houses with tall, north-facing windows. Eight of the houses are the work of William Willett Senior. At one end of Chalcot Gardens we find No.16, with its extensions designed by CFA Voysey the Arts and Crafts movement architect and furniture designer (see also p277). This house was once home to Arthur Rackham, famously the illustrator of J M Barrie's *Peter Pan* and Lewis Carroll's *Alice's Adventures in Wonderland*. The property is now owned by the singer-songwriter Rita Ora, who bought it due to this connection. At the other end of Chalcot Gardens we find No.5.

Immediately upon entering the house, visitors can't fail to notice the view from the kitchen dining area across the garden to the rear of the houses on Steele's Road. And beyond there's an uninterrupted view of the spire of St Saviour's Church with the City beyond.

"I have the original documents of the property, which are truly beautiful," says Stephanie Mercier, who hails originally from Montreal and works in communications. Her husband Nima is in finance and is also a keen photographer. "The deeds were handed to us in 2018 by the previous owner, who in turn had received them unrequested by post – they had been held in an archive for many years."

These Eton College deeds dating back to 1881 and 1882 describe the house as 'The fifth house west' from the end of Chalcot Gardens.

"I had been looking for the right property in Belsize for a long time," recalls Stephanie. "We were living in Angel, Islington. My children started to go to the Hall School in Belsize Park, and we spent a lot of time travelling up and down on the Northern Line!" So the family moved from a very busy, lively area into the relatively quieter Chalcot Gardens. The couple had been looking for at least a year before they found this ideal home. "When we first saw this

No.5 Chalcot Gardens.

place, it was like finding a pearl – these undivided houses come on the market so rarely." All this happened at the end of 2017.

The house belonged to the previous owners for well over 35 years, and much of the fabric of the building required updating to modern standards. "We redid virtually everything, the wiring, the plumbing, as well as a full renovation project," says Stephanie. "We employed an architectural firm, a husband and wife team, to design the conversion."

The beauty of the upper ground floor is the L-shape space extending from the front through to the kitchen. "We opened up the central part of the kitchen rear wall resulting in a run of three windows, creating a full-width view of the garden. It's made such a big difference," explains Stephanie. "Then down on the lower ground floor, it was very low-ceilinged, dingy,

Deed for No.5 Chalcot Gardens, dated 1881.

The kitchen/dining area with its run of three windows.

Ground floor fireplace with one of Nima's photographs.

and unpleasant." So as part of their improvements the couple decided to open it up and add a rear extension. "When we lifted the floorboards we discovered a void beneath, and so it was all there, ready for us the make the change to the floor level and extend out to the garden."

On descending the stairs to the lower ground level, it becomes immediately obvious that it is incredibly modern – a true Wow! "Our marvelous tropical fish tank goes so really well in this setting. It's a hobby that needs rather a lot of work to look after the fish, and keep the tank clean," she notes. Stephanie decided to preserve the attractive iron spiral staircase at the side of the house, which leads from the upper ground floor down to the lower terrace.

The well-positioned mature tree makes the garden. "We had a landscape gardener who worked together in conjunction with our architect to produce a synthesis between the slate floor and the garden terrace," says Stephanie. "Upstairs, we added a new dormer to accommodate the staircase to the attic we have opened up." In total, the entire project was 18 months of work. "We were so glad to be able to move in even with just with two rooms completed. Compared with living in Islington, where life in Angel is more transient," notes Stephanie, "here we see the same people regularly, and the school run is a lot easier now. Also, there is a great community around the school. It's lovely to be able to say 'hi' to people we recognize on the street. I really enjoy that." ∎

No.5 Chalcot Gardens lower ground floor and extension.

The iron spiral staircase.

The secluded garden room.

Interior of the lower ground floor.

No.5 Chalcot Gardens

View towards St Saviour's, St Paul's and The Shard.

36

Lambolle Road

A quiet street running eastwards from Belsize Square, Lambolle Road was originally named in 1876 at the request of S G Bird, the builder of many houses in the locality. However, at that time, John Galloway owned and lived at No.1 Lambolle Road and built a number of houses on the south side of the road. It is highly likely that Galloway was the builder of No.13 around 1883.

"We have always been fans of Belsize Park," says Debbie. "We love the proximity of the green spaces and we loved being able to walk our kids to school. We first lived on Eton Avenue, then moved to a north-facing house on Lambolle Road. However, having grown up in South Africa, I am always craving light and really wanted to live in a south-facing house." In 2007 No.13 became available and the couple made an offer immediately. "Although we knew we had a larger project on our hands, we could also see the potential to turn it into our dream home. Incredibly, the two main ground floor rooms were not utilised at all," says Debbie. "My late brother Saul was married to a Greek architect who was born in Zambia and understands open-plan living. Along with local architect Kasia Whitfield, they worked wonders."

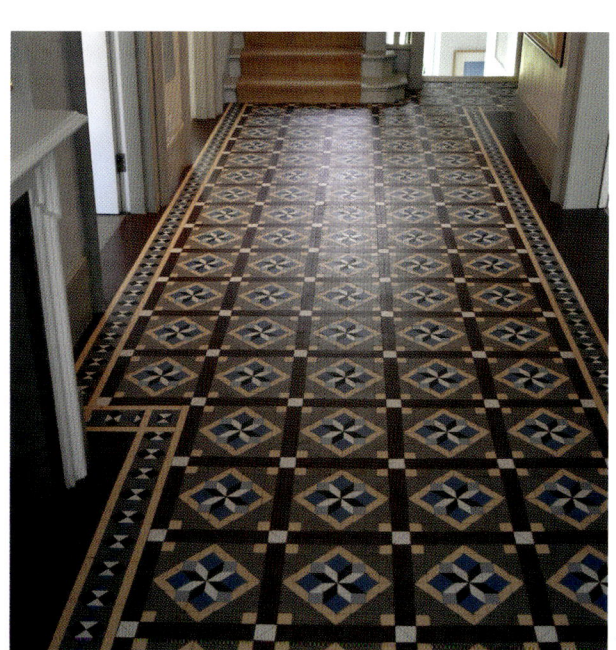

No.13 Lambolle Road has two entrances; the one at the side leads to the garden floor and gives direct access to a self-contained flat currently used as consulting rooms.

On entering No.13 through the large front door it's impossible not to be impressed by the magnificent tiling in the hallway. Debbie explains how this came about. "We discovered some of the original floor tiling in the hall, and when we decided to restore the hallway floor, we opted to replace the old floor with exactly the same pattern. The tiles were replaced tile by tile so that we could recapture the original look. It took two men ages!" The family are delighted with the outcome.

"We renovated the house in phases," Debbie explains. "We lived on the two upper floors while we worked on the lower two floors. And then vice versa. So we didn't have to move out at all."

The house is always full of friends and family and is a home with a great feel.

The hallway with its original tiling faithfully replicated.

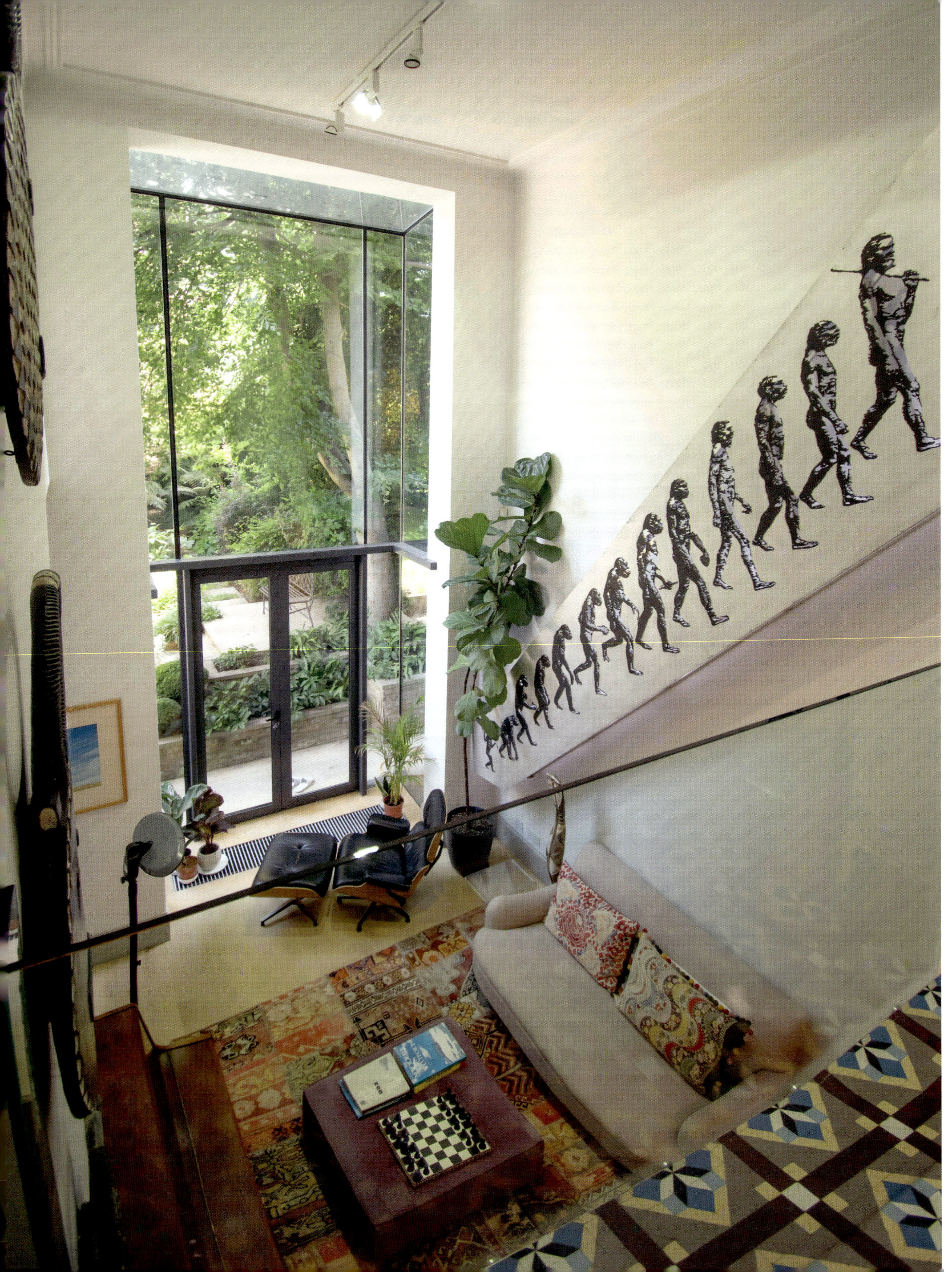

Exuding comfort and convivial living, the clean lines of the sitting room furniture offset the classical fireplace.

In 2011, together with a couple of other Lambolle Road residents, Debbie organised the street party for Kate and William's royal wedding. With tables down the centre of the road, a bouncy castle and a DJ, the event, supported by local businesses, highlighted the wonderful community spirit prevalent in Lambolle Road. "I so much enjoy living in Belsize," says Debbie. "I walk everywhere around here, say hello to many familiar faces, and it only takes me 40 minutes to walk from home through Primrose Hill and Regents Park to Marylebone or the West End."

Celebrating the royal wedding of Prince William and Kate Middleton in 2011.

The dining room combines its classical architecture with red-upholstered modern furniture and a stylish interpretation of a chandelier.

Famous people who have lived on Lambolle Road include journalist, author and broadcaster Brian Inglis; the eminent philosopher Professor John Findlay, and the artistic Aumonier family, including William Aumonier Jr and his son Stacey, the short-story writer.

Viewed from the tiled hallway above, this double-height space, created by removing a floor, accesses the rear garden through the black-framed double doors.

North House, Eton Avenue

Full of grandeur, variety and character, this Grade II-listed terracotta mansion on Eton Avenue called *North House* was built for the portraitist John Maler Collier (1850-1934). Despite a family background of politicians, Collier, specialising in the Pre-Raphaelite style, became one of his generation's most prominent portrait painters. He also became the son-in-law of Thomas Henry Huxley twice: married to Marian (Mady) until her untimely death in 1887; Collier later married Ethel. Both sisters were also artists, but it would be with Ethel that he would move into *North House* upon its completion in 1890.

With its elaborate staircase windows, *North House* was designed in Flemish Renaissance Revival style by Frederick Waller (the husband of another of Thomas Huxley's daughters). The red brick garden wall has a slightly projecting base, gate piers with enriched terracotta friezes to cross gable caps, and a panelled timber main gate. The stepped gable is one of the most identifiable features of Flemish Revival architecture. The elegant, hipped roofs have projecting swept eaves, with a moulded terracotta eaves cornice, dormers, and tall chimney stacks.

This was Collier's second house designed by Frederick Waller, the first being on Tite Street, close to his father's house (a judge and amateur artist) on Cheyne Row, attached to a mews building now accommodating The Sketch Club. *North House* is one of the first Hampstead studio houses, in the vanguard of a move away from Chelsea, where they originated.

Collier worked in this splendid high-flown studio mansion until his death in 1934, leaving the house to his widow Ethel. Unfortunately, his family couldn't maintain it during the war

The majestic main entrance comprises a terracotta round arch, with a broken pediment supported by large, enriched console brackets flanked by two narrow round-arched windows.

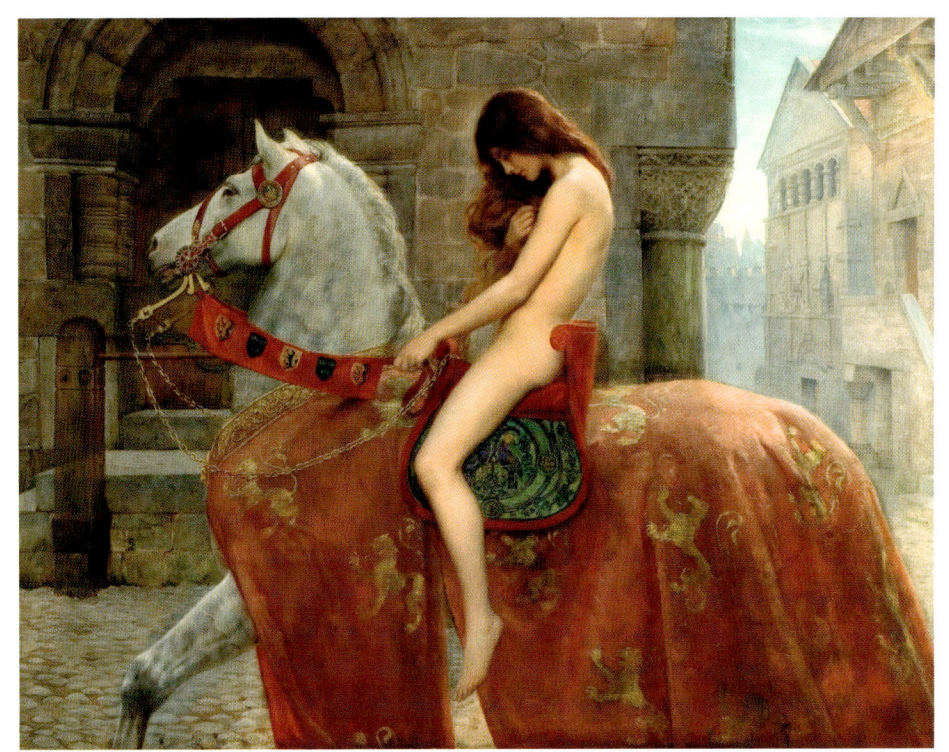

Lady Godiva c.1898, *John Maler Collier*, kind permission of the Herbert Art Gallery and Museum, Coventry.

Exterior and interior views of the elaborate staircase windows.

years, and in the 1940s, one of Collier's daughters sold the building, which has only changed hands a few times since then. Austrian exiles, primarily intellectuals, used to meet at *North House*. The building then became a school of music and in the 1970s, it was purchased by a couple who turned it into a ballet school. After that, as with so many large houses, it was converted into seven bedsits.

These days this detached mansion looks just as magnificent as ever in its red brick with terracotta dressings and its superb detailing. Terracotta plaques on the front façade are said to be the initials of John and Ethel Collier.

The present owners of this distinctive Eton Avenue building knew the area well, as their children went to school locally. By pure happenstance they noticed an advertisement in a free property newspaper for a house that had been on the market for at least two years. Their initial viewing revealed "A dimly lit interior covered with chipboard everywhere, but we could still see the potential," the owners recall. The couple worked on plans for changes to the house together with their architect, Catrina Beevor. It was a major challenge to find a solution that satisfied the vendors, English Heritage and Camden that also matched the family's vision for their future home.

"Having bought the house in 2005 we immediately planned its restoration as a family home," say the owners. In fact, it was three times the size of their previous house, and the couple needed to know precisely what the authorities would allow them to change within this listed property. An agreement was reached, and the local planners permitted certain interior changes. "We retained the basement as separate flats. However, there was a rather awful 1970s extension at the rear, and fortunately, we were allowed to replace it with something considerably nicer," say the owners. The new extension is lighter and

Remarkable Homes of NW3

more in keeping with a winter garden. It is thought that the glass studio at the front served the same function initially. "We were also able to create a new ground floor family kitchen to replace the original basement kitchen," note the owners. "All seven fireplaces have been retained; in a few cases we had to replace the tiled surrounds," they continue. "But the listing required us to restore and maintain them." Camden signed off half the house in 2007 with the bedrooms finished at the top and the basement flat also completed. At which point – and this is a familiar story of the struggle to complete a complicated restoration project – their builders went bust. Nevertheless, the family were able to camp out in part of the building while work continued for another year. In total, the rectification and restoration work took three years – clearly, a major labour of love.

North House is so named because it enjoys the north light that all artists love. This wonderfully large 5-light terracotta window, with its arched central 3-light, is encased by pilasters supporting a cornice window head with elaborate finials, plus a flanking swag frieze.

During the restoration project the couple discovered the original servants' staircase. The previous owners had removed the handrail and extended the floor over the stairs, concealing it entirely. "We also opened up the upstairs skylight as that was blocked off with chipboard," they recall. Amazingly, the original (non-functioning) gas pipes were still in place to light the chandelier.

Part of the drawing room, little changed from when John Collier lived here. Note the similarity of the American chairs with Collier's own furnishings.

"Collier used to paint in the drawing room – the room with the unusually large 5-light window," the owners point out, "and his wives also painted." The chairs in the drawing room previously belonged to the owner's grandparents from Cincinnati and are nearly the same age as the house. "Interestingly, the photo we have of Collier working has the furniture arranged similarly to the way we have chosen to arrange ours today."

The Gecko-style fireplace in the living room.

Interior view of the first floor 5-light drawing room window.

John Collier, *photo, E H Mills*, c.1894 alongside one of his canvasses in the drawing room.

The house originally had no doors on the south elevation so the garden was only accessible via the side alleys or through the carriage house (which served as a workshop for most of C20). As part of the couple's renovation project, twin garden stairs descending from the new French doors were added as well as access from the lower ground floor flat and the new extension (see next page). ∎

A delightful corner of the library.

43

Remarkable Homes of NW3

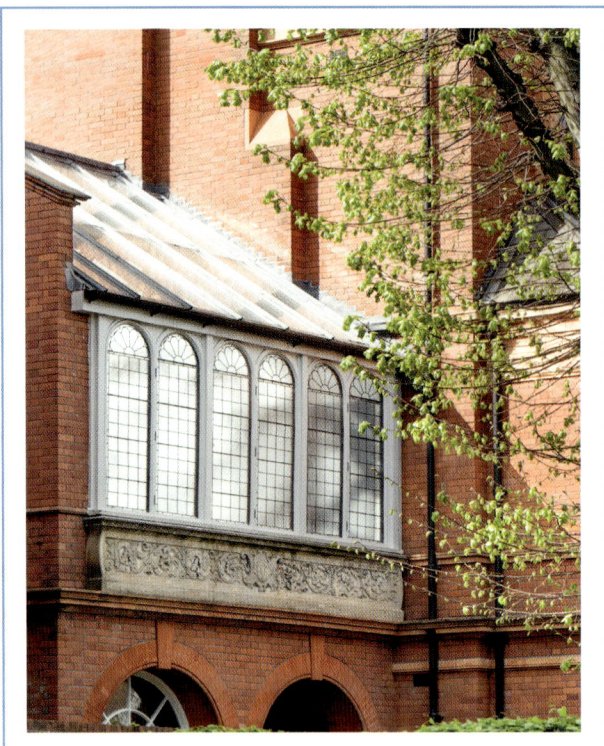

The conservatory or studio with glazed roof, beneath which are 6 arcaded lights seated on a stone base with carved panels – exterior and interior views.

Rear elevation of *North House* with part of the beautiful garden designed by Brita von Schoenaich who studied at the Royal Botanic Gardens in Kew before taking a postgraduate course in landscape design.

Belsize Park Gardens

Architectural historian Nikolaus Pevsner, writing of two pairs of semi-detached Queen Anne revival houses at Nos.83-89 Belsize Park Gardens, says this "Well-composed group of homely brick Willett houses of 1896, displays the late Victorian reaction against stuccoed pomp." Belsize Park Gardens is indeed best known for its large, matching Italianate paired villas built by Daniel Tidey, such as those elsewhere in this part of Belsize Park. In contrast, William Willett has imparted a striking individuality to each of the four semi-detached properties of essentially the same design and construction by incorporating diverse window designs, bold chimney stacks and varied, narrow gables. As a result, this group, located at the border with the Eton College Estate, makes a fine transition from the lands of Eton College and Eton Avenue to the Belsize Estate.

"We already knew the road and especially these houses on Belsize Park Gardens," say the owners of No 89. "For a long time, we had been looking for a property in Belsize with fewer stairs than our previous Georgian home in Islington. We eventually found this house, purchasing it in 2007. Interestingly, in the 1930s it was the Vietnamese Embassy." As with so many of these big houses, at some time in the relatively recent past, the house had been converted into multiple occupation, having been divided into flats for student living, and it remained that way until the late 1980s. But fortunately, these four Willett houses have all retained their original front garden walls. The owners noted other changes over the years. "No.89 differs from the other houses as it has a garage, still with its original garage doors. The others in the group have a winding pathway from the front gate leading up to the entrance. We suspect that at some point, the front door of this house was moved from its original location as we do not have such a gate or path."

No.89 also has a gable at the side – originally, the upper windows would have enjoyed views across parts of the old Eton College Estate.

The rectangular sitting room with its circular ceiling plasterwork – cornices are still present in most rooms.

"We started the restoration work on the roof first which was pretty bad. Then we re-plumbed, rewired, and re-floored almost the entire house," they recall. Unfortunately, the couple could only retain the wooden flooring in one of the rooms. But remarkably, all the fireplaces were left intact including an unexpected one in the bathroom. "We replicated the mantelpiece and surround for another room. All the ceiling plasterwork remained intact," they note. Fortunately, some of the original glasswork has been preserved within the interior doors.

Detail of an original cornice.

An unusual over-door plasterwork motif.

A lovely glass-panelled door.

The kitchen, a favourite room of the owners, enjoys access to the garden.

Staircase with its restored panelling.

"As we were able to match the panelling that is still in situ in the other three houses – which at some point in our case had been removed – we reinstated the wooden panelling to the same height as the dado in the hall, and continued it up the stairs," say the owners. "No.83, the first of the four houses, was probably built around 1896 and the last one a few years later. We found a newspaper from September 1907 under the floorboards when we were renovating, so we think this house was built last."

The owners very much regret they had not found the original brass plaque providing the location of plumbing that the Willetts installed in their homes. "The Willett company positioned the service parts at the side of the house – things like access to the utility room and larder and such. But finding our plaque would have helped us considerably and prevented the builders from drilling in the wrong place!"

The rear balcony ironwork is original, and at the end of their garden, a gate leads to another delightful triangular-shaped shared garden which was created out of land once owned by Eton College and leased to William Willett.

The large bay window of the primary bedroom enjoys delightful views over the garden.

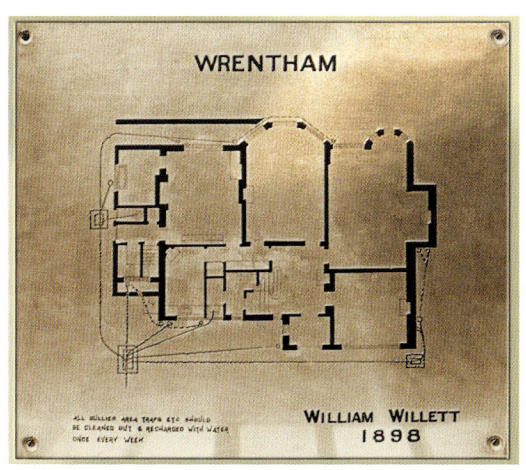

The Willetts installed a plumbing plaque like this one in most of their homes.

The main bathroom with its original fireplace.

47

Remarkable Homes of NW3

The lower end of Belsize Park Gardens near England's Lane c.1900.

The house has interesting NW3 spy connections. The KGB plan to recruit Kim Philby and the other Cambridge Spies was born in Belsize Park Gardens. Author Geoff Andrews states that No.89 was the home of Martha, the grandmother of Norman John (James) Klugmann. Klugmann was a friend of the Cambridge Five and part of the Belsize Lawn Road communists in the 1940s and 1950s. Apparently, they held secret meetings at No.89 Belsize Park Gardens. ■

Daniel Tidey's *Washington* public house sits a little further along the road on the corner of Belsize Park Gardens and England's Lane. Built in the Italianate style around 1865, listed Grade II, it retains much of its original woodwork, glass, and mirrors. However, it has a formidable history, including its name, which has nothing to do with the United States. Daniel Tidey named the pub after his own West Sussex village of Washington, and in C20, quite by chance, his great, great, great-grandson, Terry Tidey, became a landlord of *The Washington*.

The Washington with Belsize Park Gardens on the left and England's Lane to the right.

Fitzjohn's Avenue

The fine boulevard of Fitzjohn's Avenue followed the general route of the old footpath linking St John's Wood with Hampstead. Named after an estate in Essex belonging to the Maryon-Wilson family, this 1870s project was a realisation of Sir Spencer Maryon-Wilson. He was determined that by creating a 'truly impressive' road, the area should be opened to a highly desirable luxury development. Most of the mansions on the avenue were by speculative builders, anticipating sales to the wealthiest Londoners. Such desirable properties had little competition elsewhere in the 1880s, and Fitzjohn's Avenue was a huge success, widely admired as a handsome thoroughfare, frequently likened to Parisian boulevards. An 1883 edition of *Harper's New Monthly* magazine states that when the trees have grown up… the Avenue "will be one of the noblest streets in the world". Today, the mature trees and the grass verges add a delightful sense of verdant space. Fitzjohn's generous width and the scale of architecture have certainly created a powerful, lasting impact.

No.9 Fitzjohn's Avenue today. This former hostel was heavily altered in the 1970s.

Remarkable Homes of NW3

"Belsize Park has been my home for 20 years, despite my strong American accent," says Aliya Kanji, a nutritional and lifestyle consultant and property developer. She lives here with her family. "My first flat in London was the top floor of Eton Court, overlooking beautiful Eton Avenue. From there, I converted three flats into a 3200-square foot single-family home on Lambolle Road and we lived there for eight and a half years. Then, as our family grew from two to four children, we needed somewhere larger but wanted to stay within walking distance to the schools and the high street, so we decided to move to Fitzjohn's Avenue."

Built in 1887, No. 9 was ideal, but by C21 it had become a 30-person bedsit/hostel, and initially Aliya was unsure they would get permission to return it into a single dwelling. But they were successful, and working with Finkernagel Ross Architects, Aliya spent 18 months planning the reinstatement of the original character of the building on the upper four floors with a contemporary extension at the lower level. The design project was followed by two and a half years of construction work. The family were finally able to move into their new home in 2016.

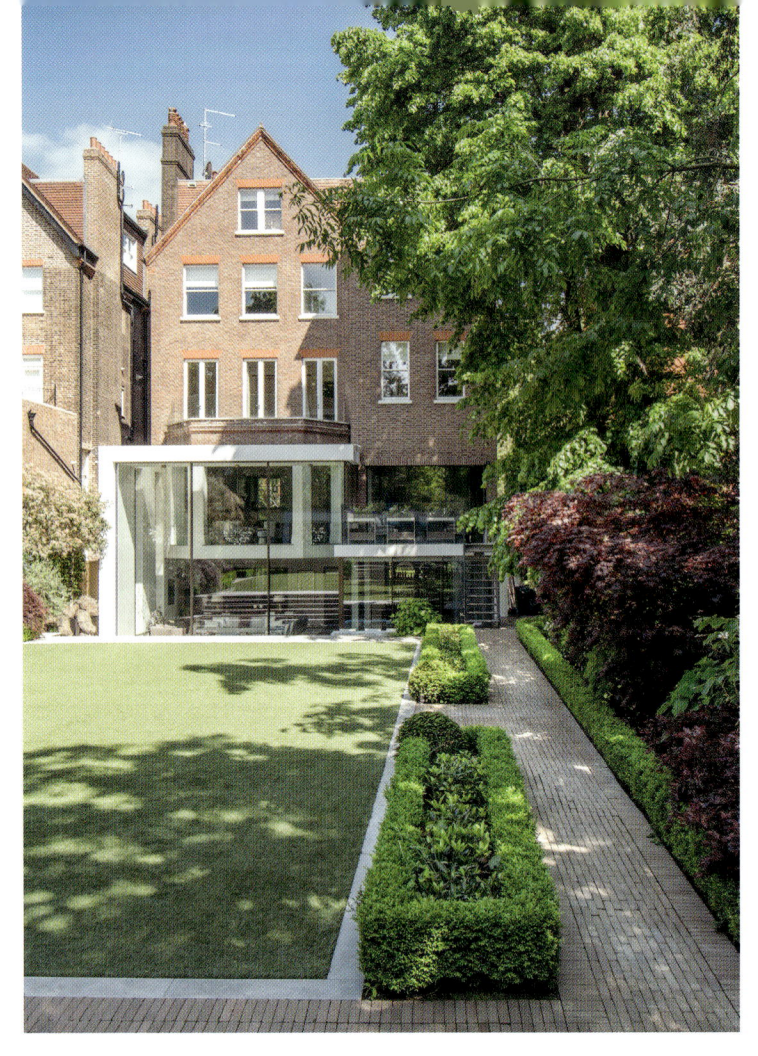

The building was stripped right back to the walls, *owner's photo*.

Aliya managing the project.

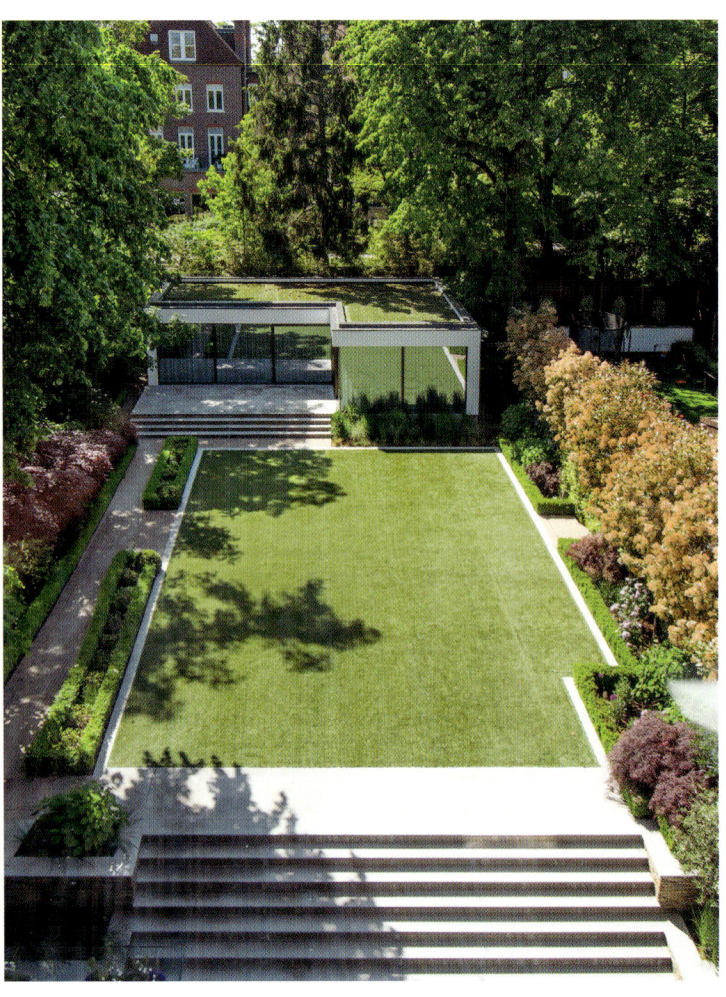

View from the house towards the garden office and gym.

The expansive upper living room – note the cut-corner wall panelling around the fireplace.

The project entailed stripping the entire house right back to its bare brick walls and removing the roof. "We removed the back of the house completely and built a double-height extension to the lower and upper ground floors," explains Aliya. "We took the six floors literally back to the studs, although we kept the façade and certain walls. So we were left with just the floors and ceilings."

Aliya acted as the quantity surveyor, project manager, and interior designer. She designed two large living spaces, one on the upper ground floor and another on the lower ground floor, both accessible to the large garden. The building at the end of the garden houses a gym on the right, an office on the left, with a kitchen and bathroom in the centre.

Aliya designed all the furniture too. For example, in the upper living room, she wanted something organic for the low-profile sofa nearest the window, "so we can fully appreciate the view to the garden," Aliya explains. "My inspiration was the work of Steven Gambrel based in New York."

The wall panelling above and either side of the fireplace in the upper living room is a cut-corner rectangular motif used throughout the house. The motif can also be found in places like the shape of the dining table, the shape of the dressing room island and the panelling on the wardrobe doors in the dressing rooms. The utility room, plant room, and climate-controlled wine cellar are in the basement.

As she is from Southern California, Aliya wanted plenty of natural light. The unusually large rear sliding windows are six and a half metres high.

The extra tall sliding doors wash the floors with light.

Remarkable Homes of NW3

The custom-lacquered piano matches the carpet colour with an appropriately-designed music-themed light fitting above.

The cut-corner motif dining table matches the wall panels, and the antique mirror features brass detailing.

When it comes to the lighting, more of Aliya's creativity is on view. The original central light's trumpet design is a natural fit with the music room. Aliya played the violin as a child and has kept her brass childhood music stand. "All four children play instruments, the violin, flute, oboe, saxophone, and of course, everyone is learning the piano," says Aliya. Her piano is lacquered blue, echoing Elton John's customised red pianos. Every detail, without exception, has been meticulously considered. "The pattern on the floors harmonizes elegantly with that on the glased bronze doors. "We worked with an interior designer on some interior architectural elements, but I was very hands-on with everything. For example, I was closely involved with the design of the three-panelled doors," explains Aliya.

The family entrance is accessed by descending the ramp on the right hand side of the house leading to an exceptionally cool boot room, where every child has their own cupboard. This lower level also provides access to an apartment for the housekeeper.

Is this an improved version of the original 1887 house? Undoubtedly so. This is truly a remarkably impressive home and does more than justice to this famous avenue. ∎

The pattern of the hall marble floor mirrors the bronze pattern on the double doors. The artwork is specially commissioned.

The lower living room, with bar and games room to the left, both with access to the garden.

The primary bedroom has separate 'his and hers' dressing rooms.

The stair lighting is a full-height drop – light floods through the entire staircase. An elevator also provides access to all floors.

Ornan Road

A sizable estate named *Ivy Bank* surrounded the eponymous villa located south of Belsize Lane. The villa, built in 1804, was occupied by Alfred Ridley Bax from 1893 (see p57). He used it as his headquarters while involved with the development of Ornan Road. This thoroughfare was allocated its name in 1873 but only laid out on the tract of land between Belsize Lane and Belsize Avenue in the late 1880s. The developer was Richard Pierce Barker, with Richard Hackworth as the main contractor. The plan was to build substantial up-market properties, but sadly, only two of the original 1888 detached houses remain. Our visit is to the imposing No.34 Ornan Road. A family of five took the decision to move to Belsize from the Mansfield area to be closer to the Underground.

"When we first saw this house in 2014, its width immediately captured our attention, as most Victorian houses are tall but narrow, making this house rather special," say the owners. "We must admit, we haven't encountered many houses like this one." During a nine-month conversion and restoration project the owners rented in nearby Belsize Avenue. "We were initially concerned that it might be busier here, but we find it remarkably quiet and peaceful," they add. Indeed, the house enjoys a rear garden surrounded by greenery and trees, undisturbed by views of other houses for most of the year.

A basement or lower ground floor already existed. The owners lowered the floor by 30 centimetres and removed several internal walls. Then they extended into the space at the rear of the building previously occupied by a brick-built music room and a traditional conservatory. The staircase down to this level was also changed because the previous one was so low that the taller family members kept knocking their heads, so something had to be done about that! "We've ended up with an overall slightly reduced footprint," the owners explain. "But the run of windows in the extension ceilings allows the light to flood into the open space, completely transforming the lower ground floor, making it the true heart of the house." And this is where we find their extraordinary kitchen.

OpenStreetMap contributors and National Library of Scotland, CC-BY-3.0. Ornan Road c.1894-98. Marked in red, the four original houses built near Belsize Lane, photographed in 1910.

Part of the extension to the left replaced the old brick music room; the section on the right replaced the old conservatory.

The relocated staircase down to the basement.

The impressive kitchen area with its suspended island unit.

Remarkable Homes of NW3

Detail of a glorious, beautifully-restored cornice.

"The kitchen furniture is by the Eindhoven-based Dutch designer Piet Hein Eek who is well known for making his furniture from reclaimed materials," note the owners. The kitchen area is quite exceptional. Its originality generates a wonderfully homely feel that permeates the entire house, enfolding the classical architecture of the upper floors.

The property had been well looked after by the previous owners. Many of the original ceiling roses and cornices throughout the house are intact, the hallway tiles are original, and despite their 130 years of life are still looking smart and bright. Some exterior iron colonettes supporting the window lintels have been recast and match the originals. So apart from the new staircase down to the lower ground floor, structurally, everything else remains pretty much the same.

As with so many families who have chosen this corner of London as their forever homes, the neighbourhood and community atmosphere are vitally important and valued. "Living here," the owners say, "we find we are much closer to places we love to visit, like Belsize Village – where socially, the Streatery has greatly helped to bring people together. And when we step out we are in the heart of Belsize Park, yet we're still relatively close to South End Green and Hampstead."

The owners have taken the time and the trouble to transform this remarkable home by brilliantly combining its classical architecture with inspiration from their own Dutch culture to the benefit of all those who live here, and to all of us who have the privilege of peeking into this interior – waarvoor wij zeer dankbaar zijn. ∎

The elegantly-curved staircase ascending from the hall with its original Victorian tiles.

Perceval Avenue

A grand villa constructed around 1875 between Belsize Lane and Ornan Road was named *Ivy Bank,* surviving until 1911. After its demise, a road was constructed across the grounds, and appropriately enough, it was called Beaulieu Avenue. Four years later, in 1915, the road was renamed Perceval Avenue to commemorate Spencer Perceval KC (1762-1812). He married the younger daughter of General Sir Thomas Spencer Wilson, Lord of the Manor of Hampstead. Spencer Perceval lived in 'damp and draughty' *Belsize House* from 1798 to 1807 when, having already served as Attorney General, he became Chancellor of the Exchequer and leader of the House of Commons. In 1809 he was elected as the British Prime Minister. But, on 11 May 1812, he was shot dead in the lobby of the House of Commons by John Bellingham, a Liverpool merchant with a grievance against the government. Perceval is the only British Prime Minister to have been murdered.

And so to No.10 Perceval Avenue. "A family lived here shortly after the house was built in the 1930s," says Markku Lonnqvist, a private equity investor in the media industry, who lives in the house today with his wife, Päivi.

"When the previous owners passed away, a developer acquired the property, and for quite a while there was little happening to the house," explains Markku. "The developer went bust. Then 18 years or so ago, a couple bought the place and completed the conversion and we bought it from them." The sad aspect of this story is that the very first developer had gutted the house and excavated the basement to install a swimming pool. Local residents still recall the house sitting virtually on stilts for some time while the works were underway. "This means that there is nothing original remaining of the place at all. When the second developers completed the work,

The housekeeper on the steps of *Ivy Bank* before 1911.

it was essentially in the style of the period around 2004!" says Markku. "So, we made our contribution, and we hope it looks much better now."

As it turns out, 'their contribution' entailed a start-again job. "We changed everything and stripped out the entire place," says Päivi. It all took a long time, awaiting planning permissions and so forth, and as a result, the couple and their twins could only move in five years ago, in 2018.

In effect, they had given themselves a clean slate to work with, and their input has left them with a house that has a wonderfully fresh feeling to it. They have infused the rooms with their own highly-creative style, while there is a nod to their Finnish origins, with a considerable use of clean lines and much joinery – some of it in a gorgeous, rich black finish. "You see, we have a place in Italy near Portofino that is all white!" says Markku laughing.

Discreet uplighting and concealed ceiling speakers, pale furnishings and clean lines create a relaxing living room.

The subtlety of the parquet floor is evident in this closer view of the living room window.

The precision and workmanship quality makes this staircase a truly masterful piece of work. Its initial sculptural design is a tribute to the creativity of Päivi and Markku.

Getting to Perceval Avenue has been a progressive journey for the Lonnqvists. "We first settled in Lindfield Gardens, followed by Ellerdale Road, Greenaway Gardens, then Belsize Grove, and Ornan Road," recalls Päivi. While they feel it was easier and less complicated to move home in the past than it is today, renovating old properties is not a new or challenging experience for this couple. "We have renovated many houses over the years," says Markku. Citing No.16 Ornan Road as an example, he notes that the house had been continuously owned by the same family for 80 years when they arrived. "We gutted the whole place, basically rebuilding it, but also replicating many of the original features, including cornices, and we completely rebuilt the staircase – it was beautiful." They are fully aware of their responsibilities to the past and future. "We are all just custodians of the houses while we live in them," is their motto, as it is with many of those who choose to live in remarkable homes.

All their attention to detail and extensive renovating experience is very much in evidence here in Perceval Avenue. "We didn't change the footprint that much," continues Markku. "But as nothing remains of the original interior, we decided on a bespoke design for the staircase. We selected a company from Japan to build it for us. The curve of the spiral was computer-designed and shipped to us in pieces. It was then assembled on site, and it all fitted absolutely perfectly."

"The handrail is bound in black leather by one of their craftsmen who came over from Japan to complete the project. And we chose the timber for the treads to match the wood of the floor," adds Päivi.

The extension at the right side of the house accommodates the kitchen. "This is a lovely bright working space with light entering from two sides and above," says Päivi. "The kitchen furniture is from Lauren Nicholas Kitchen Design on England's Lane." ∎

Here the seating fabric reflects the colours of the parquet flooring, the black wood of the bookshelves and the book jackets.

A new window at the rear of the house provides a charming view of Belsize Lane. The white building with the towers is *Hunters Lodge,* built in 1810 on the site of the original 1496 lodge on the Belsize Estate (see next page).

Part of the lovely bright kitchen.

'The Queen' in the dining room was a gift from the Platinum Jubilee in February 2022. This view shows how the panels of the sliding glass doors perfectly frame the dining table and the window beyond.

Belsize Lane in 1850, *archive*.

The turreted *Hunters Lodge* in C19. For many years the Lodge and its grounds were within the *Ivy Bank* estate; *Ivy Bank* is visible in the background.

Hunters Lodge, Belsize Lane

A stuccoed and castellated Gothic cottage orné, a rare survival for London – *Pevsner*

Undoubtedly the oldest and most handsome building on Belsize Lane, *Hunters Lodge* is one of the few early C19 houses remaining in the area. This magnificent Grade II Georgian mansion, built *c.*1810-12, is noted by Pevsner as Gothic-revival with "Ogee [double curved] windows and a varied composition of two turrets and a tall gable towards the garden, exceedingly pretty in a toy way."

As legend has it, a house has stood on this site in Belsize Lane since 1496. Later, Prince George of Denmark (1653-1708), the husband of Queen Anne, owned a hunting lodge that stood here. Three hundred years later, in 1808, George Todd, a Baltic merchant, acquired the lease of a sizable part of the Belsize Estate and from whom William Tate, a wealthy merchant of Lime Street, London, purchased the house on this site. Tate promptly demolished the old building, commissioning architect Joseph Parkinson (1783-1855) to design the Neo-Gothic lodge we see today. Parkinson's design incorporated some of the basic tenets from his earlier 1804 design of *Mabledon House* near Royal Tunbridge Wells.

In 1810 Parkinson exhibited his designs for both houses at the Royal Academy, and his design for Tate's house is labelled *Langwathby*. Unfortunately, the house would lose much of its grounds when Ornan Road was built up in the 1880s. The house became known as *Belsize Cottage*, as named on the Hampstead OS map of 1866. Later it was called *Hunters Lodge*, the name it has retained to this day. Although this iteration of *Hunters Lodge* is the oldest remaining house in Belsize Lane, by C21, it had deteriorated considerably.

Builder and property developer James Burton commissioned *Mabledon* for his own use, "An elegant imitation of an ancient castellated mansion." Between 1822 and 1830, Parkinson supervised parts of the reconstruction of Magdalene College, Oxford, *archive*.

Its present owners, who have backgrounds in finance and technology, share the home with their two children. They first became aware of *Hunters Lodge* when they saw it advertised online. It had been on the market for quite a while and was in a terrible state. "But we felt the property had huge potential," recalls the owner. "Although it hadn't been updated for more than 30 years, it had such a magical feel as if you were in a castle or hunting lodge." Unfortunately, when the couple first took over the house, there was very little detail remaining – it had been completely wrecked over the years and even the quality of the work that had been done was questionable.

The house at the end of the first redevelopment phase in 2010.

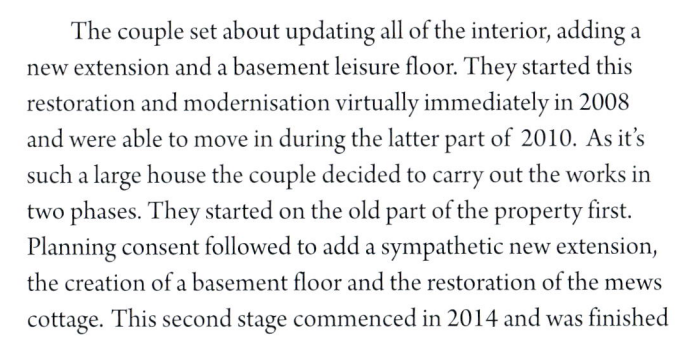

Part of the garden in 2010.

The couple set about updating all of the interior, adding a new extension and a basement leisure floor. They started this restoration and modernisation virtually immediately in 2008 and were able to move in during the latter part of 2010. As it's such a large house the couple decided to carry out the works in two phases. They started on the old part of the property first. Planning consent followed to add a sympathetic new extension, the creation of a basement floor and the restoration of the mews cottage. This second stage commenced in 2014 and was finished in 2019 – it's been complete now for four years.

Featuring some romantic Neo-Gothic extravagances, "Architecturally, the Grade II-listed *Hunters Lodge* is unique – unassuming from the outside, and surprisingly zen on the inside," the owners say. The lobby area is relatively modest, and the staircase discreet and understated. "It's a little nicer now than when we moved in. There is now a second staircase in the extension – but the Camden planners wanted the new staircase to be completely different from the original one."

The extended *Hunters Lodge* on Belsize Lane with its ornate castellated pediment and oriel bay window in 2022.

A well-preserved door to a shed now relocated in the garden.

Hunters Lodge today combines the new build elements with a modern specification and heritage features. "I'm delighted with the way it has turned out because now it is a lovely-looking building," says the owner proudly. "When you walk in through the front door it's like a little oasis – the rear garden is very private."

The magnificent upper garden and southern façade shows the towers' ogival windows (arched with a pointed crown) and their conical slate roofs. To the right is a gabled four-light oriel bay window. The triple-aspect library/reception room features wonderful ceiling coving and an inglenook-style marble fireplace.

The entire *Hunters Lodge* refurbishment has been completed to an exacting specification. The garden floor has an upper and lower level opening onto two south-facing gardens – an upper garden with a terrace and lawn, with steps leading down to a lower sun terrace.

Although this project was a major long term undertaking, the result has been more than worthwhile. All credit to the owners who have painstakingly and successfully brought this historic building back to life.

Rear view of Hunters Lodge with upper and lower garden areas, *photos Savills*. Note the towers' ogival windows and conical slate roofs. To the right is a gabled 4-light oriel bay window.

Left: part of the lower garden, *photo Savills*. Right: the preserved Georgian 3-storey staircase. Fortunately, the carved wooden balustrades with its ebonised timber handrail have survived, *owner's photo*.

Belsize Lane

Belsize Lane has changed beyond all recognition since the early C19. The houses now standing at the top of the lane were constructed between 1883 and 1890. Nos.2-26 Belsize Lane were originally named Rosslyn Gardens. Architect Henry Spalding designed No.2 *Rosslyn Heights* in 1883, and according to Christopher Wade, Spalding is probably responsible for the whole development. No.8 Rosslyn Gardens, today's No.24 Belsize Lane, was built for a Mrs Charlotte Williams Metcalf *c.*1886.

Belsize Lane in 1842, watercolour, *Edmund Marks*.

This smart, detached property is located opposite *Hunters Lodge* on Belsize Lane (see previous pages). "We were very pleased to discover this house when we did," says Nupur Ganguly, an art advisor specialising in modern and contemporary Indian art. "I grew up in Wales and came to London for work. My husband is from the Midlands, but we've always lived together in North London, particularly in Belsize Park." Previously, the couple were living in a flat on Eton Avenue. "When we started our family we realised that Belsize was the right community for us," continues Nupur. The house came up at the right time. They were impressed with the place from the moment they first saw it in 2017, thinking it rather special and immediately conducting a little due diligence on the property. "We were particularly interested as the house is in an area with such a rich history – especially in art and literature," notes Nupur.

The previous interior while charming, was rather dated. "We feel we are most fortunate to live in an area that offers so much in terms of the history," says Nupur. The previous owners had a very traditional set up with their kitchen on the lower ground floor and two reception rooms on the ground floor. The couple employed the architectural firm Callendar Howorth and benefited from an excellent team of builders. It took around nine months to get all the planning permissions in place before work could even start, followed by 12 months of remodelling. "We wanted our living spaces across both the lower ground floor and the ground floor, so we spent a lot of time redoing the interior," Nupur explains. "We were finally able to move in during August 2019, just before the Covid period."

No.24 Belsize Lane, a substantial house built in yellow stock brick with grand front bays – the segmented arched windows have attractive red brick detailing.

The kitchen is situated at the front extending into the large bay window.

The hall and staircase seen through the glass-panelled double kitchen doors.

View to the dining room.

Originally there was a bay window on the ground floor, leading to the garden, that had been remodelled at least once. "We've now extended the living room out a little, replacing the old bay and adding a skylight, which has improved the proportion of the room, and boosted the interior illumination," explains Nupur. "In addition, the lower ground floor was extended a little further, forming a terrace above. Part of the wood panelling has been retained and modernised in the dining area. "There was some original cornicing, and we employed traditional plasterers to reproduce the cornices to maintain the originality as far as possible with our aesthetic in mind," adds Nupur. "We opened up quite a lot of rooms on the ground floor as well."

The homely living room emanates a peaceful atmosphere.

Part of the delightful garden.

Although the property is not listed, it does have significance within the Conservation Area and hence required permission in to order to make alternations. "Ours may seem rather a grand house viewed from the front, especially with the steps up to the front door. But actually, it's quite modest inside, and it works really well as a family home," says Nupur. "It gives us what we want as a modern family, is not too much to manage, and is well-positioned for us to travel into work and for the children to get to school. Best of all, this is a neighbourhood we like." Nupur feels it is important to know other people living in the local area and they frequently visit Hampstead and Belsize Village. "It's lovely to bump into our neighbours; there are not so many other parts of London where that happens these days. We feel it would be tough for us to ever leave Belsize Park."

Remarkable Homes of NW3

Lord Wedderburn became the 1st Earl of Rosslyn.

The Gables, Wedderburn Road, designed by Horace Field.

Wedderburn Road

The original *Three Gables*, Fitzjohns Avenue, by Norman Shaw, *archive*.

The graceful, mature tree perfectly complements the architecture of this beautiful home.

Originating from the grounds of old *Rosslyn House*, the western part of Wedderburn Road was constructed in 1884, but the early development was only on the south side. Here we find some gracious properties designed by the highly-respected local Victorian architect, Horace Field, who also designed Lloyd's Bank on Rosslyn Hill. Formerly known as simply *The Gables*, its symmetrical composition is said to be a simplified version of Norman Shaw's grand *Three Gables* that once stood at the lower end of Fitzjohn's Avenue. Shaw's original *Three Gables* was constructed in 1881 for Frank Holl RA, a successful portrait painter. It was replaced in the 1930s by a Marie Curie Hospital, which was bombed during WWII. Despite Shaw's formidable reputation and impressive house, from looks alone, one might consider Horace Field's *The Gables* to be the more charming house. Dating from about 1886, the Grade II-listed *The Gables* on Wedderburn Road is a fabulous detached red brick mansion built in Stripped Tudor or Vernacular Revival style. Its small-paned windows are an excellent example of Field's "homely features". The doorway is centrally located and adorned with a shell-hooded gable. The house sits behind large double gates accessing a gravelled courtyard punctuated by a circular island. This features a mature tree underplanted with topiary and flowers, creating a most attractive central focal point.

Shelford Lodge, later sold to Charles Woodd and renamed *Rosslyn House,* O Jewitt 1869, later hand colour.

The grand gateway accessing the carriage drive to *Rosslyn House* before Lyndhurst Gardens was built up. Note the ball-topped column outside the lodge on the right.

Lyndhurst Road

Lyndhurst Road was laid out and developed by Henry Davidson in the early 1860s. But when *Rosslyn House* was demolished in 1896, Lyndhurst Gardens (started 14 years previously) had to be widened. This change meant potentially sacrificing Samuel S Teulon's lodge by the main gate. Researcher Roy Allen has ascertained that local architect Horace Field was asked by Charles Woodd to save the lodge in 1883. Field achieved this by reducing its footprint and rebuilding the outer wall. In Lyndhurst Road, Field was definitely engaged in designing Nos.19, 20, 21 and possibly No.22.

Offered to the current owners off-market during the Covid period, the couple completed the purchase of Neo-Georgian No.20 Lyndhurst Road in August 2021. "We knew the area previously," say the owners. "We'd been living in London for about three years in Kensington and Queens Park and have always liked this area."

No.20 stands on land that was once part of the grounds of the Rosslyn Estate. Just beyond the rear garden, a delightful detached house can be glimpsed in Lyndhurst Gardens called *The Hoo* (see next page). This grand house was also designed by Horace Field and is said by architectural historian Alastair Service to be "one of the best pieces of architecture in Hampstead."

"When we first saw this Lyndhurst Road house we were impressed by its classic proportions and timeless elegance," the owners recall. "As soon as we started to imagine how to make it into a home for our family, we couldn't help but look into its past." With a view to restoring the interior, the owners are talking to designers and architects to decide the best way to proceed.

The reduced-size lodge with the relocated ball-topped column at the head of today's Lyndhurst Gardens.

Horrace Field designed Nos.19-21 – this is No.20 Lyndhurst Road.

67

Remarkable Homes of NW3

Pictureque cottage that once stood on the old Rosslyn Estate, *archive*.

Map of Lyndhurst Road as it was prior to joining Fitzjohn's Avenue, *Ordnance Survey map 1866-70, National Library of Scotland.*

The Queen Anne style *The Hoo,* designed by Horace Field, *c.*1888, "one of the best pieces of architecture in Hampstead."

"We feel that rather than owning the house, we are just looking after it for the time being. We want to preserve it for the future, as it's a beautiful piece of architecture and a lovely place to call home," they say. The couple particularly love their double-fronted house due to the lateral space it provides. Interestingly, every floor has the same layout, with smaller rooms in the front and larger rooms at the rear. A most unusual feature is the sizable hallway that extends to the right of the front door, and accessed through a pair of tall arches. This room to the right of the front door, probably once the main hallway, features a corner fireplace, as does the room above.

The living room, behind the wisteria-clad wall, has views over the garden. The former ground-floor dining room of No.20 is now the kitchen. "The kitchen is our favourite part of the house as we love to cook," enthuse the owners, "We feel it to be the heart of the home."

The owners set out to ascertain what the house looked like originally inside and how it adapted to the lives of its occupants since it was built in 1898. "With the support of the local Camden archives, we were able to retrieve the house plans and drawings from the 1940s and 1950s. At one point in the 1950s, there was an apartment on the second floor let to lodgers," they note. "And there was an elevator accessed to the left of the front door. The house was offered at auction in the 1950s, so the auction listing has a pretty detailed description of every room. We find it all really interesting."

The main gates to Nos.19-21 Lyndhurst Road are based on design elements of the gates to *Rosslyn House*.

One of pair of splendid arches that flank the entrance hall.

A quiet corner perfect for reading, set beside windows to the rear garden.

The owners became so enthralled that while researching the architecture of the property, they learned who was living here in the middle of the last century. They have identified previous residents from the 1901 census through to the census of 1938. "It's fascinating to see how people lived over the life of the house and, of course, in those days, they had servants," explain the owners. "The Singer family might have been the house's first residents, as they were recorded in the 1901 census," they continue. "David, a stockbroker (1874-1933), was the son of the 'Reverend' Simeon Singer, best known for his English translation of the *Authorised Daily Prayer Book* in 1890, informally known as the *Singer's Siddur*. David's wife Isabel was active in the suffragette movement and held at least one meeting at No.20 Lyndhurst Road, 'under the auspices of the Hampstead branch of the London Society for Women's suffrage'. Their daughter Ruth Seruya later became a Justice of the Peace and married the chief secretary to the government of Burma."

Extensive views of the London skyline from an upper floor of No.20 Lyndhurst Road. The chimney stacks of *The Hoo* are visible in the foregound, *owner's photo*.

The Mitchell family lived here from at least 1911; the son, George Abercromby Mitchell, became a politician. The family advertised in the press for cooks and washer-uppers. The famous architect Sir Andrew Taylor and Lord Cottesloe, chairman of the National Theatre, lived next door at No.21 in the 1910s and 1970s.

"These three buildings (Nos. 19, 20, 21) were commissioned by Russell Rea MP (1846-1916)," add the owners. "We couldn't find out whether they were sold initially or rented out. Originally, Rea's son was living next door at No.21 Lyndhurst Road, and Russell Rea himself lived in the magnificent detached No.22."

Russell Rea MP, 1906.

The ancient wisteria, nearly 100 years old, embraces the rear of the house.

The wisteria seen from the first floor landing window.

Old Conduit House, Lyndhurst Terrace

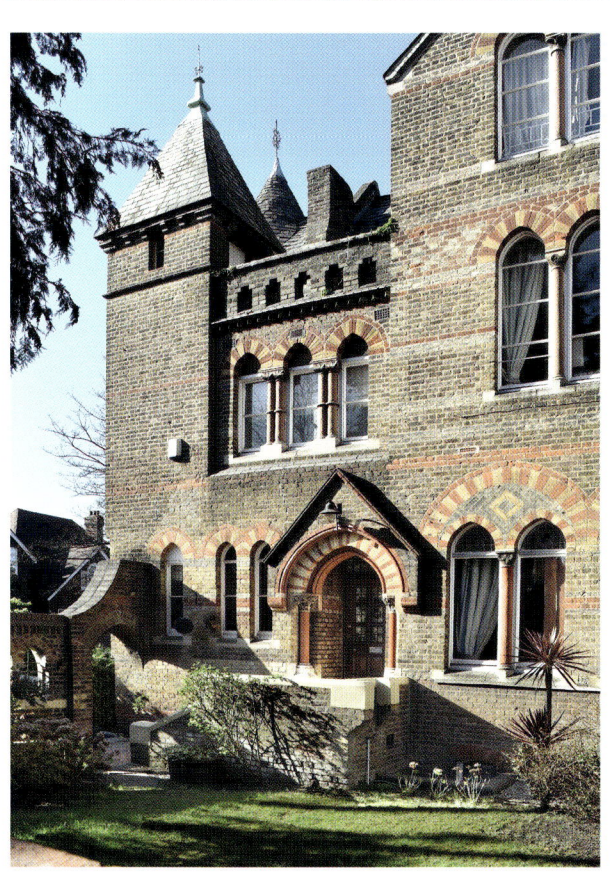

It's a delight to behold this remarkable pair of semi-detached flamboyant, turreted Gothic Revival houses located on the corner of Lyndhurst Road and Lyndhurst Terrace. Surely, they must be the largest pair of semis in London! Constructed in yellow stock brick with red and white brick dressings, bands and diaper decoration, these two listed Grade II* properties have a rather complex history. Initially, they were linked internally by a single connecting door but are now entirely independent. Today, *Old Conduit House* is the round-towered left-hand side of the building at No.1 Lyndhurst Terrace; its other half is today known as *Hall Place*, No.3 Lyndhurst Terrace.

A family affair, the two properties were built in 1864-5 for their own use, by architect John Burlison Sr (1810-1868) together with his son-in-law, Alfred Bell (1832-1895) of the firm Clayton and Bell. John Burlison Sr was a clerk of works and Sir George Gilbert Scott's chief assistant for over 25 years; his sister Jane married Alfred Bell. Scott was so impressed with the work of Alfred Bell that he took him into his firm as a pupil. And having trained both Clayton and Bell, he subsequently gave them many commissions after they had set up in partnership together in the mid 1850s.

The rectangular tower and impressive decorative brickwork of the eastern façade.

71

Remarkable Homes of NW3

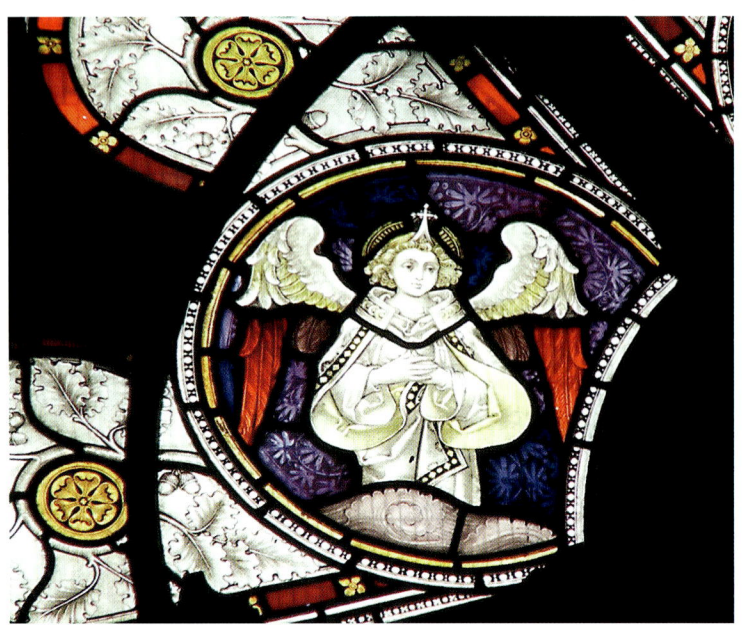

A surviving example of Clayton & Bell stained glass in St Stephens, Rosslyn Hill.

Burlinson's son, also John (1843-1891), was employed in the business side of Clayton and Bell, and in 1868 in partnership with Thomas Grylls, a fellow pupil at Clayton and Bell, he established Burlison & Grylls. Both companies, Clayton & Bell and Burlison & Grylls, were famous for the quality of their stained glass. Many of the original stained-glass windows for St Stephen's Church, Rosslyn Hill were by Clayton & Bell.

The circular tower, with its conical roof and stained-glass windows, sits adjacent to the rectangular tower with its corbelled oriel window.

Old Conduit House was thus occupied by the Burlisons and the Bells as two residences connected by that single internal door until the death of John Burlison Sr in 1868. Alfred Bell then combined the two residences into one, joining with Charles Buckeridge (1832-1873) in designing what has been described as "a wildly ornamented Gothic interior" for the newly converted single-residence building he renamed *Bayford House*. Charles Buckeridge was a student at the Royal Academy before becoming part of Scott's office as clerk of works for St Mary's, Oxford. He practised in Oxford from 1856-68 and in London from 1869 onwards. He was also the husband of Alfred Bell's sister-in-law.

The property has to this day retained many of the elaborate Gothic style interiors designed by Bell and Buckeridge. The surviving interior work, including fireplaces and of course, stained glass, is of fine quality.

After the death of Alfred Bell in 1895, the house was again divided into two, the turreted half retaining the name *Bayford House* and the other half, at that time, was named *Oswald House*. It wasn't until the artist and author Ernest Goodwin bought *Bayford House* in 1931 that the property acquired the name *Old Conduit House*. He renamed it some three years later, living there for a further ten years until his death in 1944. His widow remained in the house until 1994.

The name *Old Conduit House* is probably a nod to the old *Conduit Lodge* (see p74) that once stood on the corner with Fitzjohn's Avenue and to the nearby well. A number of pathways once led over the nearby fields to one of the most valuable resources of all – the water in Shepherd's Well. Once a primary source of Hampstead's water supply, the well was the headwater of a stream that's the main source of the River Tyburn. The narrow footpath known as Shepherd's Path runs up the side of *Hall Place* No.3 Lyndhurst Terrace. Built in the first half of the 1860s, Lyndhurst Terrace was initially called both Rosslyn Park and Windsor Terrace. The latter because Windsor Castle was said to be visible across the undeveloped Conduit fields. From 1939 Lyndhurst Terrace took precedence over these variations.

Inevitably disappearing when Fitzjohn's Avenue was built up in the 1870s, the former site of Shepherd's Well stands at the corner of Fitzjohn's Avenue and Lyndhurst Road. The River Tyburn now flows southwards in underground conduits to reach the Thames in Pimlico. A plaque located on the Thames Path near the Grosvenor pub lists all the locations under which it flows. These include Belsize Park, Regent's Park Lake and Buckingham Palace.

Old Conduit House interior, *archive image*.

The circular tower staircase with the original stained glass, *photo Savills*.

The original Shepherd's Well in 1820, wood engraving 1878, later hand colour.
The water was very pure and apparently never froze, even in the hardest of winters. Sometimes having to queue at the well in the summertime water carriers made doorstep deliveries, charging a penny a bucket.

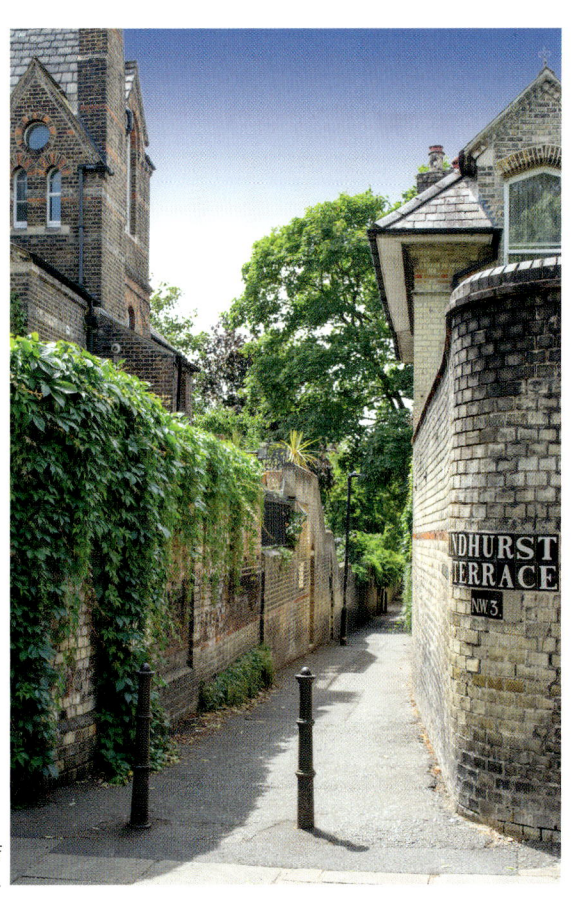

Shepherd's Path runs along the side of Hall Place, linking to Fitzjohn's Avenue.

The original *Conduit Lodge*, archive.

Conduit Lodge, Lyndhurst Road

Lyndhurst Road was laid out in the early 1860s, and in 1883 it was extended to the junction of Akenside Road and Fitzjohn's Avenue. This is where the old Shepherd's Well was located (see previous page). It is also where Shepherd's Path links to Fitzjohn's Avenue and the site of a once picturesque house known as *Conduit Lodge.*

As we saw previously (p72), John Burlison and Alfred Bell built *Old Conduit House.* But after Burlison died, it would appear from the record that in 1877 Alfred Bell acquired land from Sir Spencer Maryon-Wilson that extended from the garden of *Old Conduit House* westwards towards Fitzjohn's Avenue. A pair of semi-detached houses were built on this plot many years later. These became Nos.39 & 41 Lyndhurst Road. Interestingly, No.41 was named *Conduit Lodge*, no doubt in memory of the *original Conduit Lodge* that once stood on the corner by the old Shepherd's Well. It is this property that we are looking at here. These days it belongs to an American family. Having relocated from the United States and previously residing in Hampstead, one day they came across this house, conveniently located close to where they were living. The couple also looked at *Old Conduit House* on the corner of Lyndhurst Terrace, which, back then, was similarly priced. They recall that while *Old Conduit House* has elaborate interiors, at the time it suffered from severe dampness in the basement, requiring extensive remedial and renovation work.

Ultimately, they decided on *Conduit Lodge*, acquiring the property in 2005. Over the next 18 months the house was renovated, and during that process they found electrical sockets with unearthed 5-amp two-pin wiring dating from around 1936! Hopes of discovering the original spindles concealed within the staircase panelling led to disappointment. Outside, a massive WWII air raid shelter, large enough for six bunk beds, was removed and the rear garden landscaped.

In the early C20, *Conduit Lodge* was home to a family of renowned Doctors. Its very first occupants in the 1930s were Berthe and Carl Heinz Goldman. Fleeing Nazi Germany in 1933, he had set up a highly successful London practice. Famous patients included Elizabeth Taylor and Kay Kendall. His son, John M Goldman (1938-2013) became the world-renowned leader in studies of chronic myeloid leukaemia and a pioneer in bone marrow transplants in Europe. Considered by his colleagues as "a man you could meet once and never forget," Professor Goldman was also recognised as "a towering figure in British and international haematology."

The family finally settled in during 2007 and this they did with great flair. Inside the elegant front living room, a sizable Chinese wall hanging adorns one wall, its colours echoed by the wood cabinet below it and the handrail of the staircase. The new spindles, installed using an innovative triple grouping, can be glimpsed through the doorway to the hall. Linked by a console table and a writing corner, the rear living room's French doors open onto the garden. The inset TV above the fireplace faces the sofa, and flanked by two large bookcases, another stunning Chinese wall hanging complements the exquisite colour palette used throughout these rooms. Having transformed *Conduit Lodge* and with their children fully grown up, the owners created the Little Library book swop. Using its meticulously crafted door set into the front garden wall, local residents 'Take a book, leave a book' on a daily basis. ▪

Remarkable Homes of NW3

Belsize Crescent

D E

Belsize Crescent as it was c.1900, *archive*.

Belsize Crescent – No.21 in the centre has the white-painted chimney stack.

Belsize Crescent (originally Prince Consort Road) just about fitted into the space available. This was the very first development project in Hampstead by William Willett Sr in 1871.

Although described by Pevsner as "Rather cramped Italianate houses," the crescent has considerable consistency, with balustrading, classical surrounds to the windows, slate roofs, and barrel-shaped dormers. Twiggy, or Lesley Hornby, used to live here in the 1960s. And for many years, No.13 was the home of German composer Berthold Goldschmidt. His expertise on Gustav Mahler helped to complete Mahler's unfinished 10th Symphony in 1960.

No.21 Belsize Crescent is the focus of our attention. One of its first owners in the mid 1870s, was John H Mummery, a renowned dental surgeon who became president of the British Dental Association in 1899. Then in the late 1870s, the building became a lodging house. And so it remained until 1883. The property was divided into flats in the early 1930s. One of the residents in the 1940s was stage and film actress Vida Hope, who was friends with Dirk Bogarde. She played with Alec Guinness in the movie, *The Man in the White Suit* in 1951.

Chantal and Neil were particularly keen on this house as it was in extremely good condition even though it needed a few changes, but they were gazumped just as they were about to complete. Fortunately, the gazumper's deal fell through, and much relieved, the couple were able to acquire the house after all. "We redid the kitchen a few years ago," Neil says, "along with some modifications to the lower ground floor. Otherwise, the basic layout of the house has remained pretty much the same."

No.21 Belsize Crescent with Daleham Mews beyond.

The family's 14-year old dog Ezzie moves slowly towards a favourite chair.

View across the living room to the garden.

"Amazingly, there was no storage anywhere, so we had to take care of rectifying that. I'm pleased the kitchen is on the ground floor," says Chantal. "The flooring is Brazilian hardwood installed by the previous owner. There are some original floorboards though, on the upper floors," she adds. The metalwork on the staircase is a reproduction of a section that was recovered from the original staircase. "But we did change the sash windows in the front bay and reinstate the front bay ironwork," adds Neil. "We also decided to paint the house number on the two columns at the front as many houses have done on Belsize Park Gardens."

Moving to the rear of the house, "The garden was best described as a building site, so we completely reworked it," says Neil. The house sits is on the Crescent's curve, which means it widens at the rear giving the garden not only a rather unusual L-shape layout but also direct access to Daleham Mews through a charming gateway.

The elegant staircase with its reproduction metalwork.

Part of the delightful rear garden.

View to No.21 Belsize Crescent through the Daleham Mews gateway.

Rosslyn Grove, Rosslyn Hill

Long before the 1883-4 construction of Lyndhurst Hall Congregational Church within the grounds of the Rosslyn Estate, the site was occupied by the villa *Rosslea*. Adjacent to *Rosslea* stood an even older villa, *Rosslyn Grove*. This magnificent house, a rare survivor from *c.*1770 was built for John Stokes. According to local historian Roy Allen, the first resident of note appears to be Thomas Roberts, a broker, in 1880. Today, architect Alfred Waterhouse's Victorian church has become Air Studios, while *Rosslyn Grove*, one of the oldest houses still remaining in Belsize, is listed Grade II and known today as No.11 Rosslyn Hill. The detached villa, in brown brick with red brick dentil cornice and pediments, is arranged over 2 storeys, with an attic and a semi-basement.

As Christopher Wade explains in *The Belsize Story*, "It was probably the dower house of the Earl of Rosslyn. It was noted as a residence in the early C20 [1896-1993] when the social reformer Thomas Hancock Nunn [1859-1937] lived here."

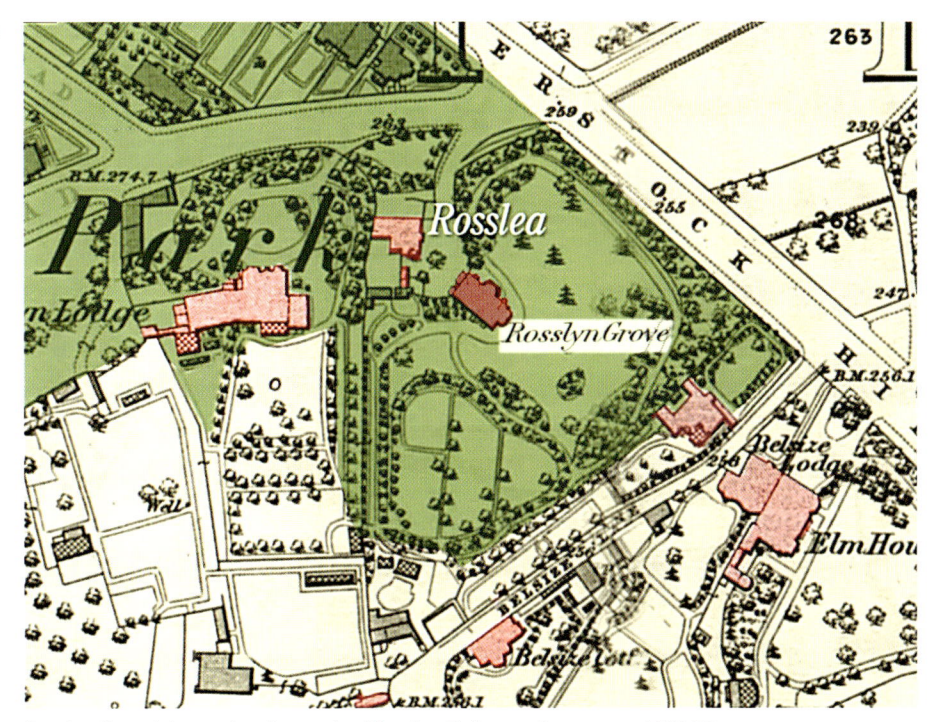

Rosslyn Grove is located to the south of *Rosslea*, Ordnance Survey map 1866-70, National Library of Scotland.

The original late C18 staircase.

Timber Doric portico, and a round-arched doorway with a patterned fanlight and panelled door.

The glorious dining room.

Back in 2009, the current owners were looking for a suitable home when one day, as they recall, "We came across an advertisement in the *Financial Times* for this house on Rosslyn Hill and thought we might like it." It seemed the vendors didn't want to use an estate agent, so they only advertised it in the *FT*. "We took a look at the details and we agreed, 'This looks perfect for us'."

When the couple decided to buy the five-bedroomed house in October 2012, the agents told them it had been used as the Manse for the Congregational Church, but there is no confirmed evidence of that claim. Some remodelling works are known to have taken place in the 1950s, but the building had deteriorated somewhat by the late 1960s. A report produced by the Historical Society on the history of the house concludes that the bay window in the living room may be the only original late-C18 windows in the property.

"The previous owners had redone the house and redecorated it back in the 1970s," the owners recall. Since then, further restoration has taken place. "We worked with interior decorator Brandon

Schubert to arrive at the current decorations and general internal design." The living room is the family's favourite room. The wall colour in the living room is gorgeous; it was chosen to be cosy in the wintertime while looking lovely and fresh in the summer.

The owners haven't touched the fireplaces, of which only one might be original. Much of the furniture in the house is family furniture and some was acquired more recently. The building does have one listed interior item – a wardrobe that has to be retained somewhere in the house as part of the listing.

"This is most the most amazing house to live in – it's truly exceptional," say the owners. "And being next door to the famous Air Studios sometimes you hear dramatic music and you think, 'Oh, I wonder if that's the new *Batman* theme'."

Having moved to Hampstead, the family has breathed fresh life and joy into this remarkable old house and they find the area a wonderful place in which to live. Working from home, the couple consider it one of life's great pleasures to be able to walk their children to school every day. They enjoy Belsize Village and often go there for lunch. "We are pleased with what has been done to create the Belsize Village Streatery – it's such a wonderful community experience." ∎

The front part of the living room – the family's favourite room.

An original late-C18 three-bay canted window and shutters in the living room.

A cosy sitting room in the semi-basement.

81

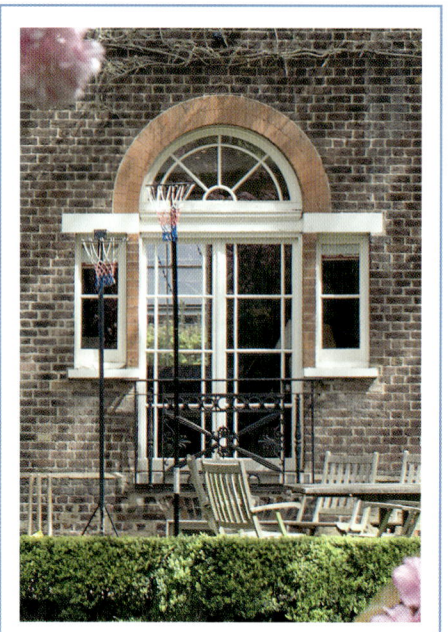

The living room's delightful early-C20 Venetian-style window with pilasters and doors to the garden.

The family dog shows off a corner of the room.

Garden view of No.11 Rosslyn Hill with Air Studios to the left.

Pond Street

The imposing front entrance to No.3 Pond Street.

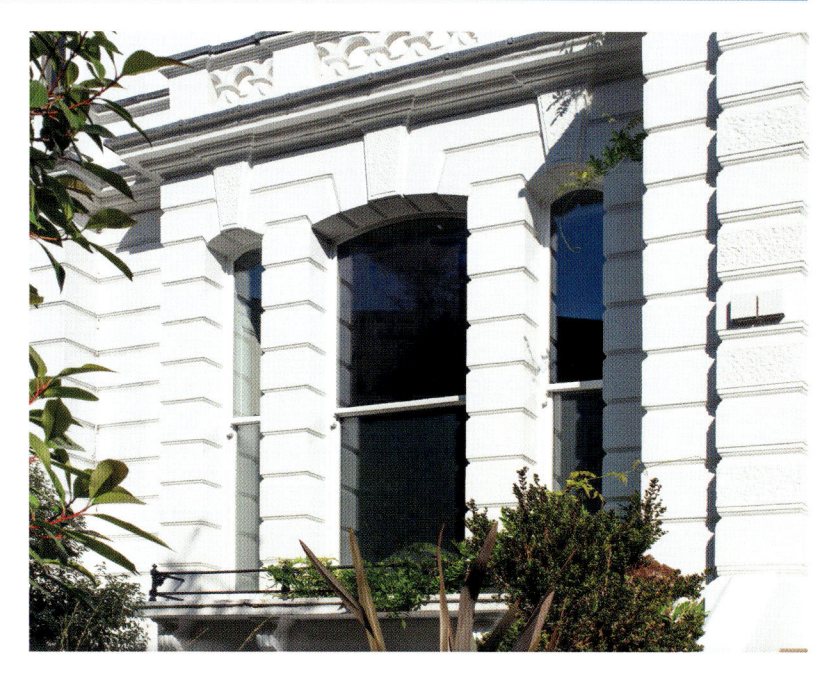

Majestically positioned at the head of Pond Street, one of the oldest roads in Hampstead, this imposing and substantial villa makes a bold statement. The street dates back to at least the early 1700s, and built of brick this stucco-fronted villa was part of the adjoining Hampstead Hill Gardens development project of the late 1860s. No.3 Pond Street is simply a magnificent, gorgeous-looking house. With its prominent external detailing, including segmental-arched windows and keystones, the property extends over four floors and has retained many of its original elements and features within.

The living room with its large windows.

One of the original fireplaces.

The internal architectural elements include extra high ceilings and wonderfully large windows that fill the rooms with daylight. The two grand reception rooms on the raised ground floor are now one large space. The floor-to-ceiling sash windows combine to make these rooms feel both elegant and bright, while the dramatically strong, dark-coloured walls create an intimate atmosphere as the light fades in the evening. Additionally, the house is replete with ornate plasterwork, wall mouldings and original marble fireplaces.

Both the marble fireplaces in the main living area are original, confirmed by the knowledge that there are similar ones in the immediate neighbourhood. It's not always easy to retain such features on a renovation project, especially when fitting new pipework and wiring. Therefore, in the end, the owners have created a modern house within a traditional structure. And in completing this project, the building has been allowed to tell its own story. When restoring the beautiful staircase for example, the well-worn stone was left bare, revealing its history and demonstrating that the house has been lived in for a very long time. ■

The Roebuck Hotel nearby was the highest building on the street when it was built in the 1860s. Pond Street grew in importance due to the discovery of the Hampstead Wells, and became the preferred route by which early carriage visitors journeyed up to Well Walk. In the early 1800s, Pond Street was home to so many 'high-class' doctors it became known as the Harley Street of Hampstead. These luminaries included Baron Dimsdale who had earned a reputation in the new field of smallpox inoculation. Then there was Dr Thomas Goodwin, who discovered another medicinal spring, called New Spa on the Heath near South End Green, and in 1804 published his findings as *An Account of the Neutral Saline Waters recently discovered at Hampstead.*

The dining area overlooking the rear garden.

The cornices in the reception rooms and the hallway are original.

Certain areas remain intentionally 'unfinished' to reveal this house's age and usage. Note the original etched glass window.

Pond Street *c.1750* long before St Stephen's Church was built, *William H Prior,* hand-coloured engraving.

85

Remarkable Homes of NW3

Hampstead Hill Gardens

The charming No.10 Hampstead Hill Gardens is built in red brick with a white painted gable end, while No.12 on the left is fully rendered and painted white.

The front door with its original stained glass.

Gently curving over the former estate of George Crispin, Hampstead Hill Gardens serves as a link between Rosslyn Hill and Pond Street. Constructed during the early 1870s, this thoroughfare enhances its surroundings with its distinctive architectural styles. Nos.10 & 12 are an attractive pair of semi-detached brick houses. No.12 is fully rendered and painted white. In contrast, No.10 displays its original red brick façade. The only subtle nod to its neighbouring counterpart is the rendered white-painted dormer that graces No.10. Step inside No.10, and you enter an interior that bears witness to its evolution as a cherished family home over nearly one hundred and fifty years.

Penelope Rowlatt and her husband purchased No.10 Hampstead Hill Gardens in 1966 for £17,750, so she has lived in the house for 57 Years. Sadly, her husband died five years ago, and this is where they brought up their children, three girls and a boy. "I was born in Highgate and, as a teenager, used to walk across Hampstead Heath and wander around Hampstead," says Penelope. "I used to swim in the women's bathing pond

Part of the living room bay.

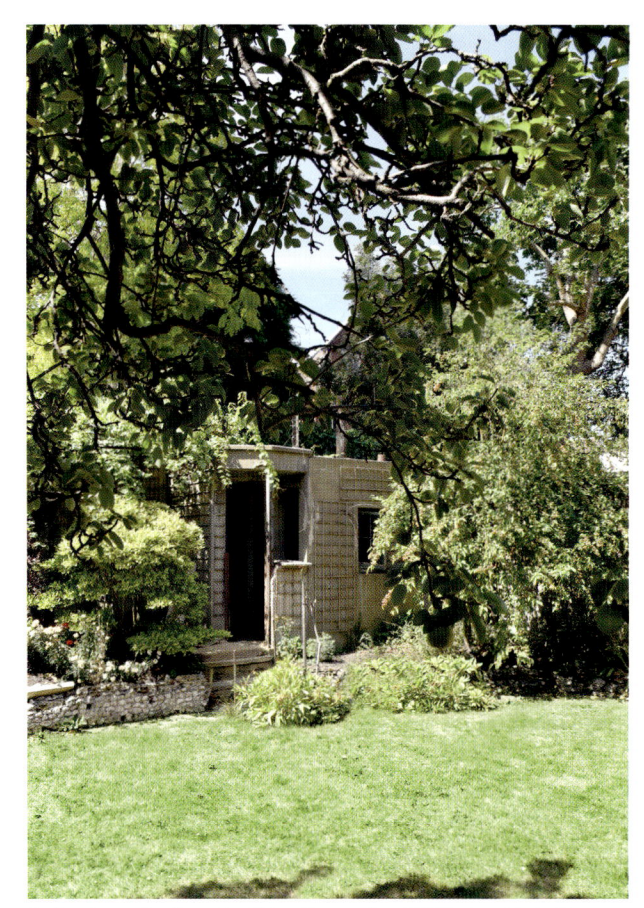

A vine is gradually entombing the surface WWII air raid shelter built in the garden of No.10.

and still walk on the Heath every day," she adds. "During the pandemic, I would go to the Heath early in the morning and encounter a bunch of people doing the same thing at around 7 o'clock. These days six of us who went on these walks often get together for breakfast at Roni's on Swains Lane."

Starting as a theoretical physicist, Penelope studied quantum mechanics, took time off to have her children, became an economist, and worked at the Treasury. While there, she wrote a seminal book on inflation published in 1993. "I have been an economist for most of my working life," she says. "After retiring, I went back to studying and this time it was philosophy of mind."

Fortunately, the house has retained many of its original features, including its attractive front entrance, with the stained glass panelling of the front door. Principally, the whole property is very much as it was when built. However, this home is of particular note as, remarkably, it has a surviving surface-built WWII air raid shelter still standing in the corner of the delightful garden. "It's extremely solidly built in thick, reinforced concrete, left pretty much as it was, and is now mostly covered by a vine," notes Penelope. "There is a similar one in the garden of the adjoining house, but it is now disguised to look like a shed."

The stucco villas at the lower end of the road were completed in the early 1870s at around the same time as Nos.1-3 Pond Street. Many of the redbrick Queen Anne-style properties on the road were constructed from 1875 onwards by Batterbury & Huxley. The semi-detached pair of Nos.10 & 12 were built just a little later than that. Aldous and Maria Huxley lived further on at No.18 in 1919, while No.14 was home to Sir John Summerson (see p17) in the 1930s.

Original architect's drawing by Batterbury & Huxley of the front elevation of a house for Andrew Miller MD built on the corner of Hampstead Hill Gardens, (today's No.12 Rosslyn Hill), *The Building News,* March 1878.

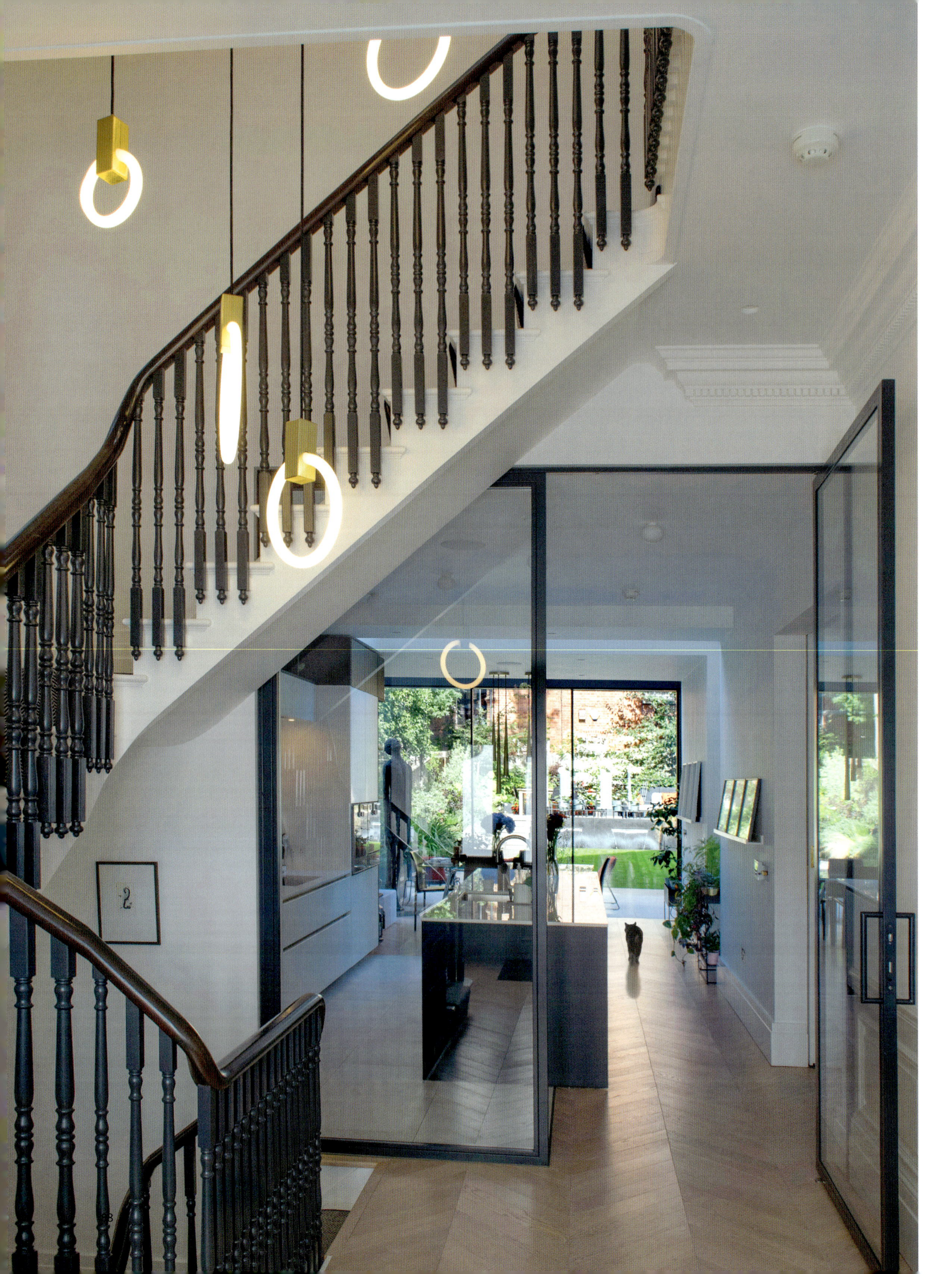
2

Arkwright Road

Standing tall on Arkwright Road, and built in the mid-1870s, the immediate attraction of this semi-detached property is its architectural detailing. The prominent front angular bay extends from the lower ground floor with a brick balustrade bridging the front porch, leading the eye to the upper floors and the contrasting brickwork.

Visitors climbing the stone steps to the generously proportioned front door of No.40 are duly rewarded with a marvellous view through the light-filled oasis in an exceptional home.

Originally from the United States, Brian Chadwick, a corporate lawyer, recalls: "We first moved to the area in 2000 when we lived in Shirlock Road." Dr Gitta Madani, a consultant head and neck radiologist, has always sought out properties that required total renovation. "We had renovated the Shirlock Road house," she explains, "but after ten years, we wanted to move on. We found an agent, Natalie Malka, who started looking around for us and came up with No.40 Arkwright Road." At the time, it was owned by a single family but was divided into three apartments. "Although one flat had been partially developed, they were all in a pretty poor shape," adds Gita. The entire house was in dire need of some major refurbishment. The ground floor was a one-bedroom flat with many small rooms and a bathroom – where the staircase is now.

"We put our Shirlock Road house on the market in 2015 and it sold in about 48 hours!" says Brian. "After that, we were able to negotiate a deal for the purchase of this entire house, as the freeholder had just passed away."

Gitta explains: "So in 2015, we were the owners of No 40 Arkwright Road. The very first thing we did was clean the place! We knew we had to gut everything, and take the building right back to its bare brick walls. We decided to live on the lower ground floor while planning the project. We used different architects for various stages of the project but the initial concept was developed with Pitman Tozer Architects in Marylebone. By the time we put in for our planning, we had spent 18 months thinking about it carefully." During this time the couple changed things around, and in the end, made the ground floor into a large, open-plan living space.

"It is very unusual to enjoy such a clear line of sight in a London house – there is nearly always a wall or two in the way," Gitta continues. "I knew how I wanted the kitchen layout – the design had to be both functional and beautiful. The colour scheme developed over time, and I made the final selections," she adds.

"The longer we lived in the house, the better we understood the possibilities, says Brian. "Observing where the sun was at different times of the day kept refining our thinking. Apart from the extension and the new staircase, we were very respectful of

View from the entrance of No.40 Arkwright Road. The owners wanted an unobstructed view of the garden from the front door.

the original house. We retained the initial proportions – especially upstairs, as the Victorians knew exactly what they were doing." And Gitta adds: "My poor 11-year-old daughter, who was promised this beautiful house, was very accommodating, because for ages she had a tiny little space with just a window into the kitchen."

"We were lucky to find Sam Malka of Invigorate Homes, a local contractor who also managed the project. We moved out in September 2017, followed immediately by the demolition guys arriving, then the work started," says Brian. "We rented a place in West Hampstead for 18 months during the works." It really was back to brick. Everything from the ground to the roof came off. "You could stand on the dirt and see the sky. There were days when we thought a strong wind could blow the whole house over!" says Gitta.

"We moved back in March 2019; and the house was coming together by July. Outside, all the external brickwork was cleaned and repointed, but the garden was not really started," recalls Brian. "The garden has been through many iterations," he continues. "The hard landscaping is version seven. The garden sloped upwards considerably; hence it was decided to terrace it at the far end. This design enabled the two delightful water features to be incorporated. Gitta

This view from the kitchen towards the front door shows how the staircase crosses the full height glass partition.

is responsible for the garden planting, ensuring that at any time there are flowers in bloom. We particularly love sitting outside in the garden in the evenings," he says.

"We absolutely love the house, there are five bedrooms plus a large study," says Gitta. "It's a truly uplifting space and a real privilege to live here. Light floods in everywhere." And Brian continues, "I love to walk around the house looking at the elements that Gitta and Paula, our interior designer from Balance Designs, created. They climbed up scaffolding to hang string models of the long drop lights that now fill the centre of the tall staircase. These pendant lights were designed by the Canadian designer Matthew McCormick. Originally, there were no stairs down to the lower ground floor. Gitta designed the full staircase featuring the spindles affixed to the outer ends of the stair treads, arranged in sets of three." A truly inspired design detail.

"As a full-time doctor at Charing Cross and St Mary's, and having a private practice I don't think I slept for four years," recalls Gitta. ∎

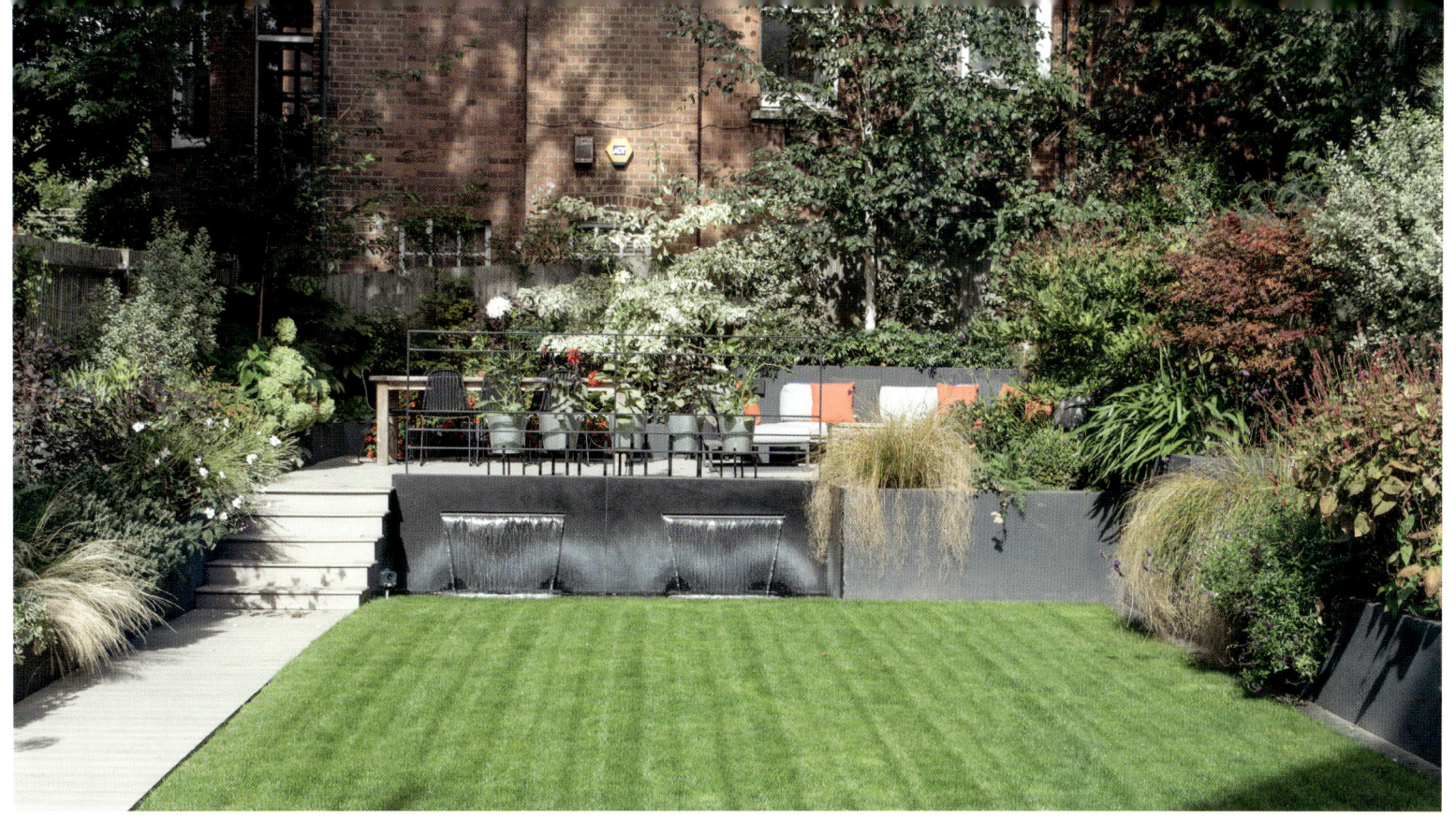

View from the kitchen to the beautifully planned garden with waterfalls on the terrace wall.

The fresh, contemporary atmosphere in the sitting room is enriched by the grey sofas with dark blue cushions complementing the interior design. A murmuration flies over the working chimney. All the fireplaces are from Chesneys and are a modification of a minimalist style.

The colour scheme extends to the primary bedroom.

At the time of building Fitzjohn's Avenue (from 1869), it was decided a route was needed between Fitzjohn's Avenue, across Frognal, linking to Finchley Road. Arkwright Road became that conduit, extended from the Greenhill Estate around 1874-78, and many of the houses were constructed at that time.

The westward development of the road continued, and most of the houses were completed by 1880. Sir Ralph Richardson lived on the opposite side of the road at No.27 in 1924.
And Hampstead's first Central Public Library (opened by Sir Henry Harben, see p25) was built at the foot of the hill in 1897.

Chester House, Langland Gardens

The origins of Langland Gardens date back to the late C19. The name probably derives from 'lang' meaning 'long', and 'land' or 'territory'. However, it is such an unusual name; who knows – there might just be a literary connection with William Langland – a poet from the Middle English period of literature and author of *Piers Plowman*. Langland Gardens runs almost directly northwards from Finchley Road to Frognal Lane and follows a virtually straight demarcation visible on the Hampstead 1866 map.

The current proprietors of *Chester House* at No.8 Langland Gardens are Olivia Barata Cavalcanti and Fabrizio Formisano. Olivia's roots are in the vibrant Brazilian city of Rio, while Fabrizio's origins lie in Italy. After residing in New York, they arrived in London in 2018 faced with the daunting task of selecting a location in which to set up home with their two children, aged 2 and 5.

Fortunately, Olivia had a friend already living in the UK and she recommended the couple consider Hampstead. In her view, not only was it a liberal, intellectual and cultural hub, its atmosphere and charm exuded all the characteristics they were looking for in a place to settle. Hampstead, she told them, is London's equivalent of New York's Upper West Side. So, after some exploration and initially renting in Bracknell Gardens, "When we weren't sure whether we were actually going to like living here or not," says Olivia, "we realised our friend was right. We decided to stay, and we just love the villagey atmosphere."

Looking for a permanent home Olivia and Fabrizio scoured various online listings. They chanced upon this particular property and thought it worth a look, despite the particulars lacking any visuals. Walking around the corner from Bracknell Gardens they were instantly captivated by the house and its feel. "As soon as I saw it I thought, 'Yes!' and we made an offer the following day," recalls Olivia.

Langland Gardens was laid out around 1891, with No.8 under construction by 1897. During this period EH & HT Cave built 17 houses on the road. One of a pair of semi-detached houses, the tall Dutch gable is a distinctive feature. The original staircase adds a unique touch to the property while the large windows illuminate the interior with plenty of natural light, resulting in a serene and welcoming ambiance. The ground floor hardwood flooring has undergone meticulous sanding and re-polishing, with its colour perfectly matched to the upstairs flooring. The first-floor primary bedroom extends from the front of the house right through to the back.

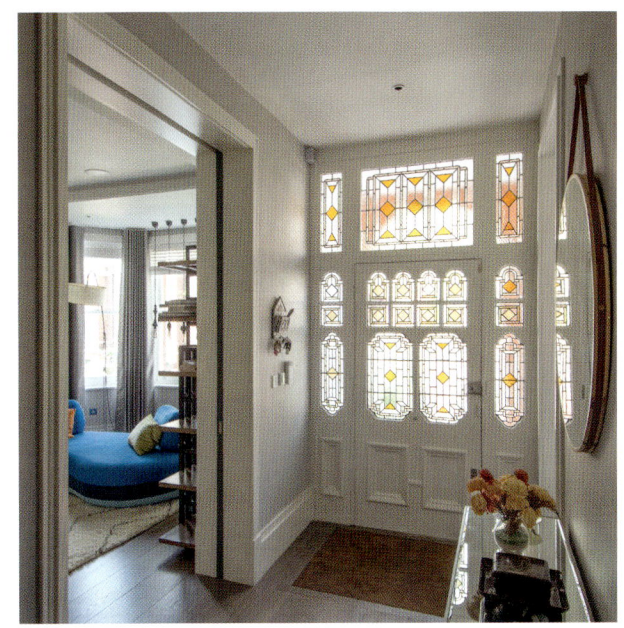

The marvellous original stained glass front door.

Books and games feature in this part of the living room that looks towards the front bay.

Full height folding wooden doors enable the division of the living room into two separate spaces.

Remarkable Homes of NW3

Full-width sliding doors and the overhead glass roof bring the garden into the dining area.

Excellent use of the structural elements increases the kitchen storage. And the sideboard's colours are cleverly balanced by the lighting over the kitchen worktop.

The living room opens up to reveal an L-shaped dining and kitchen area, with wall-to-wall, floor-to-ceiling sliding doors that provide direct access to the garden. "We used to have quite a large garden and this one is more of a terrace," observes Olivia. But although it's not as extensive as the one they were used to previously, a picturesque waterfall feature adds to the overall allure of the rear garden area, while a beautiful Magnolia tree graces the front garden.

The family also has full access to the communal Frognal Lane Gardens spanning several acres, with many mature trees, conveniently located just across the road. ∎

Cecil Beaton (1904-1980), photographer, painter and designer for stage and screen was born at No.21 Langland Gardens in 1904, and lived there until the family moved to Templewood Avenue in 1911. His work is especially remembered for his glamorous costumes for the Ascot scene in *My Fair Lady*, winning him an Oscar for Best Costume Design.

Prince Arthur Road

Running between the upper end of Fitzjohn's Avenue and Greenhill, just off Hampstead High Street, lies the relatively short eastern section of Prince Arthur Road. The road was initially laid out around 1874 with a number of substantial detached and semi-detached houses, several of which were designed by the architect T K Green.

The large, late Victorian house at No.10 is architecturally distinct from these properties. Constructed in terracotta brick with compact double gables and unusual brickwork design features, it has two front bays extending out beyond the lower ground floor. It is now the only detached house on this stretch of the road.

No.10 Prince Arthur Road has belonged to Neil Sikka and Nicola Bustin since 2011. "We started out on Goldhurst Terrace, and from there we moved to Aberdare Gardens," says Nicola, a corporate lawyer. "It wasn't easy to find what we were looking for, so we rented for a couple of years," she recalls. "But eventually in 2011 we found this house. It's a large five-bedroom property with two studies, built in 1880 with an interesting history."

Nicola explains the background. "Originally, it would have had a totally different front entrance and steps. We retained the bits we liked and removed the parts that didn't work so well for us – it took 18 months to complete the alterations, so we have only been living in the house for just over a decade." The architects John Pawson and Claudio Silvestrin had earlier remodelled the place for Victoria Miro who runs a wonderful contemporary art gallery in London.

The remodelled front door was moved to a new location at the side.

The two front bays extend out beyond the lower ground floor.

"During the time that Victoria Miro lived here she wanted some gallery space, and that included adjusting the hallway to make it wider," says Nicola. Her husband Neil Sikka, a dental surgeon by profession, is especially interested in architecture and architectural detailing. "Although the internal proportions of the spacious living/dining room are the same as the original," says Neil, "it was previously one large open space. We created the central fireplace and installed walnut doors."

These were not the only adjustments they made. "We kept the original white walls," Neil continues, "but interestingly, these were floating without any skirting, so we added the small skirting detail."

The previous large open space with the two front bays now has a central fireplace.

View from the kitchen over the first floor terrace accross the garden extending as far as Perrins Court and beyond. The rectangular light well on the right is one of two providing additional light to the playroom below.

The couple also changed the kitchen. "The massively heavy floor-to-ceiling glass doors to the terrace were installed along with the kitchen by the previous owners," notes Nicola. "They are good for protection against any noise and inclement weather, but we chose to change the layout and remodel the kitchen to take full advantage of the light and the extensive view."

The lower ground floor under the kitchen and terrace was also redesigned and is where Neil built a large TV/chillout space.

Indeed, the kitchen is bathed in light thanks to those sliding glass doors that provide expansive views across the full-width terrace and out over their garden towards Perrin's Lane in the far background.

Nicola and Neil have created a fabulous haven for their family and friends. "My children are really fond of this house and never want us to give it up," says Nicola. A true testament to the design of their remarkable home.

Prince Arthur Road was named in 1872 after Prince Arthur (the 1st Duke of Connaught and Strathearn and son of Queen Victoria) had inaugurated *Monroe House*, a home for the Sailors' Orphan Girls on nearby Fitzjohn's Avenue, designed by Edward Ellis and completed in 1869. Living at the opposite end of Prince Arthur Road was the fashionable landscape & seascape painter and friend of Charles Dickens, Clarkson Stanfield RA. From 1847 to 1865, he resided in 'this venerable house' as he referred to *Greenhill*, the corner property which shared its name with the small road linking Prince Arthur Road to Hampstead High Street. His home was later renamed *Stanfield House* and used as the Hampstead Subscription Library from 1884 (see next page).

Monroe House, Fitzjohn's Avenue.

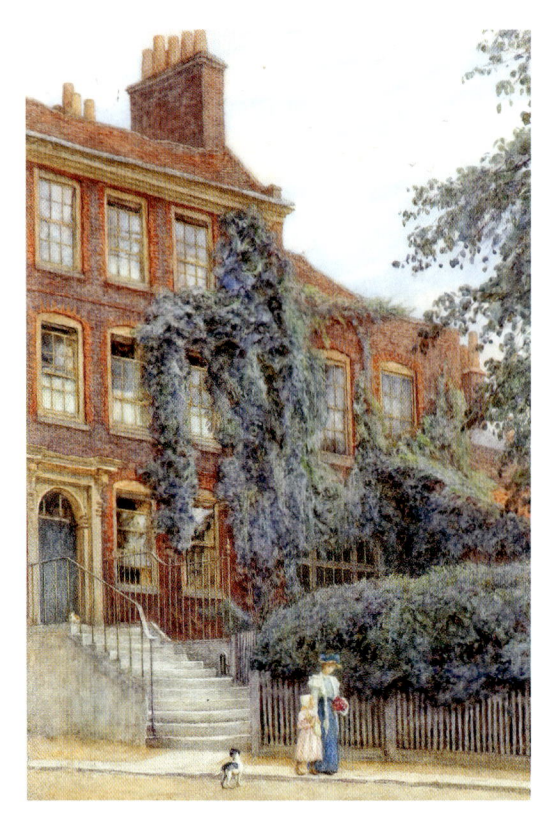

The Grade II* *Stanfield House*, by Helen Allingham RWS *c*.1899, *archive image*. Formerly known as *Greenhill*, the Wisteria covering the blocked windows has been kept in check, but the rest of the house is much the same today. Continuing around the corner, it is interesting to compare the buildings on the Hampstead High Street over 100 years apart.

Nos.82 & 83 Hampstead High Street, 1911, *AR Quinton*.

Nos.82 & 83 Hampstead High Street, springtime 2022.

Downshire Hill c.1842.

Downshire Hill north side

Sloping gently down towards the Heath, Downshire Hill is regarded as one of Hampstead's finest streets. So much so that a number of writers, musicians and painters have lived on Downshire Hill over the years. These include John Constable, who moved from Heath Street in 1826 to live for a short time further down the hill at No.2 Langham Place. He settled with his family a year later at No.40 Well Walk (see p162).

Development of the Downshire Hill triangle commenced during the Regency period, when the Lower Heath Quarter, as the area between Pond Street and Flask Walk was first known, saw significant development in the first part of C19. William Coleman was an early developer, followed by William Woods from 1817 onwards. Woods designed and built St John's Downshire Hill and likely most of the houses in the locality. And in all probability, the road was named after the 1st Marquess of Downshire (1718-93), Wills Hill, the Secretary of State for the American colonies. Resident Ian D Thompson suggests it's just as likely that Arthur Hill, the 3rd Marquess of Downshire was a candidate, and the street is probably named in honour of the peerage itself.

Downshire Hill today is a true delight. This dignified development comprises a number of stuccoed brick Regency-style villas embellished with cast-iron balconies, bay windows and canopies. Many of the houses are listed. Once described as the *Manor House* and said to be the oldest house on Downshire Hill, built c.1818, No.9 is set back from the road, enjoying a 45-foot frontage.

The reconstructed Regency-style house – No.9 Downshire Hill.

Part of the formal living room – this colour scheme has been retained throughout the ground floor and lower floor living areas.

Today there are new proud owners of this rebuilt property. These owners knew that when they bought their 'forever' house, it would need to be somewhere with six bedrooms.

While enjoying the *Belsize Walk* – the route that extends down to the Heath by way of Downshire Hill – they used to admire the varied architecture and lovely gardens. On one of their walks, the couple saw the hoardings around No. 9, sparking the prospect of settling in the area. This idea crystallised into their thinking about how wonderful it would be to live on this particular street. Then one day, when online, they saw the house was up for sale. The couple contacted the estate agent, and on entering the house, they proclaimed an excited "Wow!" It was everything the couple had always wanted. It was furnished, interior designed, and turnkey.

View across to the dining area.

The generous dining table can seat ten people with ease.

Very soon, they learned more of the history of the place, referring to the events surrounding the death in 2006 of the previous owner Allan Chappelow, whose family had owned the property since 1935. His father, Archibald Chappelow, recorded the details of his house in *The Old Home in England*: "Until about 20 years or so ago [it was] the Lord of the Manor's House. It is a well-nigh-perfect example of late Regency, built in 1823. The two front balconies, each a separate entity with its own floor and roof, are a most pleasing feature, the typical ironwork of simple but excellent design."

Allan Chappelow was a wealthy and reclusive journalist, author and photographer, but after he inherited the house, he failed to keep it in good order. One day Wang Yam, a Chinese exile, allegedly befriended Chappelow, apparently stealing his post and defrauding him. Following some suspicious transactions, his bank dispatched the police to Allan's home. Obliged to batter down the door, they eventually discovered Chappelow bludgeoned to death hidden beneath mountainous piles of papers. Wang was ultimately found guilty and sent to prison. But Wang has always denied involvement in the murder. Journalist and author Thomas Harding, who had lived five doors away at No.13a, and knew Allan by sight, later wrote a book detailing this mysterious affair. Titled *Blood on the Page*, it won the Gold Dagger prize for non-fiction in 2018. >

Imposing double doors lead from the hallway into the open-plan dining and living room areas.

The dilapidated frontage of No.9 Downshire Hill in September 2006. *Photo Adam Watson*, Historic England Archive.

The restored balconies. The view from the gate reveals how the front garden wall allows light to access the first basement level while affording it total privacy.

The family kitchen/dining area is located in the light and airy first level basement.

View onto the lower terrace with stone steps leading to the upper terrace level.

The lower level basement features a workout centre – here the pool is seen from the gymnasium.

Rear of No.9 Downshire Hill from the terrace steps shows how the upper terrace cleverly wraps around the house at ground floor level, then reaches out to access the garden and the descent to the lower terrace.

Following years of neglect, No.9 Downshire Hill was placed on the Buildings at Risk Register. Then, English Heritage and Camden Council agreed that the demolition of the existing building was justified. Numerous obstacles had to be overcome and many complaints were registered concerning the planned redesign. Nevertheless, the proposal to redevelop was granted at appeal after a Public Inquiry in 2011. Heritage Architecture Ltd (Stephen Levrant Heritage Architecture works exclusively with historic buildings and within conservation areas) was commissioned as lead architects as well as acting as heritage consultants. Unsurprisingly, all this reconstruction took a long time and the project wasn't completed until 2015. The building then stood empty for a while as the market had changed.

The present owners bought the property in 2017. They learned that while retaining its Regency style, the house is now somewhat larger internally, incorporating additional accommodation and facilities required by a modern house of this status.

This additional space was created by lateral extensions to the three floors above ground. They explain that Stephen Levrant cleverly incorporated a double basement into the structure, providing a vast family kitchen/dining area, spa, gymnasium and cinema room. As a result of Levrant's ingenious design concept, natural light extends right down into the basement levels, illuminating all the rooms.

The owners have ensured that the efforts of all concerned with the renovation project were not in vain; while creating a comfortable and happy family home, they appreciate the community spirit of Downshire Hill. Residents get together and discuss local issues like the redevelopment of the listed former Police Station and Magistrates Court, which is located at the top of the Hill.

The owners find it incredibly peaceful and enjoy the villagey feeling. They appreciate being so close to the Heath, the great pubs and so on. And then there's the wonderful sense of history with Keats Grove nearby.

No.34 Downshire Hill. the side extension on the left perfectly matches the original Regency building.

Downshire Hill south side

Peter and Lea Schwartz have put a great deal of love and attention into their home, preserving, reintroducing and highlighting its Regency features while combining it with modern design. "Lea spent her childhood in Soviet-era Czechoslovakia, and I grew up just outside of Detroit," says Peter, a lawyer, "We met when I was studying in the Czech Republic." His wife Lea is a sociologist and moved to the UK in 1998.

Before the couple started looking for their ideal property they were living at New End. "We wanted to stay in Hampstead – once you know Hampstead it's difficult to move away!" says Lea. "When we first saw No.34 Downshire Hill in 2013, it was decorated in full-blown Laura Ashley – cream carpets and wallpaper, circa 1985. "All the original cornices had been removed – except in the hallway – and the basement was damp," recalls Lea. "Another couple were looking at the house at the same time as us – they quickly ran out of the door; it felt so unwelcoming," Peter adds.

"It makes you want to cry because other houses in the area from the same period are well preserved, but we were both drawn towards its Regency architecture," continues Lea. "I like clean lines and simplicity, which appeals to me since my background is from a functionalist town

The basement levels on both sides of the house were slightly lowered, *owner's photo.*

An old outbuilding, prior to transformation.

in the Czech Republic. At the same time, I appreciate anything old, with a soul preserved and unaltered."

The problem with No. 34 is its listed status. But a big plus was that the house consisted of two distinct architectural entities. "The original Grade II building dates from 1820, while the side extension from 1920s was not affected by the listing," notes Lea. "So we were able to combine a modern approach with a traditional one in the original house." Viewed from the front, just the ground and first floors are apparent, while an additional basement level only becomes visible from the rear of the house.

Lea and Peter remained at New End for two years while the restoration and reconstruction works were underway. "The interior design concept is basically my idea; I was seeking a raw, natural, and simple result," says Lea. "We appointed McLaren Excel based on the work they had done previously, and while these architects were particularly sensitive to the period architecture of the original building, this young, progressive firm also understood our vision."

The architects specified re-using the same Douglas fir timber used for the concrete shuttering to fabricate the kitchen woodwork – the shuttering effect of the concrete and the woodwork match beautifully.

The basement levels of both the original house and the extension were lowered a little. All 3 storeys of the 1920s side extension were completely rebuilt and a new Corten-clad steel construction was added at the rear lower ground garden level which is now the kitchen-dining area. The architects designed its exterior steelwork for the rust effect (oxidation) to be sealed in. It only took six months to obtain the aged look.

The staircase descends to the polished concrete basement floor.

Concrete-shuttered walls with a timber door beyond. Lea selected the Modernist furniture, some of it custom-made.

105

The 3-storey side extension, the new Corten-clad extension with its flat roof, and its matching slate-roofed extension on the 'outbuilding' footprint. Robinson-inspired drift planting merges into the softer grassed area and then into the farther woodland area of the garden.

dissolve away the layers of the paint to reveal the original cornice in the hallway and all the missing cornices were replaced. And the original window shutters have been restored.

In the basement, a section of the wall has been stripped back to its original state, with the dado downwards painted in a lime wash. "And we had to emphasise to the decorators not to touch the basement walls so that it exposed the historic layers of the paintwork," says Lea. This truly remarkable concept was a year in the planning and required another year to complete, enabling Peter and Lea to move into their new home in 2016.

Peter's study is on the ground floor of the side extension and overlooks the grassed-over roof of the new kitchen-dining area. He says that sometimes, when sitting at his desk taking video calls, people comment about hearing birds in the background. Unsurprisingly, the birds love their garden because, following the disruption by the builders, the couple are now enjoying a garden designed by Miria Harris. Her design includes "a woven tapestry of plants," and draws inspiration from the pioneer of naturalistic planting, William Robinson (1838-1936), author of *The Wild Garden*.

Internally, some of the doorframes are original while others are excellent reproductions to match. The decorators were able to

Exposed brickwork and plaster walls reveal past layers.

There's a different feel to the building in the various areas. The rear part of the house at the garden level is exceptionally private and quiet. "Depending on our mood, we can either be downstairs at the back or upstairs in the front living room," explains Lea. "And when we emerge onto the street, what with the *Freemasons Arms* opposite, it's usually buzzing."

The result of their hard work is not only a highly successful and prizewinning conversion, but even more importantly, Peter and Lea have created a warm, genuine and edgy-yet-timeless home. ∎

Downshire Hill south side continued

As we continue down the hill, an attractive pair of white-painted stucco houses with banded ashlar plasterwork on the ground floor captures our attention. Christopher Wade describes the homes on this side of Downshire Hill as "Cottages of the early and mid-19th century variety," which adds to their allure. William Woods built many of the houses on Downshire Hill in the early 1820s and also constructed the nearby St John's Chapel. William Kerrison, another local carpenter and builder, is credited with the construction of some of the later houses, including the charming semi-detached pair where we find No.37 Downshire Hill. This house (and its partner No.38) are located virtually opposite Nos.25 & 26 which were known as Langham Place when home to John Constable in 1826 (see also p242).

More than a century later, at the adjoining at No.36, a blend of artistic ingenuity and intellectual pursuits converged in 1947. It was home to the renowned photo-journalist, Lee Miller and her husband, Sir Roland Penrose, a distinguished painter and patron of the arts. Both luminaries played pivotal roles in promoting Surrealism and International Modernism within the UK.

No.37 itself was once the home of Flora Robson, a celebrated actor of her time. Her notable performance as Queen Elizabeth I in the movie *Fire Over England* (1937), alongside legendary actors Laurence Olivier and Vivien Leigh, cemented her place in cinematic history.

The current owners were previously living in Islington, but ready to start a family, the couple were keen to avoid pushing prams around the shops! So they were naturally inclined to search for a family home near the Heath. They used a house finder to assist

Dame Flora Robson (1902-1984) in the rear garden of No.37. The garden wall and the windows appear the same as they are today. *Photo, Sasha, Hutton Archive.*

Remarkable Homes of NW3

The hall and staircase with its original arch, corbels and cornicing.

The delightful living room, little changed.

in their search and viewed eight houses before choosing No.37. When selling their home, some vendors feel the need to be satisfied that their property will be left in good hands. This was the case here, but the purchase went through smoothly because these vendors, keen gardeners, were doubly pleased; their house would become home to a family who were also aware of their responsibilities towards its beautiful garden.

The present owners arrived here in 2011 and lived in the house for about nine months, taking stock and deciding on their proposed changes. They moved out for the duration of the renovation project, expecting to be away from the house for some two and a half months, as there wasn't actually that much work to be done. But their builder, like so many others, went bankrupt, and it turned into a frustrating saga that just went on and on. In the end, it took over five months to complete the works. Despite the challenges faced during the renovation project, the couple were able to move back in just after the birth of their second child.

The house exudes a certain charm that is hard to ignore, with its original architectural details and idyllic location. Structurally, there was very little change other than adding a conservatory across the rear of the house. During that work, floorboards on the ground floor were lifted and found to be completely rotten underneath, so the entire floor needed replacement. The new conservatory has brought in ample natural light and made the space more versatile, while the new kitchen is perfect for the family.

They have changed the access to the house; now they mostly use the side door accessed via the side gate rather than the front door. There was an outdoor coal hole and vault, which is now part of the house resulting in indoor rather than outdoor storage. Additionally, an air source heat pump located at the far end of the garden provides all the underfloor heating which they say is very good at maintaining the temperature.

The family is surprised at how little they use the ground floor. They far prefer the lower ground floor garden room and conservatory, spending much of their time there and in the kitchen. The house was built before the installation of indoor plumbing, so all the bathrooms are in the side extension.

The owners have made the house their own and turned it into a comfortable and inviting home. But it's not just the interior that the family loves;

108

The peaceful garden of No.37 Downshire Hill that Dame Flora Robson loved so much.

they have two girls and the garden is a particular source of joy for them. Originally, the garden was neat and tidy, but it has slowly become wilder over time. The family have retained the essential structure but embraced the natural meadow-like look, allowing the natural beauty of the flora and fauna to flourish, creating a haven for insects and beetles. The garden is now left to its own devices over the winter months, and they're doing 'No Mow in April and May'. As the family continues to make their mark on the property and in the community, it's exciting to think of what the future holds for this home with its lovely cottagey feel. ■

The lower end of Downshire Hill, viewed from the Heath, "Hampstead Heath", detail. The *Freemasons Arms* has since been rebuilt. *G.S. Shepherd*, 1833, completed by the artist on the spot © *V&A Museum, London*.

The Wisteria-covered façade of No.17 Keats Grove – its upper floor windows flanking a central blind lunette, which together with the shared chimney stack, visually divide this pair of villas.

Keats Grove

The enchanting road we know today as Keats Grove was originally called Albion Grove, then later John Street, and was only named after its most famous resident in 1910. The road, which is actually little more than a lane, has kept many of its Regency villas and cottages intact.

Many of the north side properties date from about 1820. As does No.17, one of a pair of semi-detached houses sitting quietly in Keats Grove within a minute or two of the Heath and South End Green. The gentle curve of the bay windows, the white stucco, contrasting with black downpipes and cast-iron balconies make a most appropriate setting for the wisteria framing the façade of this delightful property.

Owners Julian Bier, a property developer, and his wife Elizabeth, a Learning Support Assistant, have two grown-up boys; one lives in Crouch End and the other in Hampstead. "As a child, I lived in Redington Road, and always wanted to return to Hampstead proper," says Julian. "When we purchased the house in September 2006, it was an absolute wreck and completely derelict, having stood empty for several years."

The couple had been looking for the ideal home over the previous fifteen years or so. "As soon as we walked in here, we knew it was the one," recalls Elizabeth. Despite the water dripping down from the ceilings, the early C20 two-storey side addition that had at one time served as a porch, and a garage with a bathroom above, they knew that the house had 'good bones'. Furthermore, the previous owner had already filed planning permissions for restoring the property and adding a new extension. So, nothing daunted, the Biers completed the purchase and then set about revising the planning permissions to include all the changes they wanted to make.

"As it's a listed building, that took a while," says Elizabeth. Overall, the renovations took two years to complete. "We moved in as soon as we could, which was in March 2008 with 90 per cent of the work completed, and the builders still in situ – but it wasn't too bad!" says Elizabeth, smiling at the recollection. As they were organising all the interior decoration and furnishing themselves, living on site during those final months enabled the Biers to fine tune everything to their taste. The result is a unique family home that fits their lifestyle like a glove.

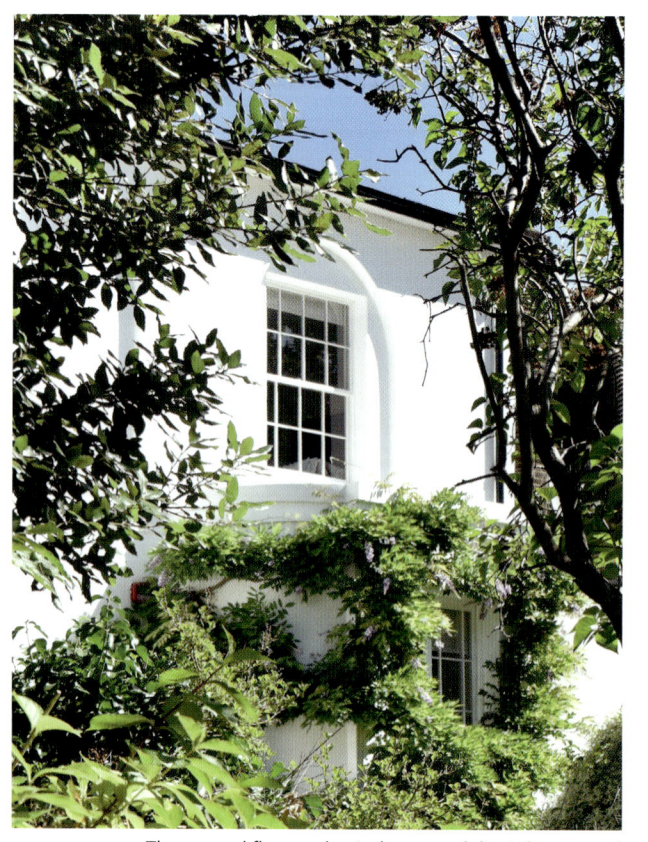

The second floor sash windows are delicately recessed in shallow round-arched recesses.

"Although we got permission to mix contemporary with the original," Julian recalls, "we had to structurally restore everything exactly as it was down to the last detail – even things you can no longer see – such as the lath and plaster walls. We weren't permitted to take out the old fireplaces in the bedrooms – we could box them in, but they had to remain," says Julian. But the couple did get planning permission for the new extension and the basement underneath, "We are not so sure that Camden planners would allow either nowadays," adds Julian.

"Although the front of the building is virtually unchanged, and we decided to keep the rooms at the front of the house pretty well as they were originally," Elizabeth explains, "we have still managed to create a contemporary feel throughout the house, and that continues out into the garden."

View from the kitchen to the new glass-covered extension leading to the patio with its figurative sculptures, and the upper rear garden patio.

The convivial dining room atmosphere is enhanced by the clever use of colour combined with the variation of fabric designs.

The front door opens onto views through the house to the rear garden's upper terrace. Stairs lead down to the basement level from the hallway on the left.

The Biers most certainly appreciate the house they have lovingly restored and also their location. "We enjoy being at this end of Hampstead; Keats Grove is so quiet, especially at night," says Julian. "From our bedroom, we can lie in bed and see the historic *Keats House*, which is just across the way," adds Elizabeth. "We previously lived on a busy corner. There's a completely different atmosphere living here compared to life in Hampstead Garden Suburb. South End Green is quite quirky." The couple find it very different compared to Hampstead High Street and Heath Street. "We can walk to South End Green in one direction and Hampstead Town in the other, which is a big plus," says Julian. "And above all, we enjoy the Heath which is just on our doorstep. We take the grandkids out there, it's fantastic."

When this house was the home of Donald and Catherine Carswell, (both mainly known as biographers) it was featured in the October 1933 edition of *Homes and Gardens*. It was then described as "A cottage in old Hampstead, standing quietly in a garden of the most unpremeditated description, and yet within a minute of shops, trams and omnibuses, is surely an enviable possession." These words are as applicable today as they were when first written.

Julian and Elizabeth have paid as much attention to their outdoor areas as they have to the interior of their house, creating two gardens of great beauty. Indeed, thanks to the clever landscaping and terracing, the front garden has brought them such privacy that it's Julian's favourite place to sit when enjoying breakfast outside. ▪

No.17 Keats Grove in the *Homes and Gardens* edition of October 1933.

The former two-storey side extension has been skilfully returned to its original purpose, minus the garage, and now serves as the principal entrance with a bedroom above.

A first-floor bedroom opens onto the wisteria-shrouded balcony.

Left: the French doors of the dining room open to the front garden.
Right: the same view in 1933.

112

Elizabeth and Julian in their front garden; the French windows lead into the dining room.

Surrounded by hedging and trees, an elegant sculpture holds court on the charming upper rear garden patio. Large pottery containers holding flowering plants punctuate the seating arrangement of this inviting space.

A house with a view. Just across the road, *Keats House* is visible from the upper floors of No.17 Keats Grove.

No.52 Parliament Hill.

The hall window next to the front door has retained its original stained glass.

Parliament Hill

The land leased from the Ecclesiastical Commissioners destined to become Parliament Hill was originally part of South End Farm. Primarily developed a few years after South Hill Park by the agricultural tenant Joseph Pickett, homes were constructed in the area slowly but surely over many years, with the roads following the old field boundaries. Parliament Hill was laid out from 1870, with houses built there between 1879 and 1892. The first homes were ready by 1881, and construction continued at about ten houses per year until 1894. The development was to carry on over Parliament Hill, but the LCC purchased the Hill for the public in 1889 and added it to Hampstead Heath.

Many of the houses on the road are in the Victorian Gothic Revival Style, with steeply pitched roofs and prominent, carved front gables. But the house we are visiting, No.52 Parliament Hill, is one of a pair of semi-detached red brick villas that were built in the 1880s. Constructed in a similar style to others on the road but distinguished from them by being on a slightly larger scale, and having a shallower pitched roof with a dormer window set at an angle to the roof rather than the Gothic-style gable.

On entering, the first impression is one of openness and the impact of the large window across the hall offering a view over London. The fabulous high ceilings and an unusually wide hallway provide the feeling of spaciousness and light that extends through to all the ground floor rooms. "You come in here, and thanks to the windows, the staircase is bright right up to the landing, as is the hallway to the left," says Roger Morley, a fund manager. In addition, pleasant arches frame the view through to the rear of the house, terminating in a central window, creating a great sightline. "We see the same people passing the house a lot – many walk past here to get to and from the Hill."

"I grew up in Suffolk," says Roger, "but I came to know this part of London because a friend had bought a flat in Primrose Hill in 1993. He needed a lodger, so I moved into his flat when I started work in London." When Roger and Sophie married, they first bought a place on Upper Park Road in Belsize Park. "Then we moved to a house in Courthope Road, Gospel Oak/South End Green," he continues, "and we remained there until 2016."

Part of the entrance hallway viewed through a rectangular archway and window overlooking the rear garden.

The staircase with a wonderfully sturdy column and curved arches.

After that, the couple and their two daughters always said that if they were to move again anywhere, it would be to South Hill Park or Parliament Hill. "Because we love the area so much and especially enjoy the proximity to this part of the Heath," adds Roger.

One day in 2016, Sophie saw that this house, No. 52 Parliament Hill, was on the market. Sophie knew the street well and was particularly taken by the fact that Nos.52 & 54 appeared very well presented. From the rear of the house, the windows look out on to beautiful views across London and St Paul's. "Delighted with the spaciousness, when we first arrived here, the house felt much wider than anything we had been used to. We agreed to buy the place in June," continues Roger, "moving in during October 2016." The interior was virtually as it appears today.

"For many years, a family owned both these houses and let them out as bedsits or small flats," explains Roger. Then in 2005, a developer by the name of Paul Castle purchased both houses. "He immediately sold this house for a decent profit to an American family with five children. The developer then did up No.54 next door intending to live there himself, but in the end, he sold that off too a few years later."

The previous American owners of No.52 had completely stripped the house. "They undertook all the renovation and restoration work, and they left their mark, as Roger hints when he says that having purchased the property from them 12 years later, "The interior has ended up with more than a hint of New England décor." In addition, there is a suggestion of the even earlier joint ownership: the lower ground floor frontage has no division between the two properties. And at one time, the back garden wasn't divided either, although that has now changed. ∎

Just along the road, No.68 was home to the poet Anna Wickham, known for her artistic salons that included Dame Edith Sitwell and D H Lawrence. And an amazingly interesting fact: Christopher Wade recalls that during an extended stay, Dylan Thomas wrote *Adventures in the Skin Trade* in Anna Wickham's bathroom!

Eric Blair, better known as George Orwell, moved from Warwick Mansions to No.77 Parliament Hill, where he lived for about six months in 1935. He was still working at the bookshop on South End Green but wanted to live near the Heath. His months in this house are said to have been amongst his happiest, since that spring he met Eileen O'Shaughnessy and they married the following year.

No.52 Parliament Hill kitchen and dining area.

The bay window area of the front living room.

An elegant living room fireplace.

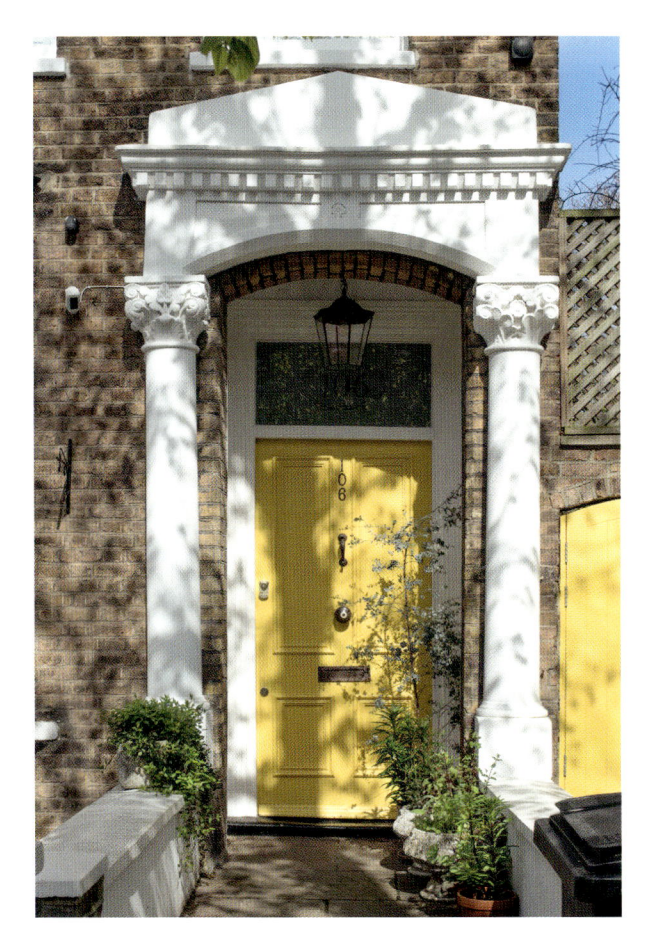

South Hill Park No.2 Pond

Seen from across the pond, No.106 South Hill Park is the house with the second white-painted bay window from the right.

At first glance, the façade of No.106 South Hill Park offers little hint of its fabulous setting. Yet this house has a garden with a stunning view overlooking No.2 Pond on Hampstead Heath. Paired with No.104, these semi-detached houses were probably built shortly after 1871. South Hill Park was developed partly by the tenant of South End Farm, Joseph Pickett, partly by Thomas Rhodes of St Pancras, John Ashwell, a builder from Kentish Town and local builder Charles S Sharp.

The current owner acquired this five-bedroom property in 2018. "The primary reason why I bought this house was for the view across the pond and the Heath," says Lloyd Amsdon, a specialist in luxury pre-owned watches. "I decided to move here as other family members are in Highgate, and I wanted to be near them but not too close! Being from Bearsted in Kent, I do like a bit of countryside, so I naturally gravitated to Hampstead."

It was quite difficult for Lloyd to find the right house. "Coincidentally, the estate agent I was consulting also turned out to be a watch enthusiast, really into his watches," explains Lloyd. "I described what I was looking for. He said if I didn't buy this house, I would regret it because these houses come up so rarely."

Indeed, No.108 next door has been occupied by over three generations of the same family for the last 56 years and counting! No.106 is particularly special because it's possible to enjoy views across the No.2 Pond from the garden without needing to be on a higher level.

Lloyd looks around and adds, "I think this location has one of the best gardens along this section of the road. When the tree in the garden is in full leaf, it partially screens the house when viewed from the pond and it makes the garden very private."

Every morning, Lloyd does a major circuit of the Heath with his three dogs. "I also enjoy fishing," he adds, "I can fish in No.2 Pond, where there are large Pike and Carp. Most of the time, I feel like I'm living in the country."

After the sale of his watch company and the change of location, Lloyd almost felt as if he had taken early retirement. Almost. Apart from his work, one of the first things he did to his new property was to reduce the height of the tall fence that stood at the end of the garden.

Then the house was completely gutted. "We ripped everything out – floors, ceilings, and walls, then put in new floors and windows – but nothing too fancy," says Lloyd. "We moved out of London during the renovation, which took about nine months to complete."

The rear of the house is in an excellent condition. Very few houses on this part of the road have arched lintels, while some homes no longer have any trace of their original rear windows. At No.106, the ground floor French windows have been replaced with smarter modern versions by Crittall. These work especially well with the rear bay window.

"There's a wonderful community around South Hill Park," continues Lloyd. "When I moved here, I was delighted to learn that the reputed watch historian and collector James Dowling lives opposite. He is a Rolex specialist and also a founder and one-time editor-in-chief of a respected watch forum. Talking of history, Lloyd is also aware of the less wonderful local events that ended badly. "I know about the one murder outside the *Magdala Tavern*, but there were, in fact, two murders on the road," recalls Lloyd. "Styllou Christofi was hanged for murdering her daughter-in-law, Dorothea, at their home, No.11 South Hill Park, on 28 July 1954."

On a less grisly note, No.93 South Hill Park was the home of guitarist John Williams in the 1970s, while No.26 was home to writer/film director Anthony Minghella until his death in 2008. He was chairman of the board of Governors at the British Film Institute between 2003 and 2007. ■

The attractive rear façade of No.106 South Hill Park.

The ground floor bay with Crittall windows opening to the garden.

Slender colonettes support each of the ground and first-floor bays.

Greenery abounds in this rewarding view from the garden across Hampstead No.2 Pond.

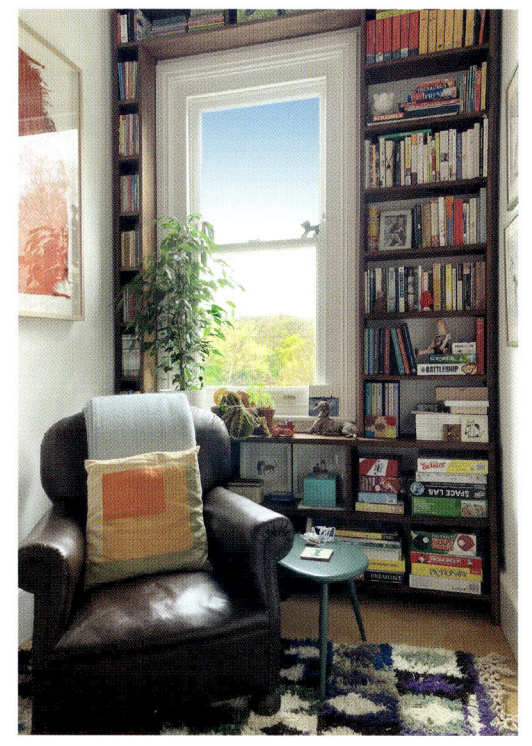

A book-browsing nook on a landing.

The hallway is separated from the living room by Crittall double doors alongside a portrait of Lyndon B Johnson.

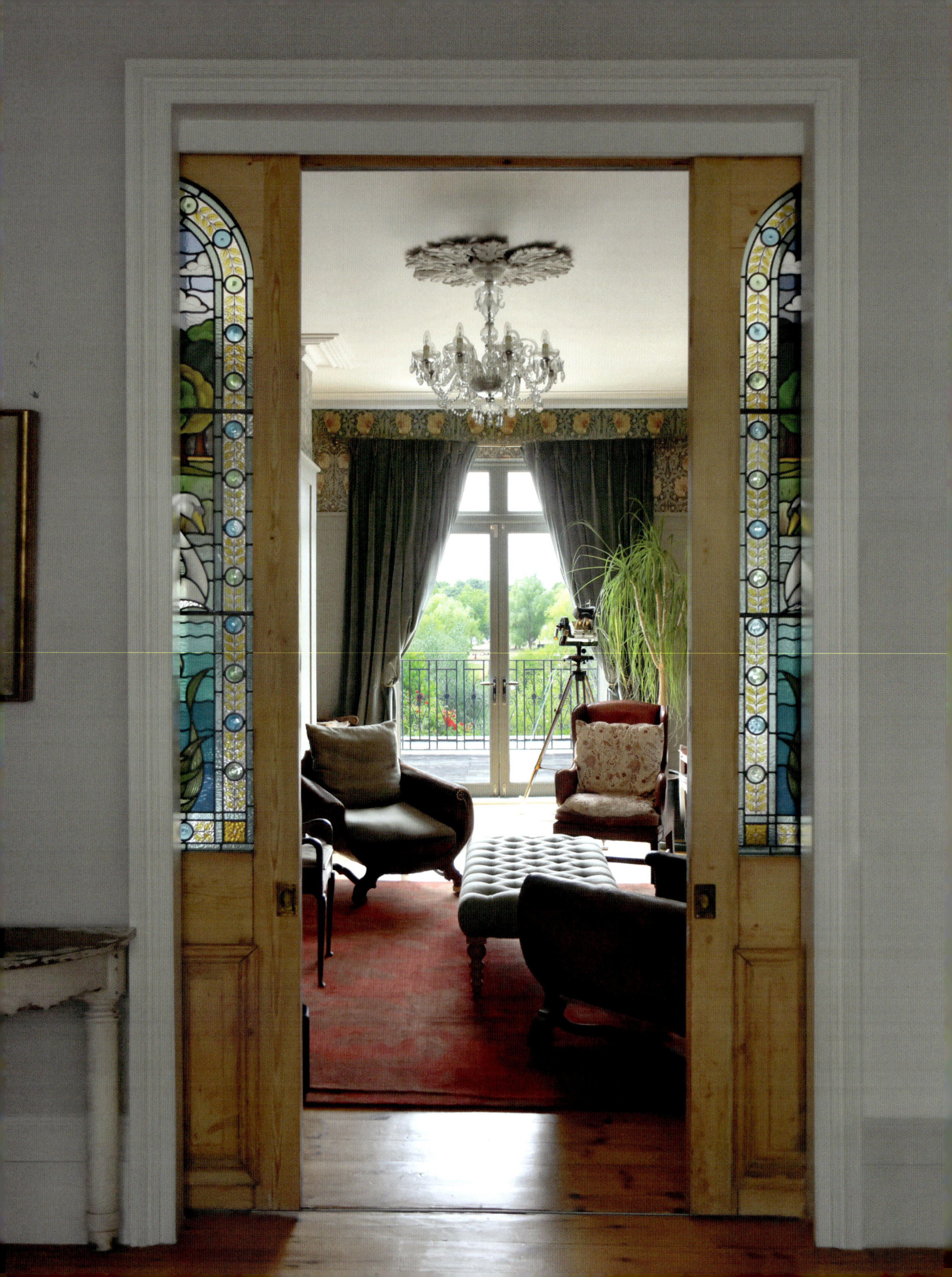

South Hill Park No.1 Pond

Imagine standing in the front room looking through these double sliding doors with their glorious stained glass panels into the living area, with its view of Hampstead Heath and beyond.

The land running northwards from today's Hampstead Heath Overground Station originally belonged to South End Farm and was developed from the 1870s onwards as South Hill Park. The first building at the lower end of the road was not a house, but the *Magdala Tavern*, which by 1868, was serving thirsty customers. Several builders were involved locally: Charles S Sharp, John Ashwell of Kentish Town, Thomas Rhodes of St Pancras, and Joseph Pickett, the lessee of South End Farm, building up South Hill Park from 1871. Pickett also constructed No.85 South Hill Park for himself, remaining there until he died in 1893, and it was he who appears to have been responsible for the part of South Hill Park where we find an outstanding house.

The paired Italianate villa is the prevailing architectural style in this middle part of South Hill Park. The current owners of No.56 have lived here for twelve years, and in that time they have created a cosy, intimate home full of charm and original detailing; the entire house exudes a homely, lived-in feel. Inevitably, the couple had to repair the fabric of the house. They had to fix all the leaky balconies that were constantly letting in water. And further, more extensive renovation work was needed. So when fixing up the kitchen on the lower ground floor, they decided to have the entire floor redone, thereby creating a wonderfully large, open area that in the summertime extends right into the garden. The family made the decision to move out during the building works. After returning and settling in permanently, they wondered why the house felt so homely and realised it must be because it's so compact. Although the Victorians knew how to design homes, it has to be rather more than that; a house also reflects its occupants. And those architectural roots, combined with their own considered redesign, have created a wonderfully calm feel to this home with fabulous views.

A few original features have survived, such as the cornices in the hallway and a delightful corbel. And many of the fittings the couple has sourced are reclaimed. One light fitting came from a Welsh chapel.

Well-preserved corbel detail in the entrance hallway.

Remarkable Homes of NW3

While the kitchen area on the lower ground floor was redesigned into one large family room, two rooms on the upper ground floor were created from one larger space by fitting dividing doors featuring lovely stained glass panels.

Of course, the house is all about its location, so when renovating, the primary focus was on the panoramas over the pond – especially from the upper floors. As the top floor bedroom looks out right across the Heath, the bed is positioned to maximise an absolutely perfect vista.

The family certainly enjoys the most incredible collection of views. There are balconies on every floor, and the garden effectively extends right down to the water. They really appreciate the possibility of swimming in the nearby Mixed Bathing Pond on the Hampstead side of the Heath, and then there's the Kenwood Ladies' Pond and the Highgate Men's Pond.

Reflecting on the quality of life that this part of Hampstead brings to the family, this building has been fashioned into a perfect house for the professions and lifestyles of the owners.

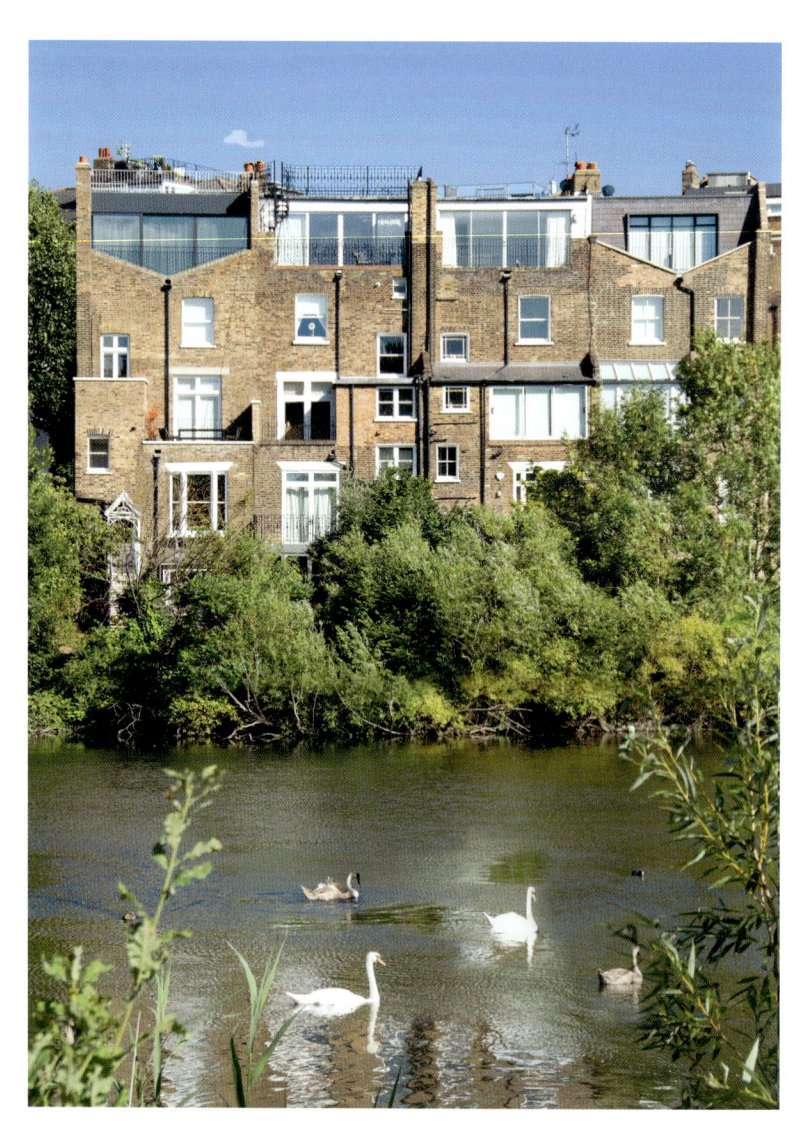

View across Hampstead No.1 Pond – the house is the second from the left.

A climb up the spiral staircase to the rooftop is rewarded with a spectacular view.

Church Row, south side, (dated 1750) depicting an air of venerable respectability, engraving *William H Prior,* 1850, later hand colour.

Church Row south side

Walking down Church Row, it's not difficult to imagine how the Georgian façades would have looked in the early eighteenth century. Leading from Heath Street to the parish church, it is not only "the best street in Hampstead," as described by Pevsner, but it's surely the most handsome. "Church Row houses were regarded as distinguished dwellings… a promenade in Church Row was akin to a walk in the Mall of St James's Park," states Thomas Barratt in his *Annals of Hampstead.* Barratt, favouring the word 'peculiar' continues: "The architecture of the houses is peculiarly restful and gratifying." They are "comfortable residences, a feature peculiarly associated with the reigns of Queen Anne and the Georges."

Church Row, north side today. Nos.5-9 are set back slightly further from the pavement than those on the south side. With railings, gates, lamps, and lamp holders, the north side houses vary in size.

123

This basement kitchen of a Georgian house of a similar age in Spitalfields shows how a kitchen in Church Row might have looked.

Church Row residents can hardly fail to fully appreciate the buildings, which cannot be changed, unlike many other properties in NW3. The majority of the residents consider themselves custodians of these homes.

Many of the houses on this, one of Hampstead's oldest streets, are by Richard Hughes, who purchased the land in 1710. Taking advantage of the popularity of the Hampstead Wells, Hughes developed the street as a speculative venture between 1713 and 1730. The brown and red brick houses mostly comprise 3 storeys with basements and attics.

These houses are embellished with panelled front doors and canopies with beautifully carved brackets. Other key features include lamps, boot scrapers, railings, and other elegant wrought-iron work, including balconettes and fanlights. This form of lunette window generally differed from house to house, and it became the custom for individual fanlight designs to be included on invitations and visiting cards. "The fanlights over the doors are full of variety of design quite in keeping with the equally varied doors," says Thomas J Barratt, and "the wrought-iron ornamental gates to some of the houses are very fine examples of the blacksmith's art."

As Pevsner points out, the Church Row terraced houses are "to a standard plan, with front and back rooms, rear staircase and closet, and retain much good panelling and joinery."

Bucking this trend is No.5 on the northern side. Built in 1728 by Hughes, the addition of its wooden weatherboarding in the late C18 changed its character,

Handsome houses of Church Row, south side today. Being terraced, residents encounter one another regularly. It is a warm, fascinatingly varied, and even an eccentric community.

and it sits almost opposite No.21, the traditional Hughes house we are visiting.

No.21 Church Row and its attached railings are listed Grade II*. It was built *c.*1720 possibly even earlier, and sensitively refaced C19 in the Georgian style. The windows have gauged red brick segmental arches, and there is white painted stucco on the ground floor with an enriched console-bracketed hood, plus a radial patterned fanlight and panelled door. Today it is owned by Erika Howard and Maurits Dolmans.

Erika is at once a portrait painter, art historian, and photographer. She especially likes to travel to remote corners of the world and capture the essence of a location and its people with her camera. Maurits Dolmans grew up in Arnhem in the Netherlands and is a lawyer. The couple met in New York and have two children, a boy and a girl. "Previously, we were in Holford Road, coming to No.21 Church Row in 2014," says Erika. "We love this street so much, and when we heard this

Fanlights were introduced to allow light into dark entrance halls, corridors, and passageways.

The Church of St John-at-Hampstead is a focal point of Church Row, little changed in 1910, from a watercolour by AR Quinton with No.5 on the right. Residents recall an onion seller occasionally standing on the corner of Church Row in the 1960s.

No.5 on the north side today.

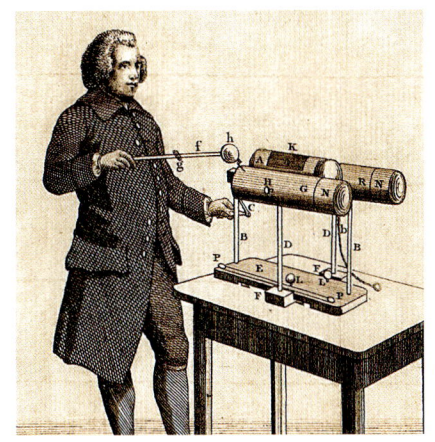

Edward Nairne and his electrical machine, 1783, *archive*.

No.21 Church Row is a complete and 'textbook' example of a relatively simple early C18 house, little altered.

house was for sale, we walked in for the first time and said, 'Gosh!' and we immediately fell madly in love with it," recalls Maurits. "For almost two hundred years, the house was owned by the Hardisty family, although in later years, the house had been leased to tenants," he continues. "When we saw it, the then owner was marketing No.21 and the rear mews house backing onto Perrin's Walk as a single purchase, but he eventually relented, and we were able to purchase No.21 on its own."

Previous tenants include instrument maker Edward Nairne (1726-1806), one of the best-known London barometer and scientific instrument makers in the late C18. John Fulleylove (1845-1908), a painter in watercolours and oils, also lived in the house. "His daughter Joan Elizabeth (1886-1947) produced the stained glass of the window of Chapel of St Mary & St John around 1920. I also know that John Constable was a friend of a woman who lived here, so he probably once sat right here in our front room," adds Erika.

Piers Plowright, the renowned BBC radio producer, was born at No.9a Church Row in 1937 and lived at No.21 from the age of eight. "We knew Piers, and he gave us a tour of the house one day," recalls Erika. "He once told us, 'The house has ghosts, but they are very friendly ones!' and added, 'You can feel the history.' Although Piers remembered only tarmac, his father said that when he first came to live there in the 1920s, the roads in Hampstead Village were all soft surface."

Dr Oliver Plowright, with his doctor's bag, leaving No.21 (where he had lived since 1945) for the last time on 15 October 1980.

A glass-paned door on the half landing reveals the original powder room where wigs were kept and could be powdered before leaving the house.

"Piers' father, Dr Oliver Plowright, known as 'Hampstead's Doctor', was also a doctor to Winston Churchill in the 1950s. "We know that Churchill had been in our dining room, which was Dr Plowright's consulting room, as had Dame Peggy Ashcroft (1907-1991), who was also one of his patients," recalls Erika. "Piers explained to us how the rooms were arranged in his day," continues Maurits. "Living here is rather special; it's a privilege to help conserve it, as we are just passing through."

The house still has many original fittings, including panelling and floorboards. It once had a service lift (or dumb waiter), but this was removed when the kitchen was moved from the basement to the ground floor. Erika, who hails from Canada, is used to large, free-standing properties and finds these terraced houses a total contrast. "In a way, elements of the terrace are reminiscent of the Dutch canal houses with their large, tall windows, high ceilings, and panelled walls," notes Maurits.

A corner of the living room.

The original staircase is typical early C18 with its decorated exposed sides, 'barley twist' balusters, and opposing wooden wall panelling.

The weatherboarded house is visible just across from No.21.

This view from the lane leading from Church Row down to Frognal Way reveals the rear of the south side, which is somewhat more irregular than originally. No.15 Church Row on the end is an agreeable 2-storey addition to the terrace by Sydney Tatchell built as recently as 1924.

These houses do not appeal to everyone as they are unable to change things around. "We haven't altered anything since we moved in as we are not allowed to, and wouldn't want to," continues Maurits. "Although we have installed some bookshelves, these are easily removable. Nothing is permanent."

The friendships they have forged since moving into Church Row are of greater permanence. "There is a vibrant local community, everyone on Church Row knows one another," adds Maurits. "We hold public affairs gatherings here in the front room. And we host home concerts here every year with the Friends of the Music in Hampstead – it's a well-used home."

"Extending out from the basement we have a long, wide vaulted cellar running beneath Church Row, which is used as our laundry room," explains Erika. "And another one which is still a coal cellar with different layers of coal, along with the original coal hole," explains Maurits. "And at the rear, there is one we use as a wine cellar. Some of our neighbours have renovated their cellars too." The terraced houses may have originally appealed to merchants as the cellars were ideal for storing sample stock.

As the historian Edward Walford records in *Old and New London*, "A part of the manorial rights attached to [Frognal Mansion] consists of a private road leading past the north side of the parish church, with a private toll-gate, which even royalty cannot pass without payment of the customary toll."

Church Row has been home to over 20 eminent people over the years, from Anna Laetitia Barbauld to George du Maurier (around 1872), as well as a number of famous architects.

No.18 was once home to John James Park, who wrote the first history of Hampstead in 1814. The historian Edward Walford lived at No.17 from 1860 to 1886; author H G Wells was in residence from 1909 to 1912, and the comedian Peter Cook lived here in the 1970s. ∎

The tollgate operated by Miss Sullivan – still standing at the western end of Church Row around 1899, *archive*.

No.18 Church Row (on the left) *A R Quinton,* and No.17 next door (behind the tree) was home to several famous residents over the decades.

No.9 Church Row façade. Right: Church Row north side. The brick house with the blue door is No.8, with virtually identical street furniture as its neighbour at No.9. The weatherboard house at No.5 sits opposite No.21 (see p125).
Engraving William H Prior, c.1860, later hand colour.

Church Row north side

Architecturally gratifying, the Grade II* listed No.9 Church Row is a terraced house on the northern side of the most handsome street in Hampstead. Constructed by Richard Hughes around 1728, with brown brick and red brick dressings, the house was re-fronted in the Georgian style during the late C19. This property is exceptional for Church Row, as it is double fronted, with 5 windows across the upper floors on 3 storeys, plus attics, a basement and 3 cellars. Outside, the street frontage has retained its cast-iron railings with urn finials. A pair of elegant lamp holders flank the decorative wrought-iron gateway with its overthrow and matching gate.

The double-plan interior features a central open-well staircase set in a hallway with full-height panelling and a dado rail. The staircase itself is closed string, with turned balusters, moulded newels and ramped handrails.

Owners Alain and Marianne have lived in Hampstead since 2012. Marianne found the house. "I saw it advertised in a magazine in 2017 and asked a French architect friend to come along with me for a viewing. As soon as the door opened I was astonished – I realised it was something special," Marianne recalls with a broad smile. "I could feel the warm atmosphere and immediately sensed the age of this house. I said, 'Alain, please come and look at it!' He viewed it the very next day."

Each time the couple return home to Church Row and open the front door they can sense the calm and nurturing feel of the house. "There are some places where you immediately feel a certain vibe, and this is one of them," Marianne says. "Maybe it's due to all the wonderful wood panelling everywhere."

While filming for the 2019 BBC production of *A Christmas Carol*, they removed all the cars from the street, vividly reminding

No.9 Church Row during BBC filming of Dickens' *A Christmas Carol* in May 2019. *Photo: Erika Dolmans.* The pair of lamp holders are clearly visible.

Church Row as seen from the entrance hallway.

Garden view from the conservatory.

the couple of the past. "You were really back to Georgian times; it was as if life had slowed down and it became agreeably peaceful." Marianne observes. "However, it is true to say that when we first visited the house we weren't fully aware of its history at that point. Even so, the feel was rather 'heavy' while at the same time very gentle, protective. It felt like being cradled."

Talking of its history, No. 9 Church Row was a Girls' Reformatory School from 1857 to 1870 and the Field Lane Industrial School for Girls in the 1880s and 1890s. "I was very concerned when I heard that Nicholas Mosley had lived here but I soon learned that he distanced himself from his father," recalls Alain. Today, the house is home to a family more focused on the musical arts.

Marianne is a French author, producer, lecturer, and specialist in classical music. She makes programmes for Radio France and is the producer of *Histoires de Musique* and *The Diary of...* on France Musique. Their three children are grown up and no longer live at home. "But they absolutely adore the house; they love coming here to stay," says Marianne.

So what did the couple do to the house? They didn't make any major structural changes. All the fireplaces are original – there is even an old range in the basement kitchen they have restored and adapted. "We concentrated purely on decorating to our taste and selecting the furnishings," says Marianne. "I only made my

The staircase with a view down to the conservatory and garden beyond.

choices after extensively reading and researching. I love looking at decor magazines, and I also read books on the Georgian era, especially studying the colour schemes."

Extending across the entire width of the house, this first-floor front room has Bolection moulded fireplaces at either end. The five sash windows have well-preserved wooden shutters and window seats. There are full-height panelling features on the doors and over the fireplaces, as well as panelling with dado moulding on the walls.

The couple find their Church Row home is remote from the bustle of the city, and "it's most conducive to my work," says Marianne. "We feel Hampstead is an inspiring place for us both." In restoring the house with such great attention to period detail and particular sensitivity to its unique ambiance, they have returned this wonderful building to its original purpose: a family haven within which creativity can flourish.

Inspiring in all respects, the subtle infusion of French chic into this ancient Georgian house has been sensitively done. The result is an elegant, comfortable and harmonious home highly cherished by the entire family. ■

The delightful front dining room.

The first-floor living room with its five large windows. Beautifully furnished, the front room is wonderfully wide – one of the reasons why the house adapted so well as a school.

Marianne writes most of her books and creates her weekly podcast for France Musique in her Church Row home.

Echoing the colour palette used throughout the home, the kitchen has also retained its original wood panelling.

Holly Walk

No.11 Holly Walk.

The wooded hillside to the west of Holly Walk gave way to development from 1894 with the construction of *Moreton*, a large mansion. Later on, a small house was built alongside the Mount Vernon footpath that first appears on the ordnance survey of 1936 in a previously tree-covered location. "This current house, No.11 Holly Walk, originates from around 1960," says the proud owner Susan Peires, an artist and a goldsmith. "But sections of the exterior wall indicate that this boundary wall must be somewhat older. *Moreton*, the house next door, remains the largest property in this area, which originally enjoyed a grand ballroom."

Older sections of the boundary wall alongside the Mount Vernon footpath.

Holly Walk extends northwards from Church Row and connects with the Mount Vernon footpath.

Susan was living abroad and wanted to come back to the UK. "My marriage had dissolved and I was looking for a place where I could feel safe but still be able to receive the grandchildren and have them come and stay," she continues. "I wanted something that spoke to me. I always loved the idea of living in Hampstead Village as I was raised in St John's Wood and lived in Highgate. So to me, this part of London is home." The garage and a small forecourt sold Susan on the house. "To be in the village with three car spaces is fabulous," she says. Many of her family members live locally, including a daughter in

The view from the delightful garden, with water feature and pond.

The lower floor terrace with kitchen beyond.

No.11 Holly Hill attic studio window.

Hampstead Garden Suburb. "There was one thing that almost prevented me from buying the property," adds Susan. "It was an odd, almost circular staircase occupying the central space." So that had to be removed, and everything around it also had to be changed.

"I acquired the property in 2019 and redid the interior in 2020, taking it back to the stud," Susan continues. It's not vastly different from the way it was before. "One previous owner had dug down and another had built upwards, but they didn't connect properly," she adds. Susan wanted her own studio, which is in the attic – a location that has proven to be ideal for her.

She lived in the house for six months before undertaking any work. She needed to know how it was to be used. "You can't get that just by simply trusting an architect or designer. The architects I selected were Philip Wagenfeld from Studio M R who did a wonderful job and Rosie Winston of Clifton Interiors. I love the place now. Every time I come home I find myself wandering around with a smile on my face saying, 'this is really nice!'" The downstairs area is large enough to host all Susan's children, whilst at the same time it's small enough for someone living mostly on their own with two dogs.

Susan has created three seating spaces, all of which get used differently. The lower ground floor has the kitchen for entertaining – an area ideal for the children, while the sitting room on the ground floor is cosy for the evenings." Susan finds that the spaces flow beautifully. "I would have never thought I would have enjoyed living in a townhouse, albeit a big townhouse on steroids. I absolutely love this place."

People enjoy coming here. I spend most of my time in the studio – it's possible to get eight women and gentlemen painting up there. I hold women's circles, art circles and various gatherings – and they always go down well." The amenities on the studio level are such that the space can easily be turned back into two more bedrooms should Susan choose to do so. This home has truly made a positive impact on Susan. "I love that I have so many wonderful neighbours," she notes, "but you can't see them from the house or the garden."

This is certainly a highly commendable conversion project, well considered and cleverly executed. ■

Part of the attic studio featuring a large circular window.

Sir Walter Besant (1836-1901).

Walter Besant's home was called Frognal End, No.18 Frognal Gardens. built c.1892, designed by James Neale, archive.

A conveyance dated 1891 indicates there was an interest in the land by the novelist and historian Walter Besant who lived nearby at *Frognal End*, Frognal Gardens. Besant served as the first President of the Hampstead Antiquarian Historical Society, he co-founded the Society of Authors and was the brother-in-law of the theosophist Annie Besant.

Just next door on the west side of Holly Walk is the listed Grade II *Moreton*, designed by Thomas Garner for Frederick Sidney in 1894. Situated virtually opposite No.11 Holly Walk is the appealing Holly Place dating from 1816, and the Watch House, the old police station.

The Watch House for the police force from 1830 in the foreground, beyond is the white-painted house where composer Sir William Walton lived in the 1930s.

Amesbury House, Frognal

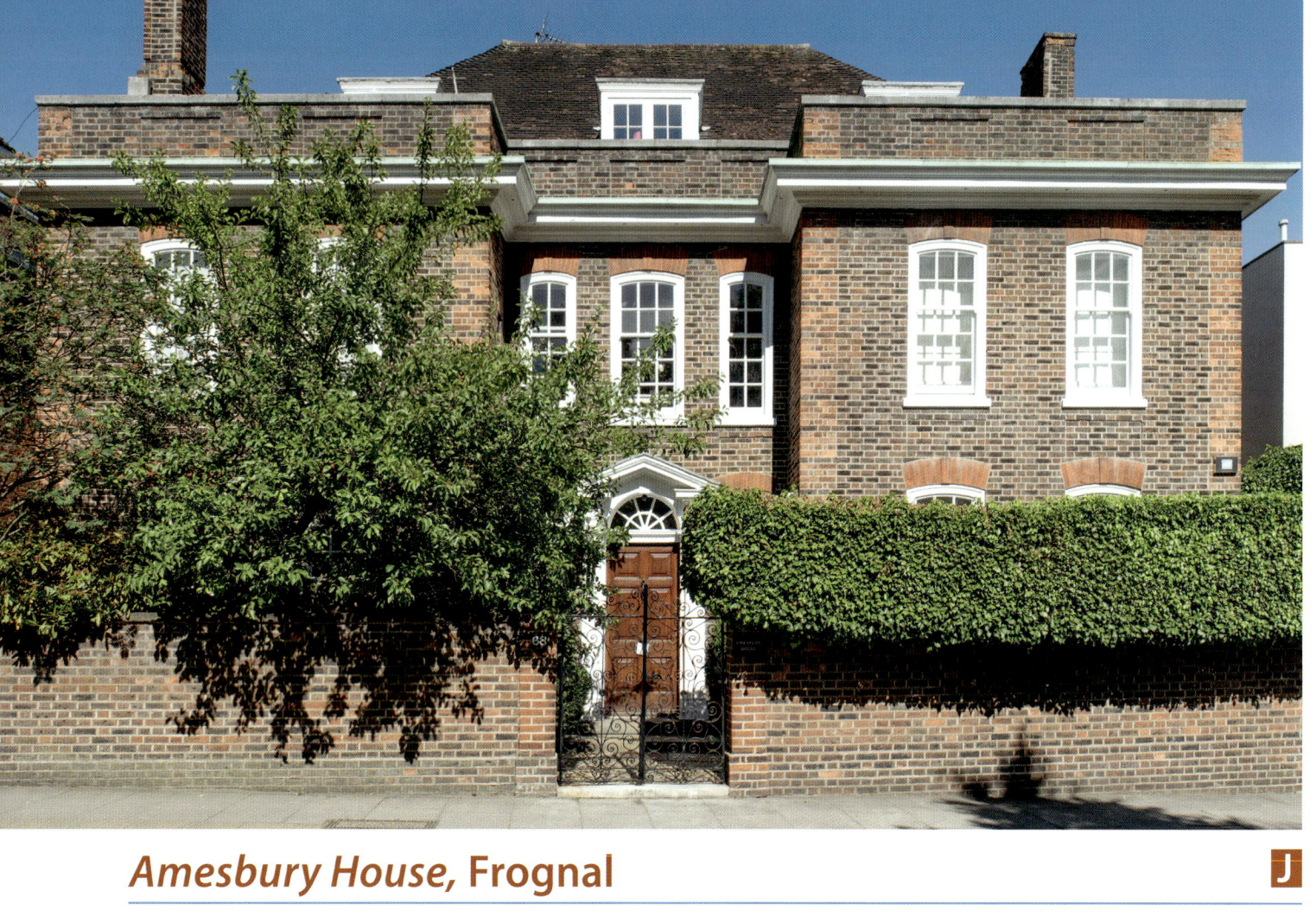

Frognal has a very long and fascinating history. Named after *Frognal Hall*, which likely existed by 1646 and was reputedly visited by Samuel Pepys in 1668. By the early C19, Frognal was described as a "hamlet of handsome residences" with groves and gardens.

The grass cutters' scythes yielded to the trowels of bricklayers when *Frognal Hall* fell to the redevelopers in the 1920s. To the south of Church Row, on a large plot of land adjoining the grounds of the old Hall, Nos.70 & 68 Frognal were built, dating from 1931. No.68 is a grand and imposing double-fronted property called *Amesbury House*. It displays symmetrical proportions and has a shallow, hipped roof with a pannelled parapet, a front door fanlight and tall windows recalling the early-Georgian style.

As designer Francine Hayes recalls: "I immediately recognised that this part of Hampstead has the same community feeling that I was used to back in my home in Brazil. Having first looked at a property at the Frognal end of Redington Road, this house was my second viewing in this area."

Frognal Hall with its distinctive cupola, looking south, in 1796, detail, engraving after Stowers.

The Amesbury Connection

"I grew up in Durrington Walls located two miles northeast of Stonehenge, and two miles northwest of Amesbury in Wiltshire," recalls Francine's partner Angus (Gus) Fraser, a futurist and progressive thinker. "I thought, what a coincidence that Francine lives in *Amesbury House* in Hampstead! When I was first shown a picture of *Antrobus House* in Amesbury I said, 'Oh my goodness, it's very much like *Amesbury House!*' And it struck me as rather odd that this Hampstead building has the same name as the small

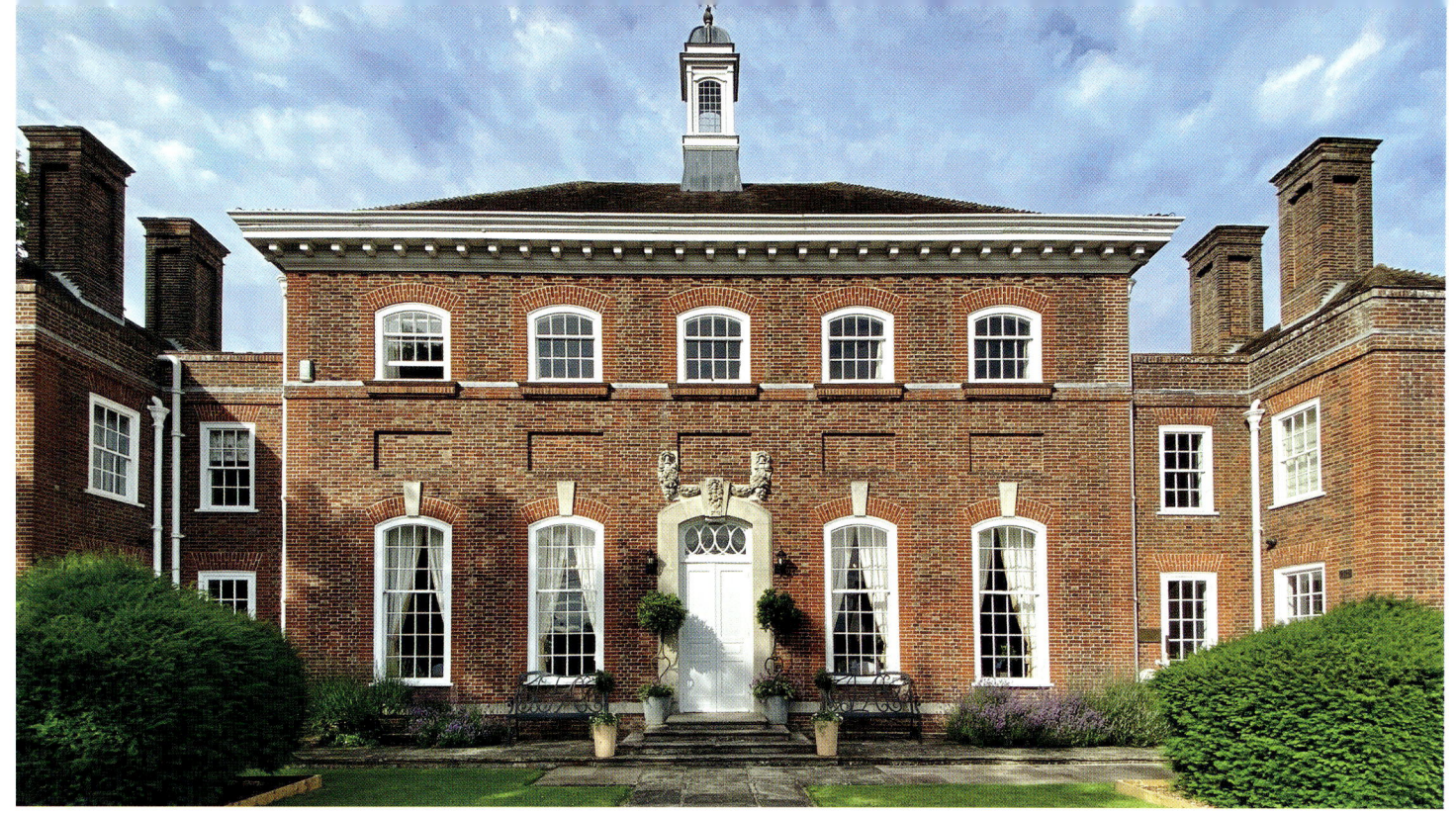

Antrobus House, Amesbury, Wiltshire, built 1924-25, and originally owned by the wealthy Antrobus family. *Photo, The Lady Antrobus Trust.*

Wiltshire town that boasts the imposing Grade II *Antrobus House.* What are the chances of that?" Gus asks.

Remarkably, these two early C20 Wrenaissance/Neo-Georgian houses are well-designed and happen to be good examples of their type. Both of their principal façades have segmented arched window lintels, rather than the more usual horizontal lintels of the period, and inset panels. Gus speculates that one of the owners had named No.68 Frognal *Amesbury House* due to connection with the design of the Wiltshire house or even perhaps with the Antrobus family. "The similarity is so incredible that anyone moving between the two houses would feel at home." As do visitors to their own house. "On arrival," Gus explains, "visitors expect the interior to be traditional and are pleasantly surprised to see that the interior has been modernised in a way that is sympathetic and age-appropriate to the rest of the house."

When the couple holds parties, they use the house to its maximum. "We can accommodate 150 people on these occasions, which are quite the event. The two main living rooms on the right side of the house were designed exactly for that." Francine is as much in love with living in Hampstead as she was when she first found *Amesbury House,* "I so much enjoy walking into Hampstead Village for my shopping and taking in the village atmosphere. And I love to hear the church bells just across the garden." And if she has incorporated her fashion and design experience into transforming No.68, it must be stressed that Francine and Gus are not simply living in the property; they have both put their hearts and their souls into it. The grand façade of *Amesbury House* hides a much-loved home. It also sits next to a house built in a completely different architectural style, as we will see shortly.

Set against a beige background, the angular mirror and consul table in the *Amesbury House* hallway strike a contrast with the softer traditional seating and rug.

The *Amesbury House* front room – ideal for entertaining.

St John-at-Hampstead just across the garden.

Part of the rear garden and terrace.

The Modernist Connection

A detailed investigation has revealed that in 1931 William Willett Ltd (Building Contractors in Sloane Square with Estate Offices at 137a Finchley Road) owned the land and the property built as No.68, and that in 1935, the Willett Company had sold No. 68 to a Mr H M Guiterman. However, the Willett Company also owned the two adjoining plots to No.68. The company built No.70 Frognal on plot 'A' in the same style as its neighbour. In 1936, when Ursula and Geoffrey Walford were looking for a location upon which to build a Modernist house in the heart of Hampstead, their solicitor, William Sturges, referred them to the Willett Company for both the land and the build. Shortly thereafter, the Willett Company offered them the freehold site of plot 'C' for £2750.

However, the juxtaposition of 1930s Modernism with the Neo-Georgian style was highly controversial, provoking strenuous objections from the neighbours. So much so that in April 1936, William Willett's Managing Director, A G Minter, felt unable to approve the building plans. He wrote, "Perhaps Geoffrey Walford should consider the erection of a house on the site more in keeping with those adjoining."

As a result, five months later at the end of September, William Willett Ltd sold the plot of land to Geoffrey Walford for the discounted sum of £2600, but withdrew from constructing this Modernist house. From the Autumn of 1936 through to December 1938, No.66 Frognal was built by Y J Lovell and Son, the contractors working from the designs of an architect greatly influenced by Le Corbusier, Colin Lucas (1906-1984).

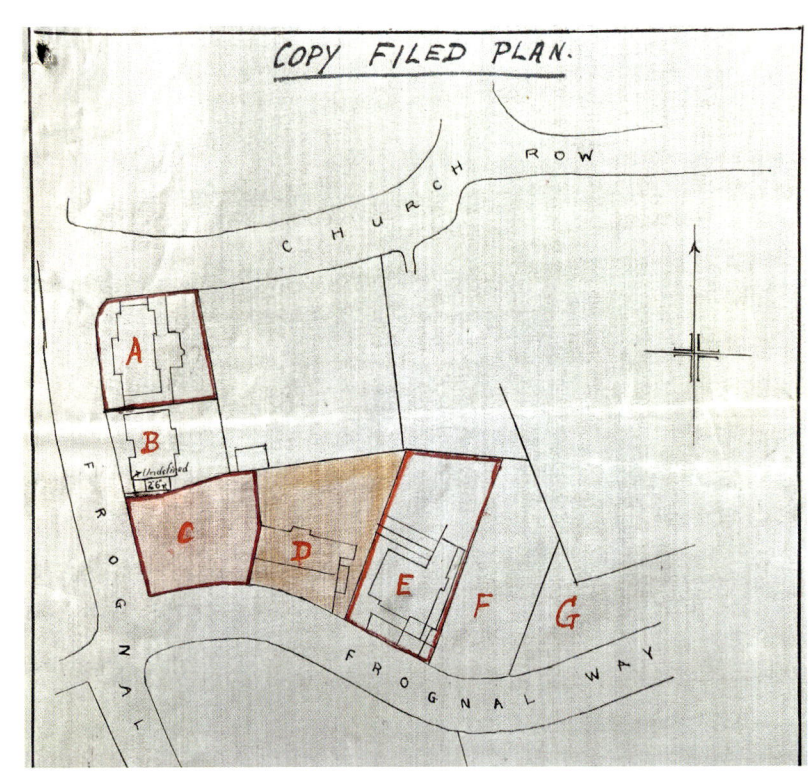

Willett plots 'A' and 'C' surround No 68, *Amesbury House,* occupying plot 'B'.

Amesbury House and the Modernist No.66 Frognal, the latter constructed on plot 'C' on the Willett plan.

In fact this international-style house was the final residential project undertaken by Connell, Ward & Lucas. Constructed "in the extreme idiom of the day, now something of a classic," according to Pevsner, the concept included the freestanding ground floor red pilotis made of reinforced concrete.

Yet, despite all its architectural merits, the 'Frognal case' as it was known, continued to be the cause of considerable dissent. Even though it was built just after the arrival of another Modernist house round the corner in Frognal Way, No.66 did not receive the same amount of admiration. If Maxwell Fry's first London building, *Sun House,* at No.9 Frognal Way was considered to be 'one of the most important embodiments of the modern, international movement of the 1930s in Hampstead', No.66 Frognal, although essentially in the same vein, was considered less than charming. Its reinforced concrete façade was totally at odds with its brick-clad neighbours, and the house was criticised for being an attempt to 'épater les bourgeois'.

Today it is seen differently. Described by the architectural critic Ian Nairn as the "best of [Connell, Ward and Lucas'] pre-war houses in England" – which Nairn states, is "tantamount to saying the best pre-war house in England." No.66 is now a listed Grade II* award-winning building which we visit next. ∎

Frognal Modernist House

J

Continuing on from the previous pages, we now take a closer look at the exceptional building at No.66 Frognal, designed by Connell, Ward & Lucas and built by Y J Lovell and Son in 1938 for the Solicitor Geoffrey Walford. The current owners were looking for a modern house in Hampstead and used a property acquisition agent to purchase the building.

On coming to view, the prospective owners walked up the stairs into the living room to find the floor flooded with light. The effect was breathtakingly beautiful, but sadly the whole place was in an extremely dilapidated state due to the lack of maintenance. It needed a severe overhaul to bring it up to current standards.

Undaunted, the new owners commissioned the specialist architect John Allan of Avanti Architects to design and specify an entire scheme of repair, upgrade and alteration works. "Initially, we weren't fully aware of the extent of John Allan's expertise and experience in this kind of project," they note, but that soon changed. At the time, Allan was the chairman at Avanti Architects and had worked on numerous similar projects. "We were fortunate to have him – he is a true expert," they recall. "English Heritage and the National Trust have a very high opinion of John Allan's work, and once he was on board, the project simply developed." The couple quickly understood the extent of his expertise, and the smooth running of their

Even though Walford only lived in the house for a few months, the curved front door, originally painted bright yellow to match his Rolls-Royce, remains the same colour – as have the rasberry pilotis.

138

own project reinforced their notion that they were truly fortunate to work with him. The owners are delighted with the result of their extensive renovation project. Ensuring that nothing was overlooked, they did everything they could to restore the house beyond its former glory.

Located at the far end of the original living room on the right is a 'curtain store' where the curtains would be pulled back out of sight. Geoffrey Walford, the original owner, could draw out seven different sets of curtains across the entire run of windows according to changing moods. The magnificent sliding glass screens opening to the 1st-floor terrace were retained and refurbished.

The architect installed shadow gaps around the stone, while the louvres adjacent to the living room entrance, for example, are a lovely detail intended to register the slightly different status of this from the kitchen entrance wall beyond the central fireplace.

Overall, the project took four years, with the couple living just up the road for the first two. This was followed by two years of living in the house while the works were completed. Originally it had cork floors and was freezing cold in the winter. Now that the building has underfloor heating, lots of insulation and double glazing, it's very comfortable.

A rectangular swimming pool was installed by the previous owners just before the house was listed Grade II. The new owners had the option under the listing to remodel it. John Allan cleverly stepped the pool down from the mass of the house and introduced the curve. His brilliant design takes the whole experience of swimming at home to another level.

Louvres in the living room.

The living room is east facing, enabling the family to enjoy the sun in the morning.

A piloti in the hallway.

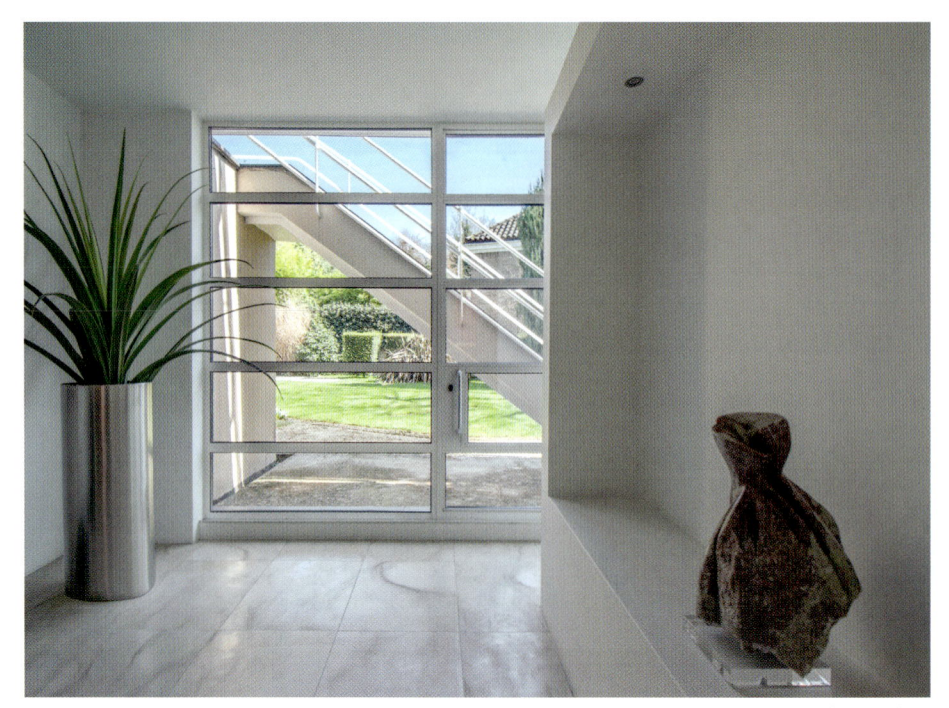

View to the garden.

The reconfigured swimming pool design now perfectly complements the architecture of the house.

The rear elevation today. All the alterations and additions by the present owners had the approval of English Heritage as they were considered to be in a manner sympathetic to the original design, now listed Grade II*.

Exterior photograph of the original house showing the upper floor's extensive terracing. *Archive image,* Connell, Ward & Lucas, *c.*1938.

Twenty years on from that project, it's time once again for more maintenance work to be undertaken to protect the original investment. The owners stress how fortunate they are to live here as the current custodians of the building. Many people like to look at this style of home but generally don't want to actually live in such a house. But for those like this couple, who truly do love the space and the light that Modernist houses afford, it's ideal. They use virtually all of its 5000 square feet. And with its three bedrooms and six bathrooms, this remarkable home is extremely easy to live in.

It is amusing to sometimes hear the comment, that given the outside staircase at the front of the house, this building must be a block of flats with two apartments on either side. But the Avanti project, in recessing the new upper enclosure in frameless glazing behind the column line, restores the deliberate asymmetry of the original design.

The project won both a RIBA Award and a RIBA Conservation Award in 2005. Avanti Architects have sought to make No.66 Frognal a state-of-the-art C21 home that can also once again be recognised as an outstanding building of its period.

Remarkable Homes of NW3

Shepherd's Well, Frognal Way

Priory Lodge, built c.1747, illustration J P Emslie, 1899.

The earliest house on Frognal Way is considered to be No.11, built by Albert Farmer. This house was owned by a Mrs Jane Flood, who, together with Earnest Farman, also held other plots of land nearby. They sold some of this land to William Willett Ltd in July 1931. And one of the houses built on this land, is *Shepherd's Well*, No.5 Frognal Way.

This detached property was designed by Adrian Gilbert Scott (1882-1963) as his personal residence with title passing to Scott on 27 May 1930. A specialist in ecclesiastical architecture, Adrian Gilbert Scott CBE was the son of an architect and the grandson of the prolific Sir George Gilbert Scott, who had famously designed the Albert Memorial and the Midland Grand Hotel at St Pancras Station.

A house called *Priory Lodge* once stood on part of the Frognal Hall Estate, located opposite what is now Frognal Lane. It was here, in this house, where Samuel Johnson compiled *A Dictionary of the English Language*. And while living at the lodge, he also wrote much of *The Vanity of Human Wishes* (published 1749). "Mrs. Johnson, for the sake of country air, had lodgings in Hampstead, to which Johnson occasionally resorted," recounts Anna Maxwell in her book *Hampstead: Its Historic Houses, Its Literary and Artistic Associations* in 1912. She continues, "The land south of Frognal Lane still lay in lovely fields, rich in every variety of foliage. Artists came from afar to sketch the picturesque 'Haunted Court' Frognal Priory, which stood, buried in trees, not far from Priory Lodge." Described by Johnson as the "small house just beyond the church," this charming house was finally pulled down in the 1920s, and the land redeveloped.

East of Frognal Lane lies Frognal Way, which was initially laid out in 1924 on the former grounds of *Priory Lodge*. Already mentioned as the location of Maxwell Fry's Modernist *Sun House* (see p137), today, the lane is a wide unadopted, gated thoroughfare.

Priory Lodge (coloured red) once stood opposite Frognal Lane.

No.11 Frognal Way built in 1925, with the *Sun House* visible in the left background. *Photo, Tony Murray.*

142

Standing guard as the first house by the entrance to Frognal Way is this fine-looking, Grade II house *Shepherd's Well*. The dormer windows, porch and garage frontage are later additions to Adrian Gilbert Scott's original design.

The style and design of *Shepherd's Well*, with its handmade bricks, red pantile roof, and white-painted wooden sash windows, is said to suggest the influence of Lutyens. Reassuringly, much of the exterior remains as it was designed, although the dormer windows were added later, as was the garage. The porch is also a further addition. The staircase and other key features within the house are substantially as they were originally, and the layout of the entrance hallway and the ground floor rooms remain the same.

Naomi, the daughter of Adrian Gilbert Scott, fondly recalls living at *Shepherd's Well*. In 1984 she wrote that her father had "Designed everything right down to the door handles. The bricks were made in Holland, and the tiles and the double staircase came from Italy. The doors of the drawing room and the dining room were specially carved from Magnolia wood by an Italian craftsman."

The current owners were looking for a permanent residence in Hampstead. Hunting for the ideal place, they viewed many houses over a period of two to three years. Not wanting a school commute by car, they needed to be within walking distance of their childrens' schools in Hampstead. They were particularly attracted to Frognal Way due to its unique, detached houses and asked their estate agent to try to find them a property on the road. Fate intervened in 2003 when No.5 came up for sale.

The family fully appreciates the house's architectural lineage. The fact that Adrian Gilbert Scott had imported so many beau-

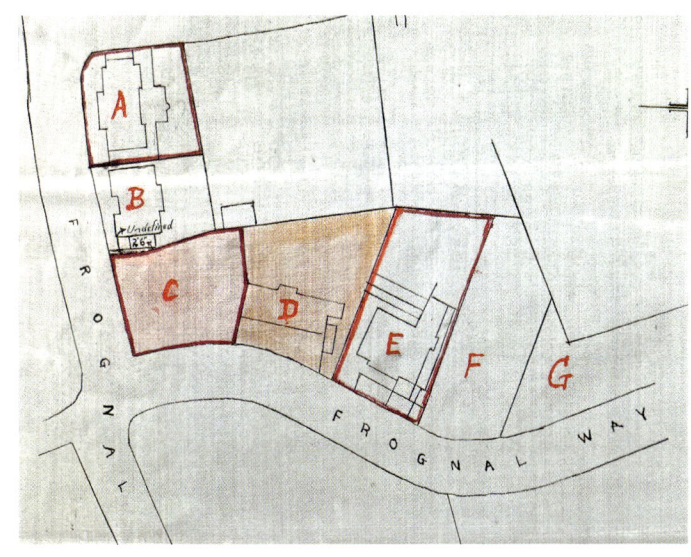

Shepherd's Well is the plot marked 'D' on the William Willett Ltd plan.

tiful elements into the house, including his favoured double staircase (a preference shared with his distinguished grandfather, George Gilbert Scott) is, for these owners, a constant pleasure.

The owners enjoy living in what is virtually a country lane, even though it's in London, as they had previously lived on a relatively busy road. And they particularly value the fact that there is an open view of the house from the road. As there are so many architectural gems hidden away behind walls and fences, it is wonderful for passers-by to be able to see and enjoy the building.

The imperial or double staircase from Italy. The first flight rises to a half landing and then doubles back into two symmetrical flights.

An original magnolia wood doorframe and magnolia door beyond.

Detail of the silk wallpaper.

The dining room walls are hung with hand-painted silk wallpaper.

Due to its Grade II listing, there are some things the owners would wish to change. But they fully understood the limitations of listed building status when they bought the house and are aware they are preserving it for future generations while enjoying the benefits of living in such a remarkable house in an enchanting location. ▪

Frognal Way

J

As we have noted on previous pages, it was Mrs Jane Flood who, together with Earnest Farman, also owned other plots of land on Frognal and Frognal Way. They sold some of this land to William Willett Ltd in July 1931. And it is another of the houses built on this land, No.7 Frognal Way, which is the focus of our attention here (see the plan on p143).

Set between *Shepherd's Well* and the *Sun House*, No.7 Frognal Way was built in the early 1930s by William Willett Ltd and designed by Oswald Milne, then aged 40.

The old *Priory Lodge* in 1911 as seen from the grounds, with the parish church of St John-at-Hampstead in the background, *A R Quinton*.

No.7 Frognal Way with the church of St John on the left.
The house stands on the plot marked 'E' on the William Willett Ltd plan.

Remarkable Homes of NW3

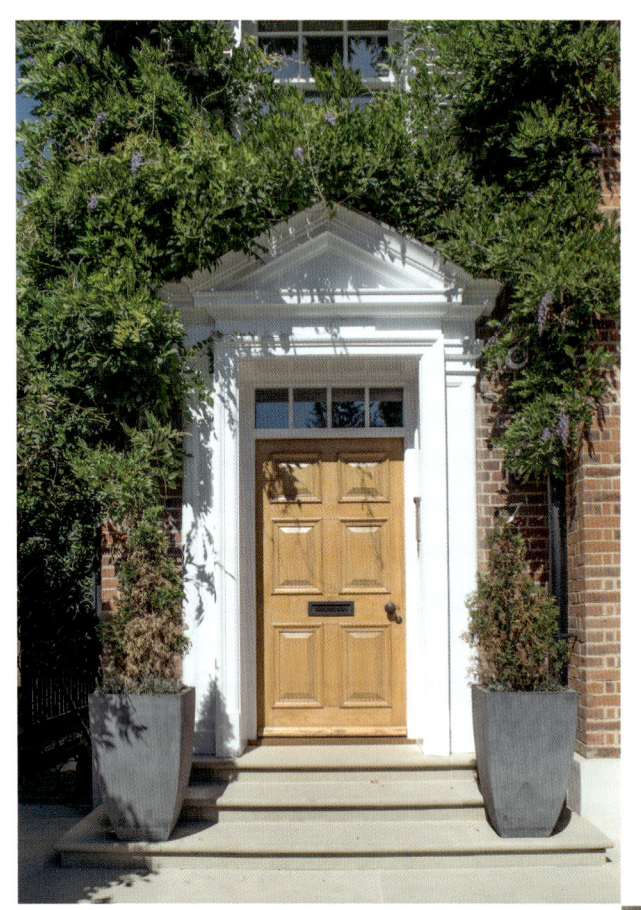

Traditional balusters and hardwood stair treads.

Sliding doors access rooms in the new basement.

French windows in the delightful dining room.

The renovated conservatory opens to the terraced garden.

The son of an architect, Oswald Milne lived from 1881-1968 and had been employed for two years as an assistant to the highly-regarded Sir Edwin Lutyens prior to setting up his own practice in 1904. From 1906 to 1910, collaborating with his father, he designed some of the Mayfair Claridge's Hotel interiors. Milne himself succumbed to the charms of Hampstead and, on moving here, also fulfilled civic duties. From 1937 through to 1953, he served various council functions, including that of Mayor of Hampstead from 1947-49.

The present owners of Milne's No.7 had been patiently keeping their eye on this lovely property for some time. Renting locally, they purchased the house when it was placed on the market in 2009. Working closely with their architect Peter Phillips and his partner Krysia Swierkosz, they embarked upon designing the layout of the new interior. This project was a significant undertaking involving considerable restructuring work while sensitively retaining the style of the original house.

All in all, it took three years before the new owners could move in. Virtually everything in the interior had been gutted, and a new basement floor was created.

Very little was done to the exterior as the property is in a conservation area, although there is a new kitchen extension. Set at right angles to the house, the renovated conservatory, now with a lowered floor, opens out to the terraced garden. Neither the extension nor the conservatory are visible from the road. The overall result is an exceptionally well conceived and beautifully executed family home that remains in harmony with its surroundings.

Interestingly, the neighbouring churchyard surrounding St John-at-Hampstead is particularly noted for its beautiful collection of flourishing plants.

A few elements of the original house have been preserved including this charming iron side gate.

Frognal Way *continued*

No.4 Frognal Way viewed from the east.

Frognal Way is a wide, unadopted thoroughfare laid out over part of the land of the Frognal Hall Estate and *Priory Lodge* in 1924. The development has been described as "the showpiece of inter-war Hampstead housing" by architectural historian Andrew Saint. And, without doubt, the houses on Frognal Way vary considerably in style and character. Located virtually opposite No.7, here we are looking at No.4 Frognal Way. Dating from 1934, Pevsner describes this attractive and rather unusual property as "Hollywood Spanish-Colonial". The frontage displays a central block, framed by two angled wings set slightly below ground level.

Steps lead down to the front entrance.

The flying or 'winged monk'.

The rear aspect on the other hand, comprising two long sides set at right angles, is above ground level. This change is due to the descending contour of the land, leading out onto a generous garden. The garages are located to the right of the house.

A flight of steps leads down to the front door in the central section of this 2-storey property. Above the entrance are three small round arch windows with columns – almost Palladian in style. And most notably, an intriguing plaque with a bas-relief

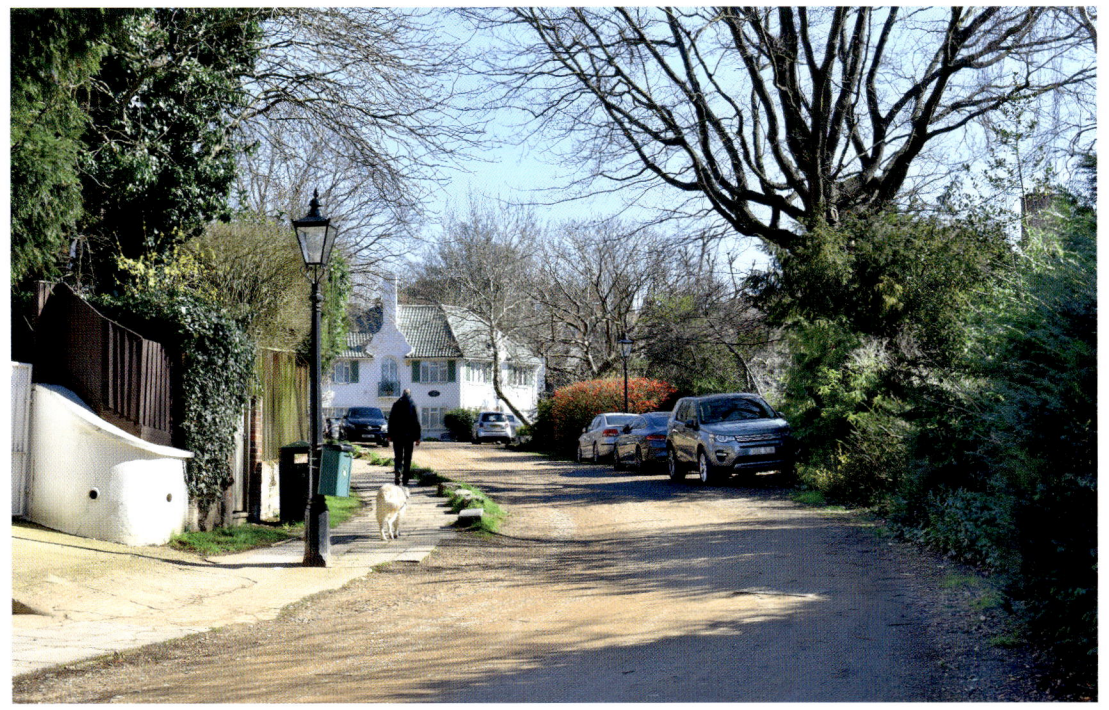

Looking eastward from the location of No.4 Frognal Way.

Blue Tiles Frognal Way, designed by R L Page for Dame Gracie Fields.

Dame Gracie Fields in 1973, *photo Allan Warren* CC BY-SA 3.0.

depicting what looks very much like a man wearing a skull cap and a winged cloak, along with the date 1934. It might even be portraying a winged monk, as originally suggested by historian Christopher Wade.

Leaving No 4, we turn towards Church Row, and another unusual house comes into view. Designed by R L Page, the original colour of the roof gave it its name, *Blue Tiles.* This South African Dutch-styled property was built specifically for the multi-talented artist Gracie Fields (1898-1979), said to be the highest-paid film star in the world in 1937. ∎

Remarkable Homes of NW3

Frognal Close

No.2 Frognal Close.

Just south of Frognal Way, we find Frognal Close, comprising six brick-built Modernist houses designed by Ernst L Freud in 1936-7 for his client Ralph Davies and completed in 1938. This enclave of houses is arranged around a cul-de-sac that leads to a small square planted with green shrubbery. Each block of two semi-detached dwellings has a front door and a canopy at either end. Raised bands in buff brick dress the windows on the upper storey. Freud's development is part of a modern group of buildings in NW3 that include the *Sun House* on Frognal Way and No.66 Frognal (see p138). Tucked away just off Frognal, the building we are visiting is the Grade II semi-detached No.2 Frognal Close overlooking the square. The property is owned today by a couple who have lived here for many years. "I used to live in Belsize Crescent at No.20 at the time when Twiggy was living opposite us on the Crescent," says the owner. So architecturally, this house is significantly different.

"I've been an architect since 1971," he continues. "I set up my own practice in 1978, acquiring this house in 1984. It now seems to have been relatively cheap, but then it was a seen as an enormous sum, particularly for such a run-down piece of modern architecture." The development was only 46 years old at that time, but it was already in need of care and attention.

The light-filled dining/living area extends to an L-shaped sitting room beyond.

"Back then, this was quite a viable little close, but now it's lost a little of its original crispness, although it is wonderfully quiet." Needless to say, the house has been changed by each generation that has owned the property. The kitchen and the floor above it are not original, as is evident from the rendered white exterior. The couple added this extension in 1989.

"This parcel of land was once part of *Frognal Priory* which had fallen into disrepair," explains the owner. "After we bought the house, I found a terrace about three metres below the level of the current one. It was clearly original, complete with its terrace tiles and no doubt belonging to the old *Frognal Priory*."

"The close is a development by Sigmund Freud's son who had trained at the Bauhaus, so being Austrian and trained in Europe he designed in metric dimensions. Therefore the whole building is metric, which in 1938 must have been an interesting experience for the English builders used only to imperial dimensions. It also meant that he needed to use metric bricks," recalls the owner. However, the internal structure comprises imperial bricks as its core with just a surface skim of metric bricks as a cosmetic finish on the external face. The interior was constructed with a cellular arrangement of lounge, kitchen, dining and sitting rooms, although some walls have been altered since then.

"The project was aimed at the bourgeoisie, the middle class at the time, with a call system for the staff and the kitchen clearly separated from the rest of the house. We still have the buzzer box," adds the owner. As well as building the kitchen extension, he rebuilt the garages at the side. "The metric bricks we used were specially imported from Belgium, therefore the bricks on the new garage look exactly the same as those in the main house.

The view from the garden terrace, the white extension was added by the owner.

Prospect from the kitchen extension towards its semi-detached neighbour, No.1.

The owner comes from a school of architecture where Bauhaus was king. "The buildings are quite severe and academic in appearance on the outside," he explains. "But as soon as you enter, light pours in, and the place takes on a very different feel – the interior reveals a totally different house. My wife hated the whole idea of the architecture at first, but she has now got used to it and truly loves our home."

The living accommodation on the ground floor flows beautifully from one room to another. It's just two stories – a single staircase leading to the corridor and bedrooms occupying the entire upper floor. "In that regard it's lovely, says the owner. "Although on the other hand, its construction is terrible because the building has no cavity – it's an old-school solid external wall building. As a result, the heating bills are horrendous. We have improved that by changing all the original Crittall windows as part of our renovation work and by insulating the flat roof, which is also a terrace."

From Belsize to Bauhaus, the owner's alterations and additions, together with its original architectural credentials and the cherishing care of its present owners, ensures that No.2 Frognal Close continues to hold its place along with the other remarkable modern homes in the area. ∎

The first-floor corridor still looking crisp and fresh.

Manor Lodge, Frognal Lane

From the side, this view only offers a partial glimpse of the building behind the wall. The dual-coloured stock brick building has 2 storeys, attics and a basement.

A fitting home for the manorial bailiff, this detached house, constructed around 1813, was the summer meeting place of the Court Leet and Court Baron of the Manor of Hampstead well into C20. It stands as a beautiful example of a surviving Georgian property in Hampstead. The first occupant of No.40 Frognal Lane, recorded in 1815, was John Thompson, a retired auctioneer known as 'Memory Thompson' for his impressive knowledge of London. *Manor Lodge* later passed into the estate of Sir Spencer Maryon-Wilson, and in April 1880 it was sold to the architect Basil Champneys (1842-1935), who lived here until August 1882. In more recent times, from 1956 to 1986, it was the home of the much-loved actor Dame Peggy Ashcroft.

In the late 1980s, *Manor Lodge* and *Manor Farm* (the neigbouring property at No.42 Frognal Lane) were owned by Peter Hill-Wood, former Chairman of Arsenal Football Club, according to the current owner of the property, who knows much about the history. We learn that *Manor Lodge* had changed hands again in the late 1990s, when it was bought, along with No.38, by a Russian owner. No.38 was sold on and in turn demolished (the current owner is now rebuilding on that site). *Manor Lodge,* meanwhile, was furnished in the French classic style while under Russian ownership.

"When it comes to the architectural development of *Manor Lodge*," the owner says, "the Georgian windows visibly define the original rectangular 2-storey Georgian house. And its original entrance was through the round-arched doorway with French windows and fanlight positioned on the garden side."

The original house entrance was through this round-arched doorway.

Manor Lodge, viewed from the garden, offers a much better idea of its status; the differences between the 1849 Victorian extension and the original 1813 rectangular Georgian build with its original central round-arched doorway are evident.

The dining room is located within the original Georgian part of the building.

The dining room occupies the former hallway of the Georgian house as revealed by the round arch over the French windows.

From the early 1840s until 1848, the house was sublet and occupied by George Chater, a wholesale stationer. After obtaining a direct lease in 1848, Chater extended the house in 1849 – his Victorian extension can be identified by the smaller Italianate windows. George Chater's family enjoyed his enlarged residence until 1871.

The current owner has conducted a full restoration of the interior with the blessing of the assigned conservation officer. "The staircase is a reinstated replica of the original. It's based on some rediscovered details of the balusters and a handrail," the owner recalls. "During the strip-out, our architect found a small section of what we believed to be the original staircase which had been boxed in. From this sample and his research, he proposed a design which Camden's heritage officer, Antonia Powell, subsequently approved." Fortunately, besides the extensive improvements already completed, the owner has obtained consent to make further changes and reopen some of the original fireplaces. He has also had the time to take stock of the exterior surroundings. "One of the best things about this property is its privacy; there are only a handful of houses in Hampstead that offer this level of seclusion," he notes.

'If music be the food of love…' the music room piano placed within the bay window of the Victorian extension.

A study desk deliberately offset from the window allows for the benefits of natural light and eye focus change while working.

Then comes that heartfelt observation made by so many Hampstead home owners: "I enjoy the fact that when you look out of the window, you could be anywhere rural or at least semi-rural while being just a five-minute walk into the heart of Hampstead and a fifteen-minute drive into the centre of London." The owner's passion for this very old and remarkably beautiful house and its grounds is evident throughout this restoration project, and his last words to us reveal the heart of the matter. "And most especially, I love the house itself due to the beautiful Georgian architecture."

Concealed at the end of a long driveway and unseen from the road No.42 Frognal Lane hides a grand symmetrical, red-brick mansion. Writer and architectural historian Alastair Service notes it's "A remarkably strong composition – rising to four gables and a crowning central group of four chimneys." Then called *Manor Farm* and described as "very snug and solid," it was built on the site of old farm buildings in 1881 for the gifted architect Basil Champneys then living at *Manor Lodge*. Champneys lived at *Manor Farm* from 1882 until his death in 1935 while designing glorious buildings of which the Rylands Memorial Library in Manchester is but one example. In 1894 *Manor Farm* acquired the name *Hall Oak*.

Today, both names are used, although *Manor Farm* is the more usual appellation.

Chesterford Gardens

Located on the western side of the quiet, secluded, tree-lined Chesterford Gardens, this beautiful house at No.16, with 3 floors plus a basement, is in excellent condition and looks superb inside and out. Its key external features include the French windows that give onto a single-span central balcony that links the two full-height bays. In addition, there are three magnificent dormers. Above the hedge line separating the house from the street a distinctive band of dark blue brickwork is just visible. This band delineates the boundary between the basement and the ground floor.

Researcher Peter Wenning has ascertained that in the 1901 census No.16 Chesterford Gardens was home to the Rowe family with their six live-in servants. But after WWII the house was converted into flats and eventually occupied by squatters. It remained divided until the end of the century, only reverting to single-family ownership when Karsten and Barbara Moller became the new owners in 2000. The investment banker and his wife restored the property and lived here until 2007, when it became the home of Jules and Cheryl Burns.

Jules Burns, a media and television professional and ex-Director of Liverpool FC, was born at No.13 Redington Road. He met his wife Cheryl, also born in Hampstead, at St Jude's youth club in Hampstead Garden Suburb. Cheryl is a choreographer and professional dancer who previously performed in theatre and on TV. Now retired but still teaching

A corner of the reception room looking out onto the rear garden.

Part of the main reception room.

exercise classes, her efforts to do anything to get people moving have been awarded with a British Empire Medal – she jokingly describes this honour as standing for 'bossy exercise mistress'!

"We moved to the north and lived in Manchester from 1976, and I later became Operations MD at Granada Media," explains Jules. The couple returned to London in 2000, buying a house on Gayton Road in Hampstead. After leaving Granada in 2002, Jules and two other colleagues started a new business, All3Media in 2003. Then in 2007, Jules and Cheryl came across No.16. "We were immediately taken by the interior finish and all the lovely woodwork," says Cheryl. "It was so unusual we went for it! The house had been extensively remodelled internally after having been a squat."

The restoration of this double-fronted house back to single occupancy was accomplished with first-class rebuilding work, which included the precisely executed external brickwork pointing. However, that conversion was completed over two decades ago. "We also had to do quite a few other things, such as replacing the roof and upgrading to double glazing," adds Cheryl.

"One advantage of a large house is that there's room for visiting family members who come to stay, and there's plenty of wall space everywhere for our pictures," says Cheryl. The house is also perfectly suited for hosting the various fundraising events the couple hold, both for different animal charities and also for the arts. "We host concerts – pre Covid we held two or three concerts a year and the garden is perfect for these gatherings."

Extensive panelling and woodwork on the staircase viewed from the ground floor.

This view from the first-floor landing shows the panelling and barley twist balusters to advantage.

The beautiful solid wood doors and door frames match the staircase.

Prospect to the southwest from a rear bedroom window.

The garden loggia with its Doric-style columns.

Chesterford Gardens was laid out on land originally owned by the Maryon-Wilson family. Work began after the 1896 application for the construction of a new route to connect Redington Road with Frognal Lane. Local builder Edward Michael built a house at the junction of Redington Road with Chesterford Gardens, as well as others on Chesterford Gardens itself. Nine houses were constructed between 1897 and 1900. This phase of development included No.16 Chesterford Gardens, built on the western side by Edward Michael in 1900. Four further houses on the road were constructed to a similar design, one of which featuring a Tudor-style variation. Quennell may have designed some of the houses including Nos.5-11 on the opposite side of the road. No.18 Chesterford Gardens next door was the last home of the Victorian artist Henry Holiday (1839-1927). Holiday was part of the Pre-Raphaelite school of art, as well as an accomplished landscape painter, stained-glass designer, illustrator and sculptor. ■

The Well Walk area

Winding southwardly from the heath, there is a charming little grove in Well Walk, with a bench at the end; whereon I last saw poor Keats, the poet of the "Pot of Basil," sitting and sobbing his dying breath into a handkerchief,—gleaning parting looks towards the quiet landscape he had delighted in—musing, as in his *Ode to a Nightingale.*
– William Hone (1780-1842) *Table Book*, Vol 3

Samuel Taylor Coleridge would sometimes come over across the green fields, by way of Millfield Lane, from Highgate, to have a chat with Keats on his seat at the end of Well Walk; and when he last shook hands with him here, he turned to Leigh Hunt, and whispered, "There is death in that hand." And such was too truly the case; for John Keats was in a consumption; and he went abroad very soon afterwards, to die beneath the sunny skies of Italy.
– Edward Walford from his *Old and New London*

John Keats, silhouette, *Charles Brown*, 1819. Keats lodged in Well Walk in 1817.

"As Well Walk stands to-day there is little of the old Wells element left," recalls Thomas Barratt in his *Annals of Hampstead*. "The grand old trees still remain at the upper end of Well Walk the trees under which … in the years between 1817 and 1820 Keats sat and mused in complete abandonment to poetic inspiration." As Barratt reminds us, "The *Wells Tavern* marks the site whereon in Keats's time stood *The Green Man*," and "the site of the Wells and Great Room, or Pump Room as it was often styled, is now partly the entrance to Gainsborough Gardens, Wellside, Well Walk, being built on the remainder."

Located on the opposite corner of East Heath Road and Well Walk, we find No.50 Well Walk, *Klippan House*. Built in 1881 and originally known as *Thwaitehead,* it is a remarkable building. Set at an angle to the corner with East Heath Road, *Klippan House* is now considered one of the best Victorian houses in Hampstead with its red brick façade, large stone mullioned windows, and the pleasing first-floor open fretwork balcony. It was designed by Ewan Christian (1814-1895)

Nostalgic view of Keats Seat (now replaced) at the far end of Well Walk, *O Jewitt, c*.1869.

The imposing Grade II *Klippan House*, No.50 Well Walk, built 1881-82, was undoubtedly influenced by the Domestic Revival style made popular through the work of Richard Norman Shaw (1831-1912).

Klippan House, garden frontage, *photo: Nick Kane.* The house has been fully restored internally and externally by Belsize Architects. Of note are the massive and spectacular ribbed chimney stacks.

and built in 1881 by Cornish and Gaymer of Norfolk for the architect's own residence. Ewan Christian previously lived in Eton Villas during the 1850s. He is particularly noted for designing the National Portrait Gallery, completed shortly after his death. Alastair Service notes of Klippan House: "Its design is subtle, the volumes and the complex roofs play with each other as one moves around it, and there is much lovely metalwork on the exterior."

By 2010 this lovely house was falling into disrepair. Belsize Architects were commissioned to return it to a single-family home and bring back its former glory. The exterior was carefully restored, including the elaborate glazed panels. Sadly, a frieze along the 1st-floor band was not wholly recoverable, having been rendered over during earlier restorations. It originally read: "God's Providence is Mine Inheritance" – as noted by Christopher Wade, most apt for a church architect. However, the 'shadow' of that inscription remains beneath the render awaiting possible restoration in the future. Nevertheless, some fine internal features have survived, including high-quality joinery, a few original windows with patterned lead work, oak-panelled doors, and fireplaces in an Arts and Crafts-related style.

The Hampstead Spa

John Duffield secured the Wells Trustees' approval and was granted a lease of the land, excluding the Well, from 2 June 1701 at £50 per annum. Duffield immediately built an imposing Long Room on Well Walk. It housed an actual pump room at the northern end – where the chalybeate water was taken. The Pump Room led to the Assembly Room for partakers to rest and to enjoy the entertainments – the establishment could accommodate up to 500 people.

The gardens to the southwest had lawns and pathways interspersed with flower beds, an ornamental pond, and a bowling green. As a result of its chalybeate waters and fresh air, the health resort of Hampstead soon became a pleasure destination. Hampstead "arose into a place of crowded and fashionable resort, teeming with amusements, dissipation and folly," wrote John James Park in his *Topography of Hampstead.* The original Long Room site is now marked by a plaque on the wall of *Wellside,* a house that adjoins the main entrance to Gainsborough Gardens.

No.46 Well Walk is early C18, with Gothic features added at a later date, it stands on the other corner of Gainsborough Gardens. We pay a visit to Gainsborough Gardens on the following pages.

Tablet on *Wellside* recording the site of the old Pump Room in the Long Room at the entrance to Gainsborough Gardens.

Well Walk, *by E H Dixon,* showing the Long Room incorporating a Pump Room. This was demolished in 1882, making way for the present-day entrance to Gainsborough Gardens. No.46 Well Walk is in the foreground.

Wellside, Well Walk stands on the corner of today's Gainsborough Gardens. In the 1960s it was the home of economist Baron Balogh, "of Hampstead in Greater London".

No.46 Well Walk is "of exceeding charm," according to Pevsner. "It has a pretty Gothic oriel, tripartite window above, and porch with clustered columns." This corner house originally adjoined the spa's Pump Room and Long Room.

A 1911 image of Well Walk with the commemorative Chalybeate fountain constructed by Henry S Legg in 1882, *archive*.

Today, the well head is still flanked by its steps, but no longer delivering chalybeate water. Located virtually opposite the fountain is No.40 Well Walk (see next page).

161

Remarkable Homes of NW3

The dignified and popular *Wells Tavern* on Well Walk with its elegant, round-arched first-floor windows.

The Grade II three-story *Wells Tavern* with cellars replaced *The Green Man* c.1849, which itself replaced *The Whitestone* of the Wells Spa period.

John Constable had a commanding view of London from No.40 Well Walk, centered on St Paul's Cathedral. Soon after moving in he wrote to his friend John Fisher, "Our little drawing room commands a view unequalled in Europe – from Westminster Abbey to Gravesend."

Among the first Well Walk residents, John Constable's family was to suffer the tragic loss of his wife Maria to tuberculosis the following year, 1828 – but it remained the family home for John and their seven children until 1834.

"I love every stile, and stump, and lane in the village," said Constable, "as long as I am able to hold a brush I shall never cease to paint them."

The Grade II Georgian townhouse at No.40 Well Walk, was leased by John Constable from the summer of 1827 until 1834.

Gainsborough Gardens

The Long Room, Well Walk in 1879 from a watercolour, *J P Emslie*. The house at the end was added later.

A talented and artistic man, Legg designed almost half the houses, including the charming gardener's lodge, built in 1886. One of the houses in the Gardens was built in 1895 by local builder Charles B King for Henry Legg himself. In addition to enjoying the right to access the central garden, common to all residents, that house has a covenant stipulating the right for an unrestricted view of the gardens from its front windows. We also have on record that E J May built Nos.3 and 4, and that Nos.11-14 were designed by Horace Field in the early 1890s.

Once John Duffield turned the Gainsborough gift of six acres into the Hampstead Spa, and 'taking the waters' in Hampstead became fashionable, the area also began to be coveted as a place in which to live permanently. From then on, substantial developments around the spas occurred. After some 180 years, the *Long Room* was finally demolished in 1882, making way for the present-day entrance to Gainsborough Gardens. And a year later, the Wells trustees laid out Gainsborough Gardens on the southern side of Well Walk. This 1883 project was overseen by its surveyor, Henry S Legg.

©Openstreetmap Contributors theundergroundmap CC BY-SA 2.0
Plan of Well Walk and the neighbourhood in the Spa period superimposed over a modern map. The black outline is the boundary of the 6 acres given by the Gainsboroughs, based on a drawing by George Potter in 1904. The Long Room is defined as a grey rectangle, the Wells Gardens are pale green, the bowling green area is a darker rectangle, and the central oval was the approximate location of the ornamental pond.

Occupying land once part of the original spa's pleasure gardens, Legg's Gainsborough Gardens houses surround an oval-shaped area that once had an ornamental pond Gainsborough Gardens is regarded as a scheme of significant architectural and historical interest, thanks to the balance between the houses and the surrounding open garden space set out by Legg. Railings originally encircled the garden but were removed in the 1940s as part of the war effort. The central oval is now an open area surrounded by many beautiful trees.

The Lodge, built for the gardener.

Part of the central garden.

at one of the houses." The present owners have lived here in Gainsborough Gardens for six years, having bought the property in 2017. The house still retains some original chimneypieces, most of the joinery is original, as is the attractive staircase with its arcaded balustrades. The owners consider themselves extremely fortunate to live here, as the house is ideal for them in so many respects. They stress that it is remarkably well conceived, the interior layout is excellent, every room has a specific feel to it, and with energy flowing from one room to the next, the result is an delightfully creative environment in which to live and work.

Gainsborough Gardens Ltd oversees all its care and maintenance, as well as matters concerning parking, arrangements for builders, etc. Two major events are held every year, a summer party and a fireworks party for the residents of this private, gated estate which has become a highly desirable enclave in which to live.

House in Gainsborough Gardens, *The Builder*, 1885.

We are visiting one of a superb pair of Grade II semi-detached houses which stand on the southern part of Gainsborough Gardens. Built of red brick in the Domestic Revival manner, the architectural details include rubbed and moulded-brick details, red sandstone dressings, gables rendered in pebbledash and clay tile roofing. The house features an impressive gable set flush with the front elevation, with a small triangular pediment above the window. Designed by Henry S Legg and built in 1888 this elaborate house was once the home of Arthur Bolton (1864-1945), architect and architectural historian and curator of the Sir John Soane's Museum (1917-1945). The women's suffrage campaigner Elizabeth Knight lived next door in 1933. According to *The Times* in 1934, residents "enjoy privacy and quietude as there are gates and lodges, and few, except an occasional visitor out of curiosity, enter the gardens unless to call

The hallway and staircase with original ceiling plasterwork.

There is also the added advantage of the original basement – today it's used as a family workshop, but at one time, it had been converted into a separate flat. Unfortunately, the house suffered from some further inappropriate changes during the 1960s and '70s. Windows were changed, and original details were lost. So the current owners are reinstating many of the original features and, over time, hope to rectify most of the errors. As with all such projects, a great deal of work is involved in preserving the fabric of the building. They describe this as an endless but entirely worthwhile task and have vowed to continue their work to preserve the house for the next generation. ∎

The home we are visiting is to the right of this pair on Gainsborough Gardens. The original ironwork of the front steps has been preserved.

Original stained glass illuminates an ante-room.

Rear view of the house with its square bay and balcony above.

The wonderful square rear bay window.

Also on Gainsborough Gardens, No. 9 was the London home of David Cornwell (1931-2020). Better known as the author John le Carré, he often frequented *The Wells Tavern* with his wife and friends.

165

Cottage doors on Flask Walk.

No.75 Flask Walk, early 2022.

Rosemount, Flask Walk

With rendered front and some mid-C19 detail – *Pevsner*

Located on the corner of New End Square, we find the imposing *Rosemount*. Set back from Flask Walk and approached by steps, this detached Grade II house dates from *c.*1812 and has a most interesting history. The building is a double-fronted Regency property comprising 3 storeys and a semi-basement. While it appears to be a large house when viewed from the front, it is in fact only one room deep. Although the house had been restored in recent years, the current owners renovated the entire front façade in the summer of 2022. The superb portico is now returned to its former glory. It also features a magnificent fanlight over the front door.

The grand prostyle Doric portico with dentil cornice is now fully restored. The round-arched doorway has a fluted surround, and a magnificent radial fanlight over a panelled front door.

167

Restored metalwork on the window guards and splendid portico.

Part of a restored cornice.

Well preserved original fully-working shutters.

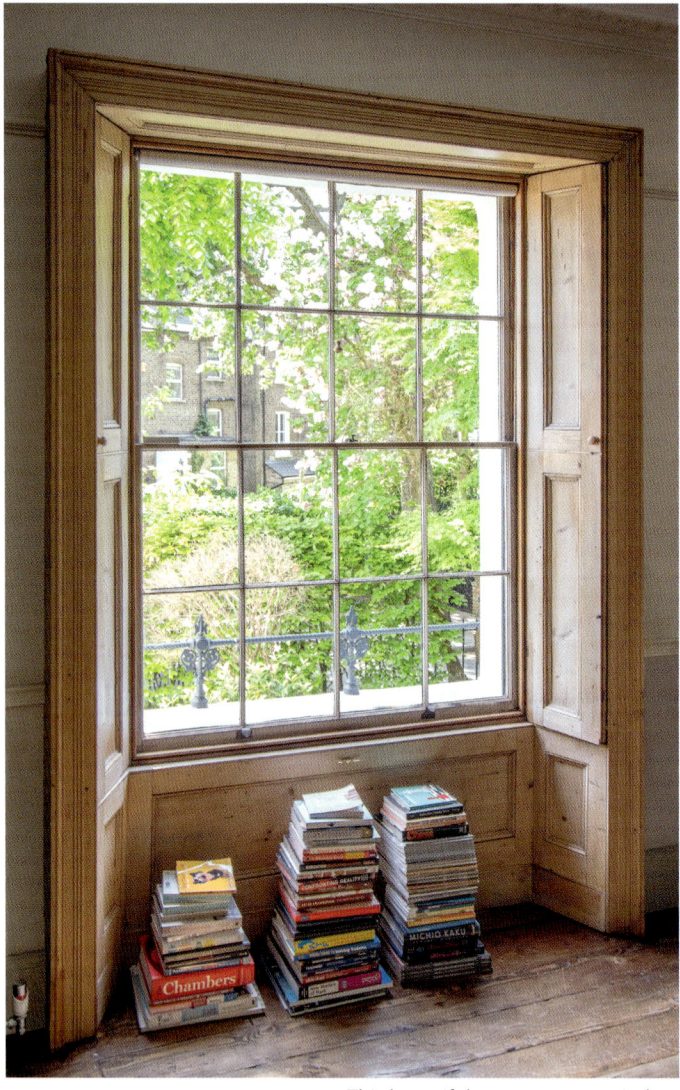

This beautiful 8 over 8-pane window frames the garden and piles of books.

The house's fabulous Regency windows with their delicate glazing bars are beautifully balanced. The owners note that the original metal counter-weight system, embedded in the surrounding frames, has survived; this has the effect of the sashes being so light that they can almost be opened with one finger. Restoring the exterior ironwork was a recent project. "The ironwork had been painted over numerous times," says the owner, "so we stripped it right back – now the definition of the metalwork is fully revealed."

A primary feature of this property is the spiral staircase, a rather practical option as the house is so narrow. This staircase extends right down to the semi-basement. Here, the original stone steps to the semi-basement level are

The family cat gazes down the spiral staircase, *owner's photo*.

This lower section of the spiral staircase retains the original stone steps.

said to be from part of an old tavern on the site that predated the building of *Rosemount*.

Interestingly, the adjoining house, now No.40 New End Square, stands on the site of what was once the *Hawk Tavern*. This hostelry was established sometime between 1748 and 1759 but rebuilt in 1815 following a fire. It had reopened by 1827 and traded until 1860 when it was converted into private ownership. Alfred, Lord Tennyson made it the home for his mother in the 1860s, linking it via an opening in the wall to No.75 Flask Walk. In the 1860s, *Rosemount* was once home to Captain Richard Jesse, who was married to Emilia, Tennyson's younger sister, so no doubt Tennyson visited the house occasionally during his trips to London from West Sussex.

More recently, after WWII, *Rosemount* would become the family home of the publisher Douglas William Service, whose eldest son Alastair Service (1931-2013) was the architectural historian and Secretary of the Family Planning Association. The family moved to *Rosemount* from Alastair's birthplace at *One Oak*, the Arts & Crafts house at No.16 Redington Road (designed by A H Mackmurdo in 1889). ∎

A glazed door accesses the delightful courtyard, *owner's photo*.

The recent conservatory with the adjoining white stucco No.40 New End Square.

Rosemount is located just across from the Queen Anne Grade 1-listed *Burgh House* on New End Square built *c.*1704. Now a museum, the house is named after The Rev Allatson Burgh who helped prevent the Lord of the Manor from building on Hampstead Heath.

Remarkable Homes of NW3

Heathside

K

On leaving Gainsborough Gardens by the south eastern entrance we find a lovely Grade II-listed cottage aptly called the *Cottage on the Heath*. Built in the Vernacular Revival style, until the 1930s it was the former stables for the corner house No.6 Gainsborough Gardens c.1885, designed by Henry S Legg.

The ground floor of No.6a, the *Cottage on the Heath,* is constructed in red brick in Flemish bond with the upper floor tile hung in alternating bands of plain and fish-scale tiles. The outer wall of the cottage forms part of the boundary with the Heath.

On turning the corner and continuing along Heathside – a gently-curving roadway connecting to East Heath Road – a truly delightful scene comes into view.

No.6 Gainsborough Gardens, side elevation.

The Grade II *Cottage on the Heath* on Gainsborough Gardens, viewed from Heathside.

170

Heath Lodge, to the left of the tree, is a delightful, low-built, Grade II Regency period cottage with an extensive front garden and a magnificent landscaped garden at the rear.

We arrive at a fine pair of handsome bow-fronted C18/early C19 cottages in a beautiful front garden setting. Positioned to the west of this pair, the delightful semi-detached *Heath Lodge* is built in yellow stock brick with elegant central bays, bowed to full height. The original continuous first-floor iron balcony has been attributed to James Wyatt, possibly indicating that the Lodge might date from around 1775. And the former coach house to the lodge has become its garage.

These remarkable dwellings – *The Cottage on the Heath*, along with *Heath Lodge* and its neighbour – enjoy such a wonderfully discrete position, that although located virtually on Hampstead Heath, they offer their owners the feeling of living deep in the countryside. ∎

Heath Lodge has historical associations with Prime Minister William Gladstone (1809-1898) who is said to have visited in 1893. Leaving office in 1894, Gladstone was the only prime minister to have served four non-consecutive terms.

An elegant cast-iron balcony dated *c.*1775 is visible above the ground floor window.

East Heath Lodge, East Heath Road

What could be more enchanting than awakening to embrace sunrise over Hampstead Heath in the early hours? Nestled amidst this magnificent natural setting we find the Grade II *East Heath Lodge*, an architectural gem. With its origins rooted in the late C18, this is one of a pair of semi-detached houses. Comprising 5 storeys including a basement the house was built in multi-coloured stock brick with red brick dressings, undergoing alterations around 1820. At 1st floor level, the two verandas are endowed with attractive tented canopies, while the recessed sashes of the original windows on the two upper floors are adorned with white shutters.

A captivating tale whispers through its walls, recounting the residence's past inhabitant – the mistress of its original owner, who resided in the neighbouring property on East Heath Road. Once united by a secret passageway that linked these two abodes, the passage has since been discreetly sealed, concealing its clandestine history for eternity.

A blue plaque commemorates Sir Arthur Bliss, the renowned composer and Master of the Queen's Music, who lived in *East Heath Lodge* from 1929-1939.

The house is now under the proud custodianship of the owners, Lisa Glynn, a specialist Couples Psychotherapist, and Richard Glynn, a successful company director specialising in business transformation.

Sir Arthur Bliss, 1891-1975
photo, Herbert Lambert.

East Heath Lodge, southern elevation.

The double-aspect ballroom on the first floor.

"The previous owner was the well-known TV personality Esther Rantzen, who had lived in the house with her husband and children for over 30 years. "The property was on the market for ages," explains Richard. "Esther, the previous owner, only wanted to sell her house to a family, ideally one with dogs. We turned up for a viewing with our three children, and we all fell in love with it the moment we walked through the door. We could see what an exceptional family home it was. The house has the most gentle atmosphere." But there was a problem. It was on the market for much more than the couple could afford. And although Esther had partly renovated the house in the early 1970s, the property required a considerable upgrade.

Remarkable Homes of NW3

A corner on the half landing.

"Esther was prepared to be a little flexible as we fitted her requirement of being a family," says Richard. "We also promised that we would include dogs once we arrived. We further agreed to extend the handover process so she could hold a Jubilee party in February 2012, which she dearly wanted to do. As a result, we reached an agreement that suited us all."

When, in 2012, the couple got down to the restoration, they worked on the project for the best part of a year. "The house was built around 1785, so when we commenced work on the place the structural engineers said, 'You do know there are no foundations to your property, don't you?' Indeed, the basement was damp,"

Part of the original 1780s wine cellar.

continues Richard, "so we tanked the interior up to 6 feet above the basement skirting." That said, the basement still retains all its original flagstones and its wine cellar.

All the plumbing and electrics were changed or updated, with much of the restoration project in the hands of Retrouvius, who sourced many recovered items and materials. Their manifesto states that at the company's heart is the belief that good materials and well-made things are precious, whether quarried stone or a piece of expert joinery. "Lisa chose the décor and selected all the furniture and detailing in conjunction with the advice of Retrou-

A set of the old Unilever House copper-faced elevator doors.

174

vius," explains Richard. "Then, when it comes to innovative doors, we have two sets of the original lift doors from the old Neoclassical Art Deco Unilever House," Richard adds proudly. Acting as decorative mirrors, these doors are installed in the ballroom on the first floor, a large room that benefits from double-aspect windows overlooking the Heath. Then, on the ground floor, "the dining room cabinet doors are repurposed display case doors previously from the Natural History Museum," says Richard.

"The marble in the main bathroom and the kitchen is reclaimed from the old flooring of Heathrow Terminal 1 building (opened by Queen Elizabeth II in April 1969). "The people from Retrouvius sourced all of these things for us, including a variety of other materials. Interestingly, John Pawson was the architect of our previous project, so we have moved from absolute minimalism to this historic building," continues Richard. "We obtained planning permission to restore the rooms to how they were originally," Richard says. It's also of note that the living and dining rooms have 'brother and sister' fireplaces.

"When we look out from the front window, we could easily be in the middle of a forest. We feel virtually on the Heath," explains Richard. "We have planted three silver birch trees in the garden, one for each of our children."

A welcoming upper floor guest bedroom. Lisa chose the décor and colour schemes with the advice of Retrouvius, and has carried her preferred colour palette throughout the house.

Restoring such a remarkable home has been an incredible journey for this couple, who clearly couldn't be happier living anywhere else.

A flight of the colourful staircase.

The cabinet doors are repurposed from the Natural History Museum.

Remarkable Homes of NW3

The Logs and *Foley House*

The Logs, Well Road, *illustration, W E Hodgkin.*

This remarkable building, *The Logs* on Well Road, in seen here in an illustration by W E Hodgkin as published in *The Builder* in November 1868. The entry reported that Burnham bricks with Portland stone dressings were used on the exterior alongside polished granite and red Mansfield stone.

Pevsner describes *The Logs* as exhibiting "Yellow, red and black brick and excrescences in all directions, arches pointed and round, motifs Gothic and Frenchified, and a remarkable wilful tower with château roof." He also called it "a formidable atrocity".

Virtually impossible to miss on the northern corner of Well Road and East Heath Road, *The Logs* is a wonderful combination of Gothic and French architectural styles with some Italianate thrown in. An eccentric mix of designs and details, this Grade II structure, dating from *c*.1868, was designed by J S Nightingale and built by Charles Till of Hampstead for the civil engineer, developer, and Justice of the Peace for Middlesex, Edward Gotto.

From 1860 Gotto was in a 30-year partnership with Frederick Beesley to form the engineering firm of Gotto and Beesley, with contracts for major drainage and water supply projects worldwide. Built to what is said to be partly his design and for his own residence, Gotto later added another wing to the north side of his property in 1876.

Reporting on various details in 1868, *The Builder* records, "The hallway, vestibule and conservatory are paved with Minton tiles. All the rooms are accessed directly from the hallway. The drawing room, dining room and library feature pitched pine ribs. The Portland stone staircase leads to the main bedroom suite which overlooks the Heath." *The Builder* also notes the chimneypieces were specially made by Mr Mitchell of Brompton Road, and Arrowsmith's parquet was used for the floors of the principal rooms.

Since the demise of Edward Gotto in 1897, this characterful building has attracted the famous and artistic to its doors. Appropriately enough, for its location, in Victorian times the drainage expert was replaced by the plumbing expert when the renowned maestro of the Royal Flush, Thomas Crapper (1836-1910) moved into *The Logs*. However, in 1951, this massive house was internally subdivided into separate large properties. The two components illustrated in *The Builder* of 1868 (the left wing and the principal façade with the tower) were assigned

The Logs, viewed from East Heath Road and Well Road stands tall, surrounded by its front and rear landscaped gardens – but alas, the original ironwork on the château-style roof is now missing.

addresses on Well Road, Nos.19 and 17 respectively. Most fortunately, the original triple-height entrance hall and grand central staircase had been preserved within No.17.

Some 18 years after that, in 1969, the writer and actor Marty Feldman and his wife Lauretta bought one of *The Logs* properties and lived there until they left the UK bound for Hollywood. They had been equally charmed by the architecture, the village atmosphere of Hampstead, and its proximity to central London. For much the same reasons, when he was only in his twenties, the singer-songwriter Boy George bought No.17 in the 1980s. He has owned it ever since, and in 2022, led by F3 Architecture & Interiors in conjunction with Kelly Hoppen, a thorough refurbishment project of No.17 was completed that included a new extension into the rear garden.

Also associated with *The Logs,* we turn the corner and come to *Foley House* at No.11 East Heath Road. Believed to be the residence built for John Duffield the first Wells Spa manager in 1698, but recent dating suggests *Foley House* (see next page) was built after 1762 and probably even nearer to 1771. ›

The distinctive gate to *The Logs,* No.19 Well Road.

Remarkable Homes of NW3

This grand, detached property apparently takes its name from Captain Foley who lived here in 1805-8. Interestingly, the house was leased to Edward Gotto of *The Logs* the 1880s. Gotto added the porch and made other improvements. The brown brickwork house features a round-arched central doorway with open dentil pediment and Roman Doric columns with a patterned fanlight. Pevsner notes the "Mid-C18 three-bay front with bay window," as well as the "Venetian windows left and right," plus the "Early C18 stables, weatherboarded." The interior is noted to retain some early C19 features and has received later additions. The property was bought from the Wells and Campden Trust in 1990. *Foley House* is owned by Pink Floyd's drummer Nick Mason.

Foley House c.1840, George Childs.

Framed by a brick archway, the double wooden doors, marking the entrance to the front garden of *Foley House*, were added by Edward Gotto.

The Grade II *Foley House*, No.11 East Heath Road, from the corner of Well Road.

Redington Road

An introduction to the area

Meandering gracefully for just over half a mile from Frognal to West Heath Road, this thoroughfare follows the undulating contours of the Hampstead hillside. A variety of detached and semi-detached houses abound.

Redington Road was set out in 1875, following the Maryon-Wilsons' gradual relinquishing of their Hampstead estates. Christopher Wade posits that the road's name is probably a tribute to the illustrious Irish administrator Sir Thomas Redington (1815-1862). Such a claim appears well-founded, considering the close Irish connections held by the chief developer, George Washington Hart. CHB Quennell was Hart's leading architect and According to Alastair Service, Quennell "Produced series after series of excellent designs, most of them of two subtly varied styles, with occasional larger houses of spectacular inventiveness interspersed among them." Over sixteen years, the partnership resulted in around 100 houses in the area.

A distinctive house on Redington Road.

An attractive Neo-Georgian house dating from 1905 designed by CHB Quennell. An unusual feature is the central dormer window with chimney stacks on either side.

Following the curve of Redington Road houses date from 1906, and although altered over the years, the house shown here was possibly designed by CHB Quennell.

Also standing on a gentle bend on the eastern side are two listed Grade II detached properties designed by Quennell in 1908-09. The run of houses from Nos. 54 to 64 comprise "A mixture of brick and tile-hung vernacular houses with others in a brick classical mode for variety," as recorded by Alastair Service.

A fine house on the gentle curve of Redington Road.

This grand red brick property features a central entrance with an early C18-style scallop shell hood on shaped brackets and a part pattern glazed panelled door.

This house features some lovely red brickwork detailing in a "witty travesty of classical decoration," says Alastair Service. The ground floor right-hand bay forms an entrance porch, the pilaster forming a pillar, with two columns supporting an entablature.

Redington Road south

No.11 Redington Road.

The homes located at the Frognal end of Redington Road and nearest to Hampstead Village were among the first properties to be developed on the road. Here we are visiting one of a pair of semi-detached Edwardian houses, where the present owners are Fritzi Kain, originally from the Netherlands, and her husband Raphael, who is German. "We bought No.11 Redington Road in 2017," says Fritzi. "The previous owner was James Dodd," she continues, "and before that, the house was owned by the academic Francis L Carsten, Professor of Central European History. I believe the house dates from at least 1915."

When the Maryon-Wilson family started to sell off their Hampstead estates, there was a conveyance of land dated July 1887 between Spencer Maryon-Wilson, Herbert and Edward Kelley, and Reginald Herber Prance (1824-1912). Prance became head of the company Robert Prance and Co, one of the leading firms in the Consol Market, the Grand Trunk Railway of the Canada Market, and the India Rupee Market. As a wealthy stock broker, Reginald Prance purchased a sizeable estate in Stanley Pontlarge, Gloucestershire, most of which is still in the family. So acquiring this land was most likely part of his investment portfolio. As the Prance family researcher Mike Williams records:

> At one time, Reginald [Prance] was a very rich man and gave large sums to the church. He helped build St Stephen's Church and gave the organ. To Hampstead Parish Church he gave a new organ, choir stalls and decorated the chancel. At Christ Church, Hampstead he enlarged and remodelled the organ which his father had given.

The land conveyance included a requirement to fence off the 11 Redington Road plot within six months of July 1877. The house itself was constructed later.

Reginald Herber Prance (1824-1912), *archive*.

A corner of the comfortable and cosy library.

Previously, Fritzi and Raphael lived in a flat on Canfield Gardens on other side of Finchley Road. At the time, they had two small children and were upsizing. "We were looking for a house for quite a while," says Fritzi. "But not necessarily in Hampstead; we were concentrating more on the Belsize Park and South Hampstead areas."

When Fritzi first moved to London, she stayed with a relative on Heath Drive, so she knew the area. "I needed a place from which my children, when they are older, could walk easily to public transport. We also wanted a lateral kitchen and dining space, not on the basement level." The agent found this house, which ticked all the boxes, but when the couple came for a viewing, they realised it was in a rather dilapidated state. "Nevertheless, we went ahead and bought the place anyway. We found an architect, and immediately the building underwent a ten-month renovation," Fritzi recalls.

"We moved into the completed house in December 2018." Fritzi and Raphael remained in their flat for the duration of the works. "We didn't need to make any structural alterations, but we did change the position of some of the doors, creating a double door from the hallway to the living room, for example."

The elegantly-furnished living room, *photo, Julian Abrams*.

The original staircase with its classical detailing.

The enlarged doorway from the hall to the living room. The hall floor was re-laid with tiles from the long established Victorian Tile Company.

Fritzi worked with Andrea Benedettini Interiors to create a warm and welcoming family home with an understated, timeless elegance and feel. "We had the sofas specially made by an upholsterer, and the lamps are from the Chelsea Design Centre," says Fritzi. A charming fireplace has been retained in the hall. Interestingly, the extension from the kitchen/dining room that many people often add to their homes was unnecessary here, as it was part of the original house design. "But we added the larger windows overlooking the garden, and we also created a sightline through to the garden from the hallway."

The result of this admirable project is a delightful period interior blended with contemporary furnishings. Fritzi and Raphael have every reason to be happy in their elegant Redington Road home.

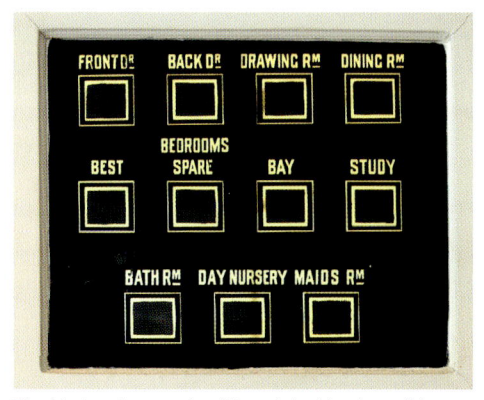

The formal dining room can seat ten.

The kitchen/dining area with its large windows.

The kitchen has retained its original butler call box, still in an excellent state of preservation.

Front elevation of No.39 viewed from Redington Road.

Redington Road continued

Standing proudly on the corner of Redington Road and Oakhill Avenue, this large Edwardian building at No.39 is a restored free-style Arts and Crafts home dating from 1903. Alastair Service says that architectural author Susan Beattie established it was built by Bull and Esdaile and likely designed by Walter William Bull, a pupil of the *avant-garde* Arts and Crafts architect James MacLaren. One gable has a relief sculpture in plaster, while two others have large lunette windows.

Sadly, by the end of the 1980s, the entire house had fallen into a severe state of disrepair. The property was bought by a developer who intended to knock it down to rebuild the site with three new flats plus three garages at the back. The Redfrog residents association objected and, as at the time the market was plummeting, the project failed, and the house was put on the market.

"We purchased the property in 1991," says Izak Uziyel, an electrical engineer with a master's degree in industrial engineering. "We completed the major restoration project and moved into the house in 1994." Izak's wife Freda, originally from Poland, came to the UK in 1978. Freda is an art historian and specialist in contemporary art. "When we were living in our house in Finchley in 1991, Izak visited Hampstead," says Freda. "While driving past No.39 one day, he saw that the run-down wreck on the corner with Oakhill Avenue was for sale." Freda had an idea. "Maybe we can buy it if it's not too expensive and spend some money restoring it. I came over to take a look, only to realise it was a total disaster – a ruin. There wasn't even any easy way to see upstairs – no staircase, no floors, nothing!"

The turret with its looped brick and stone balustrade topped with a cupola.

Finding themselves the new owners of a derelict building with its collapsing walls, floors and ceilings, the couple set about a reconstruction project with energy and determination. *Owner's photos.*

"The house was for sale by Savills in 1991," continues Izak. "As the result of the failed developer's impending bankruptcy, the bank had put it in the market." It was due to be auctioned. "I told the agent 'I don't like auctions, but I have an offer he may wish to accept prior to the auction'. They asked for £750,000, and I offered £700,000, which was accepted. But, of course, it was going to cost us a great deal to rebuild the house."

Over the next four years the property was remodelled entirely, not simply restored – it was virtually rebuilt. "The building had been unoccupied for over 15 years," explains Freda. "The brickwork was a total mess, and even the lovely stonework of the window surrounds had been painted over." The couple designed the reconstruction project together while working with architect Scott McGregor, who prepared the drawings. "We also had a structural engineer, especially for technical issues," adds Izak. "The architect produced a physical scale model, so we all knew what we were aiming for."

In searching for the best way to reconstruct the building, the couple located a variety of reclaimed elements. The house has an original cartouche dated 1903, whereas the number 39 plaque on its front wall is a replica in stone of the original. They bid for items at auctions such as Sotheby's in Billingshurst, a leading auction house for paintings, sculpture, fine art and antiques. They also acquired reclaimed architectural items from Lassco in London.

"We went to auctions in France which were held in a town near Versailles," continues Freda. "The tiled floor in the kitchen, for instance, dates from the 17th century – having once graced the floor of an old monastery in France."

C17 kitchen floor tiles from a French monastery.

Izak and Freda are fervent art collectors, and artworks are to be seen throughout their home. Wonderful light permeates everywhere and the ample space combines to provide an excellent setting for their collection. "I decided to buy some beautiful 19th-century Neo-Rococo carved wooden panels that I thought could be made into doors," Izak explains. "We had sufficient panels to make double-sided doors for both the ground and first floor, and they were made into lovely doors by an Italian artisan found by our architect."

The imposing staircase with its specially-commissioned curved metalwork.

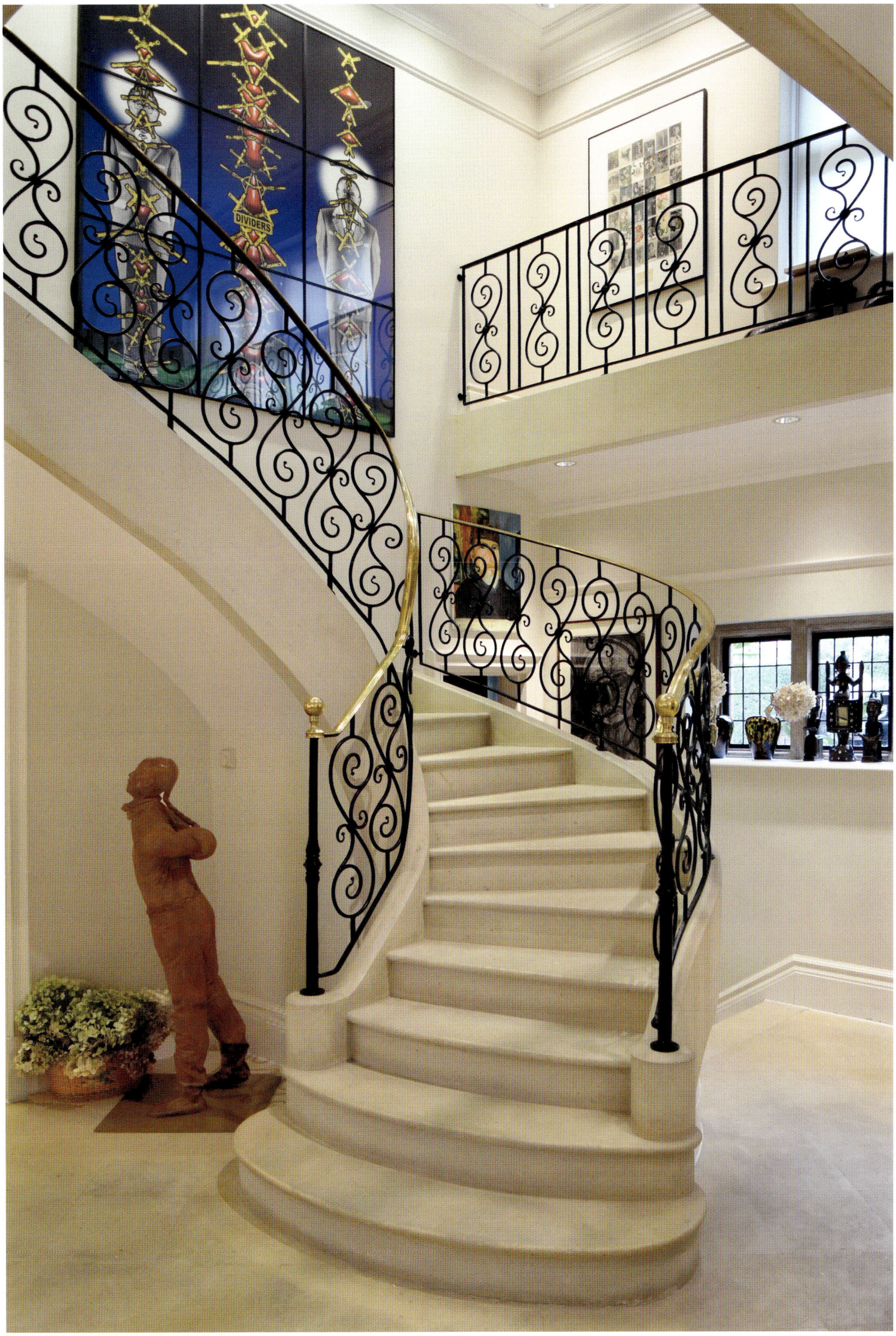
DIVIDERS

Remarkable Homes of NW3

The original internal stairs would have been wood, while the new staircase is built in stone and designed by Izak. "We wanted the curved metalwork to be in one piece for each side of the staircase," explains Freda, "but there were no British companies that could produce the curve in one piece."

Recalling that the ironwork in Poland was excellent, Freda contacted a Polish developer hoping to find a solution. Through this developer's help, as it turned out, the only people who could manufacture this metalwork in one piece was a family-owned company in Austria – and they did a magnificent job at a most acceptable price.

While searching for exterior stone steps to complete the garden layout, they found a rather grand, sweeping flight from a French château that worked out perfectly for them. Freda designed the entire garden. "We created the terracing at the same time as we built the swimming pool," explains Freda, who also takes care of every aspect of tending the beautiful garden herself. The couple has been living in the completed house now for 26 years. And 15 years ago they added a gallery area downstairs. "The result of all this work is very eclectic, which we feel is right because the Arts and Crafts style was also eclectic," says Freda.

"People say that while our house might be described as rather 'posh', they find it very welcoming," adds Freda. "It feels homely and comfortable – a real family abode, having brought up our three girls here. They are all grown up now, with two living in America and one here in the UK."

As well they might, Freda and Izak have created a home and a garden from passion, imagination and an abundance of flair.

This grand flight of wide stone steps leading down into this splendid garden was relocated from a French château.

188

The square bay with its first floor balcony overlooks a wide ground floor terrace, edged with a magnificent stone ballastrade, which in turn overlooks the garden below.

The two large lamps on either side of the front porch of No.39 Redington Road were an excellent find.

The Wabe with its roof terrace and varied window styles.

The Wabe, Redington Road

This most unusual Edwardian-era house was once owned by Dr William Garnett (1850-1932). He designed *The Wabe*, No.66 Redington Road for his family in 1902 and they lived here from 1903 for its first ten years. William Garnett, a celebrated academic and mathematician, was appointed demonstrator in experimental physics by Professor James Clerk Maxwell when Cambridge University's Cavendish Laboratory was first opened. Garnett was inspired to build this somewhat eccentric house, adopting a variety of architectural styles ranging from Scottish Baronial to elements of Art Nouveau and the Arts and Crafts movement. Said to be William Garnett's dream house, Garnett designed it with children in mind – he had three sons and two daughters.

He named the property as a tribute to Lewis Carroll's poem *Jabberwocky*. In the poem, The Wabe is the fictional grass plot around a sundial where the slithy toves are to be found (slithy means lithe and slimy, while a tove is a creature that combines aspects of a badger, a lizard and a corkscrew).

Pevsner considers *The Wabe* a "maverick design". While Alastair Service more usefully describes the building as "odd…big bay windows project with total disregard for visual composition,"

Every room has at least two large windows.

Stunningly beautiful – bluebells abound in springtime.

and "a wide terrace on top of the house gives it a flat roof surrounded by Tudor crenellation and complex chimneys." A set of small steps accesses the terrace, and the views extend as far as the South Downs via Earls Court.

Garnett sold the property in 1913 to industrialist Harold Ellis and his wife, Mina Benson Hubbard, a noted Canadian explorer and a campaigner for women's suffrage. Hubbard's guests included Emmeline Pankhurst and Isadora Duncan, who once danced here at a fundraising event for the cause. Other guests at that time included George Bernard Shaw, Rudyard Kipling and H G Wells.

The character-filled interior is highly noteworthy, with a variety of window designs and abundant period details. The timbered, double-height top-floor games room/study is just one of the many remarkable spaces, while the most fabulous of all has to be the grand room on the ground floor with its magnificent double-height stone mullioned window, (see next page) overlooked by a minstrels' gallery that William Garnett designed as a small ballroom.

Following the acquisition by a Bond Street tailor, Philip Osner and his wife Pearl, the house was converted into apartments in the 1950s. The Osners lived on the ground floor, turning a living room into a bedroom and workroom.

The house is filled with light – there are windows everywhere – each one unique.

Remarkable Homes of NW3

charity concerts and dances for up to 75 guests, with a band playing in the minstrel's gallery. They also hosted numerous guests, co-stars and friends, including David Bowie, Arthur Miller, Jamie Lee Curtis, Farrah Fawcett and Rod Steiger. Five wedding receptions, including that of their daughter Nina, were held at *The Wabe*.

Interestingly, *The Wabe* is only the second house the couple owned. Tom says *The Wabe* never felt too big for them, and they both knew the house was extraordinarily special with an atmosphere of great warmth, impossible knowingly to create – it was innate.

The care they took in cherishing their home has been rewarded in turn by the house. Although they had never envisaged leaving *The Wabe*, there came a moment when it became clear to them both that they needed to move on. When the couple decided to downsize, Kara gave a dramatic performance describing her home's fabulous history. In 2019 they sold *The Wabe* to the very individual film director Tim Burton – so it seems that this remarkable home continues to choose the owner most perfectly fitted for its dramatic setting. ∎

The ballroom with its double-height mullioned window.

But the divided house was rescued in 1985 when Tom Conti and his wife Kara Wilson purchased it and lovingly restored *The Wabe* into a single occupancy family home once more. They recall that when they first viewed it they immediately fell in love with the massive garden, games room and wonderful ballroom – although the rest of the house was all front doors and kitchens. The fireplaces had been ripped out and blocked up, but Tom and Kara reinstated four working fireplaces, including a beautiful Art Nouveau fireplace in the kitchen. Original radiators were sandblasted and painted. There were eight bedrooms, although Kara used one as an office and another became a screening room with a projector. Tom's workroom was the games room of the original house. You can peer down into the ballroom from the primary bedroom windows. And the ballroom is where Tom and Kara held

William Garnet used this as a games room with its wonderful exposed timbers and leaded windows.

All The Wabe photographs courtesy Charlie Smith, London REA.

Templewood Avenue
Comfortable, large detached houses – *Pevsner*

The driveway to No.15 Templewood Avenue.

Templewood Avenue first appears on Hampstead maps as late as 1909. The road name derives from Great and Little Templewood, two local farms on land believed to have been owned in the Middle Ages by the Knights Templar. Running between Redington Road and West Heath Road, this broad, tree-lined avenue with its red-bricked pavements, adds to the green and leafy character of the area. The houses are Neo-Georgian in style, mostly in red brick and with brick quoins, decorated chimneys, and projecting open porches.

"If these suburbs must be built over then let the architects and builders work together and make the consequent bricks and mortar as much at home with their surroundings as possible." Thus spake CHB Quennell, who held firm views regarding the suburban streetscape. He gravitated towards designing buildings in suburbs like Hampstead and Highgate, where good trees were allowed to remain in situ. Working with the builder George Washington Hart, Quennell's designs have played a major part in shaping the character of parts of the area.

Alastair Service regards No.15 Templewood Avenue as "one of the most striking houses in Hampstead." It is most certainly an elegant property, set back from the road by a short driveway

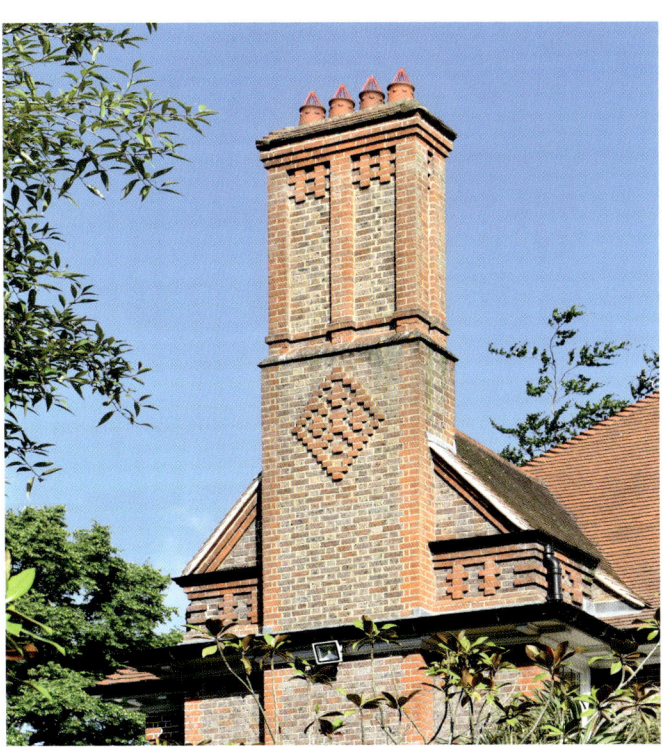

A tall slab chimney-stack with brick patterning and overhanging bracketed eaves cornice.

Remarkable Homes of NW3

Wider view of No.15 Templewood Avenue showing the red-bricked pavement.

Front entrance to No.12 Templewood Avenue.

and now listed Grade II; this detached house by Quennell was constructed between 1905-09 by George W Hart using plum-coloured brick with red brick dressings and rusticated quoins. The hipped roof displays wonderfully detailed chimney stacks.

This house is of particular note as the property is at least three times deeper than the part visible in the photographs, as its frontage was set at a 60-degree angle to the road. (Part of *The Wabe*, No.66 Redington Road, was constructed in a similar fashion, at 50 degrees to the road, see p191).

A half-courtyard on the right of the house provides access to the front door. "From this courtyard," says Alistair Service, "steps and a path lead around the terraces of the lyrical garden past the front of the house and to the far side. This garden side elevation of the house is very complicated, a composition of many varied windows and a romantic loggia balcony off the drawing room." ∎

Some notable people have lived in Templewood Avenue over the years, including the celebrated photographer Cecil Beaton. From 1911 to 1922, he and his family lived at No.1, which was then called *Temple Court*. No.12 Templewood Avenue was originally built for the Maples family, who lived there until 1966. Maples & Company was once the largest furniture retailer and manufacturer in the world.

Oakhill Avenue

Known initially as Barby Avenue, the road was developed around 1907 before being renamed Oakhill Avenue. Nestled towards the upper end of this picturesque thoroughfare stands the delightful No.2a. In 1958, following a transfer of land from the Maryon-Wilson family, the house was constructed during the early 1960s, occupying a plot that was once part of the original garden belonging to No.39 Redington Road (see p182).

Reflecting on their initial encounter with the property in 1989, the owners fondly recall standing in the formal garden, captivated by its appeal, and thinking, "This is truly delightful!" At the time, the interior design reflected the architectural trends of the 1960s and required substantial updating. Opting to rent a property locally on Redington Road for eight months during the renovation process, they finally settled into their newly-transformed home in 1990.

Pointing out a tree in the garden, the owners share an intriguing historical insight: "All of this area was originally Glebe land – it belonged to the church." Indeed, these Glebe lands were fields specifically acquired by religious authorities to provide additional support for the parish priest.

No.2a Oakhill Avenue entrance hallway and stairs.

Remarkable Homes of NW3

A corner of the charming light-filled sitting room.

The couple greatly appreciates the original build's exceptional craftsmanship and the impeccable eye of the designer. "Structurally, we decided to preserve the hallway, including the staircase, just as it is now," they explain. "But we did decide to enlarge the original tiny kitchen into a much more practical space." Additionally, they extended the house slightly on either side and added a sunroom. "We were meticulous in our approach to maintain the overall balance of the house," they remark. "Now, we enjoy a sensibly sized four-bedroom home that effortlessly accommodates our needs. The most significant change for us was expanding into the loft space," they add. "Initially, when the architect presented the plans, we thought it didn't need to be that large! However, we are now grateful that we followed the advice. The result provides us with a generously-proportioned floor area, which we utilize as a gym, offering the added bonus of stunning views across the rear gardens of Redington Road."

The front aspect of the property exudes undeniable charm, which is enhanced by the beautiful trees, attractive planting and numerous skilfully arranged pots for evergreens, herbs and flowers. Their seasonal planting elicits many compliments from passers-by. ∎

The living room from the bar area.

Springtime view from the top floor of No.2a Oakhill Avenue looking towards Redington Road.

A corner of the well-tended rear garden.

The attractive façade and front patio.

Elisabeth Schwarzkopf, the operatic soprano, lived diagonally across the road at No.3 Oakhill Avenue with her husband, Walter Legge. An influential recording executive, Legge was the founder of the Philharmonia Orchestra, and in 1960 their house served partly as the headquarters of the orchestra.

Greenaway Gardens

Laid out in 1914, Greenaway Gardens gently curves its way between Oakhill Avenue and Frognal Lane. Originally forming the western boundary of Frognal Park, the road was named after the children's book illustrator Kate Greenaway (1846-1901), who had lived nearby at No.39 Frognal (a house designed for her in 1885 by Richard Norman Shaw). The first houses built on the west side of Greenaway Gardens enjoyed commanding views over the Frognal estate. But those grounds have long since given way to the developers, and today, the only signposts of a past when *Frognal Hall* and its parklands dominated the locality are the various roads prefixed with the name Frognal.

No.5 Greenaway Gardens is one of those first houses. Constructed in 1915 on the western side of the road near the corner of Frognal Lane, this grand residence, built of red brick on 2 principal floors, enjoys a splendid lateral aspect and is perfectly balanced by its imposing frontage and driveway.

Jeremy Smouha is in fund management and has a company with his brother in Geneva. He is the CEO of the firm in London. Jeremy and Sabine met in St John's Wood. "I was brought up in Geneva," says Jeremy, "and Sabine was born and raised in Paris. We moved to the UK in the 1980s. My grandmother lived with her mother on Rosecroft Avenue and my father was born in No.20, making our grandchildren the sixth generation in Hampstead," he adds.

This is the couple's third house. "We had just married," continues Jeremy, "and we lived in *Bracknell Cottage* on Frognal Lane for a while.

©Openstreetmap theundergroundmap CC BY-SA 2.0
Historic map of the grounds of *Frognal Hall* and Frognal Park with Greenaway Gardens added.

When the grandchildren visit, all the furniture in this part of the living room is pushed back to provide more play space.

I hadn't thought of Hampstead, but Sabine had an aunt who lived in Cannon Hill, West Hampstead." The couple then moved to No.29 Heath Drive. "It was a beautiful Quennell house, ideally proportioned internally," adds Jeremy. "We would take a walk around here pushing our prams from Frognal Lane to Greenaway Gardens, and I often thought that one day, if all goes well, we might be able to have a house here." Years later, with their family of two daughters and a son growing up, they were rapidly outgrowing No.29 and moving became a necessity.

Then two seemingly unconnected events occurred. On a walk around the neighbourhood the couple visited a summer garden open day at No.5 Greenaway Gardens. "We found it to be an absolutely enchanting garden," says Jeremy. Then quite unexpectedly, that very house appeared on the market three months later. "Bids were invited, together with a letter to accompany the offer as to why we wanted to live in the house," recalls Sabine. "Surprisingly, we won the bid, and it all went through. So we went from *Bracknell Cottage*, then to Heath Drive, and finally we arrived here." That was October 2001.

The living room with French windows accessing the garden.

Remarkable Homes of NW3

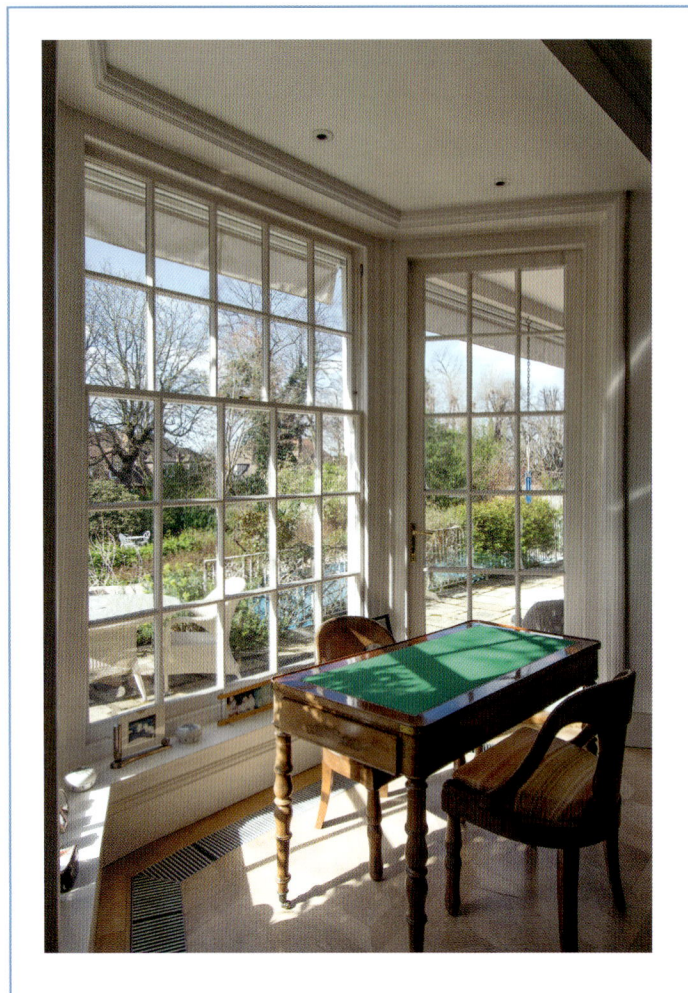

This beautiful and imposing home with two sets of French windows opening onto the garden. The swimming pool can just be glimpsed on the left of frame.

Everything in the building needed an upgrade to modern standards, and the improvements included adjusting the height of some of the doors and doorways. "We appointed an eminent architect who specialises in Grade I & II listed buildings. We needed the works to be completed within six months so we could settle in before our daughter's GCSE exams," Jeremy recalls.

Their architect created a very clever internal link that runs along the rear of the house. This quasi-invisible 'passage' seamlessly connects the living room at one end of the house to the kitchen at the other while allowing the space in the two bay window areas to be fully utilised. "Sabine designed the decorations and the furnishings," says Jeremy. Sabine is a gifted designer and co-founded Prettysac, a business of haute couture bags and accessories selling in London, New York, Paris, Geneva and online.

The previous owner, Helen Marcus, a renowned prima donna (under her maiden name Helen Lawrence) with a voice of immense range and power who performed at the Royal Opera House, had installed a grand piano in the living room. On her retirement from the stage, and despite her roles within The Heath & Hampstead Society (she variously held the position of Chair, Trustee, and Vice-President), Helen also found time to design and nurture the remarkable garden at No.5 that had so enchanted the present owners back in 2001. "The garden she created is extraordinary; she tended it for three hours every day," says Sabine. "And the lateral aspect of the house, with its expansive views of the garden from all its rooms – there are six bedrooms and two studies – makes this place so wonderfully attractive," she adds. "It's like a country house in London, and it is so easy to live in."

Indeed, this beautiful and imposing home has been lovingly cared for over time by everyone living within its walls. ∎

Bracknell House, Bracknell Gardens

Bracknell Gardens takes its name from a Maryon-Wilson estate in Berkshire and was originally laid out from 1905. The houses were built starting at the Frognal Lane end by various builders, including William J King. Four very substantial houses were built a little later on the western side nearer to Heath Drive. One of these, standing opposite Oakhill Avenue, is No.31 Bracknell Gardens – re-named *Bracknell House* in 2003 by the present owners. It is a sizeable Neo-Georgian property designed by Randall and Pile and built in 1921.

The previous American owners undertook an extensive reconstruction, refurbishment and interior decoration programme executed to an exceptionally high standard in the early 2000s. This seven-bedroomed house, with en-suite bathrooms, is set behind security gates and a carriage driveway and extends over 4 floors. The impressive triple-height entrance hall leads to a double reception room, music room, dining room, and kitchen/breakfast room, beyond which is the family room. Descending to the basement, the leisure/entertainment floor houses the cinema, swimming pool and gymnasium.

An array of contemporary features include the extensive use of limestone, oak flooring and Italian fixtures and fittings. Notably, the refurbishment project introduced a passenger lift and most interestingly, a centralised vacuum system in the basement plant room with wall-mounted vacuum inlets in each room. The previous owners went to a great deal of expense and

The majestic triple-height entrance hall.

effort to redesign the interior to suit their family's needs. Regrettably, they were denied the opportunity to enjoy their new home when they had to move back to the USA for work reasons.

Today's owners are Professor David Gartry, a senior Consultant Ophthalmic Surgeon at Moorfields Eye Hospital in London, and his wife Lily, a qualified Optometrist. They both studied Optometry in the same class in Glasgow Caledonian University in the late 1970s. David went on to study Medicine at UCL/UCH and then trained in Ophthalmology at St Thomas' Hospital and Moorfields Eye Hospital. He was the first eye surgeon in the UK to perform laser refractive surgery (PRK, in November 1989 at St Thomas') and was to become one of the foremost experts in the field. In 1995 David was appointed as a Consultant Ophthalmic Surgeon specialising in corneal, cataract and laser refractive surgery to Moorfields.

Lily and David have been living in or around Hampstead since they were married in 1980. Initially, they rented an unconverted flat in Southhill Park Gardens. They then bought their first home, a three-bed flat in West Heath Road, then a semi-detached house on The Hocroft Estate, and finally a detached house in Alvanley Gardens before the opportunity arose to purchase *Bracknell House*. "With three rapidly-growing sons we were looking for something bigger," Lily recalls. "One day, I brought a brochure home for a beautiful house and showed it to David. It seemed absolutely out of the question for us at the time, but David was rather intrigued so we decided to take a look." They both had the same impression when they first arrived for a viewing. "When you enter the grand hallway you're immediately taken by the amazing natural daylight coming from above and from the dining room opposite," relates Lily. "It was so spacious, light and airy, we both fell in love with the house at first sight and put in an offer!"

It was accepted but the vendors had already returned to Palo Alto in Silicon Valley, so there was no direct contact with them. "Coincidentally," says David, "I was speaking at a conference in Anaheim the next day, just a few hundred miles from Palo Alto, when we received the bad news that foreign buyers had gazumped us!" Lily acted really quickly to organise a survey the same day, after which they made a counter offer comprising virtually simultaneous exchange and completion. "I also gave the vendors a call early the next morning as I was very local to them in Anaheim," says David. "The vendors said that they would be far happier for a family to live in the house (that they had designed so carefully to be their own family home) and

Part of the bright, double-aspect living room.

The open and light dining room.

Remarkable Homes of NW3

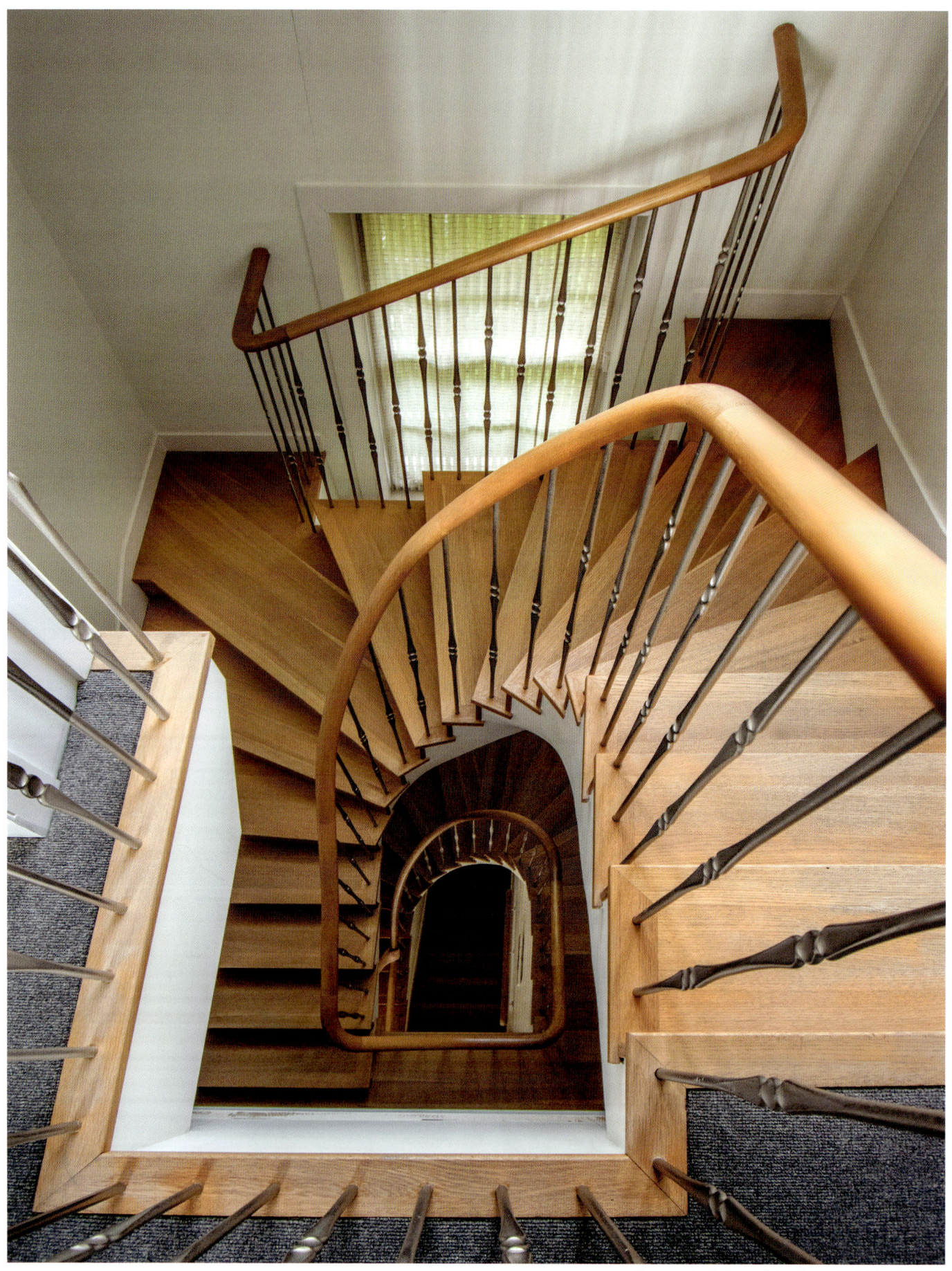

The amazingly beautiful staircase in Californian oak.

Bracknell House rear garden view.

said that if we could 'meet them half way' on the price, it would be ours." David agreed, at which point the vendors replied: "It's yours – our word is our bond". The personal touch of a local phone call made all the difference. They were sure it was meant to be.

"When we first moved in, during December 2003, the builders had only just left and it felt like a new build with that fantastic 'new house smell'." Nothing major needed to be done – just some minor exterior re-painting and a few windows were replaced in the same Neo-Georgian style. "The modern (very American) open-plan interior was left exactly as it was, but I put a lot of effort into the furnishing," recalls Lily. The couple brought furniture from their previous homes, but because *Bracknell House* is so much larger, they needed more than they had acquired gradually over the years."

Our sons are very musical and we love having a music room with the grand piano we brought from Alvanley Gardens. Quite often, when the boys come to stay, they gravitate to the piano," says Lily. "The Chinese Guzheng, a plucked zither, was brought all the way from Hong Kong by my youngest son and it has pride of place in the music room."

The family has been enjoying *Bracknell House* for almost 20 years now. Lily remembers driving past the house when it was being re-developed by the previous owners. There were seemingly endless workmen, builders, scaffolding and skips. Lorries would regularly hold up the traffic during the hectic school run. "Very inconvenient at the time but never, ever, did I think that one day we would actually be living here," she muses. "Yes, I agree, and it's turned out to be a wonderful family home for us," David says with a big smile. ∎

The music room with the Guzheng in the foreground.

Heath Drive

Up there among the best homes designed by CHB Quennell (1872-1935) in Hampstead is the Grade II house at the corner of Heath Drive with Bracknell Gardens, No.33 Heath Drive, built by George Washington Hart in 1905. Regarded as an excellent example of his balanced Arts and Crafts detailing, the most notable features of this outstanding design are the protruding six-angled bays and the bold, double gables rising steeply to the right of an unusual four-arched open porch that unmissably forms the corner.

Purchased from the Maryon-Wilson family, the land for the build also provided for a four-stall garage with a chauffeur's flat above and a large garden initially incorporating an orange grove, a tennis court and a greenhouse. Astonishingly, to this day, the house has only had three owners since its construction. Lloyds' senior underwriter Harry Calkin (1861-1926) lived in the house from 1911 until his death in 1926, with his wife Margaret remaining there until her death in 1936. After a hiatus, the place went to auction in 1937, with the second owners of the property, Peter and Peggy Farebrother, buying it for just over three hundred pounds sterling.

Over fifty years later, Ronald and Linda Boschetto, the third and current owners, arrived in 1989. Ronald Boschetto, an American, remembers how the house was arranged when he and his British wife Linda first came across the property. "Interestingly, when Linda and I bought the first floor flat in August 1989, Peggy Farebrother, the woman who owned the house since the 1930s, was still living here," says Ron. "Peggy had sold off a portion of the land behind the house for development and converted the building into the three flats, retaining the ground floor, the basement and the remaining garden for herself."

By 1999, Peggy had reached a point where she was unable to live in the house any longer, and the couple purchased Peggy's ground-floor apartment, planning to leave the top floor as a separate flat. Then six months later, the house was listed Grade II. The regulations that were thereby imposed on any conversion work complicated their intention to return the house to single occupancy over time. It wasn't until 2003, having bought both the top flat and the freehold, that the couple could embark on the necessary round of complex planning applications.

"We expanded the basement to extend to the full width of the house and to a total depth of 12 feet, fully tanking it and waterproofing to hold back the Hampstead water," Ron recalls. This project was also to underpin and thus preserve the property from any future subsidence prevalent in the area. "We have a pump in the garage that runs much of the time to pump water out into the drainage system to keep it dry," Ron adds.

The original late 1800s wall lamp in the porch, which was two feet long, was stolen one day, probably to order. The brickwork still has the markings of where it was located.

The original hall in 1906. The staircase had 52 steps to the top of the house, *photo, H W Bennett.*

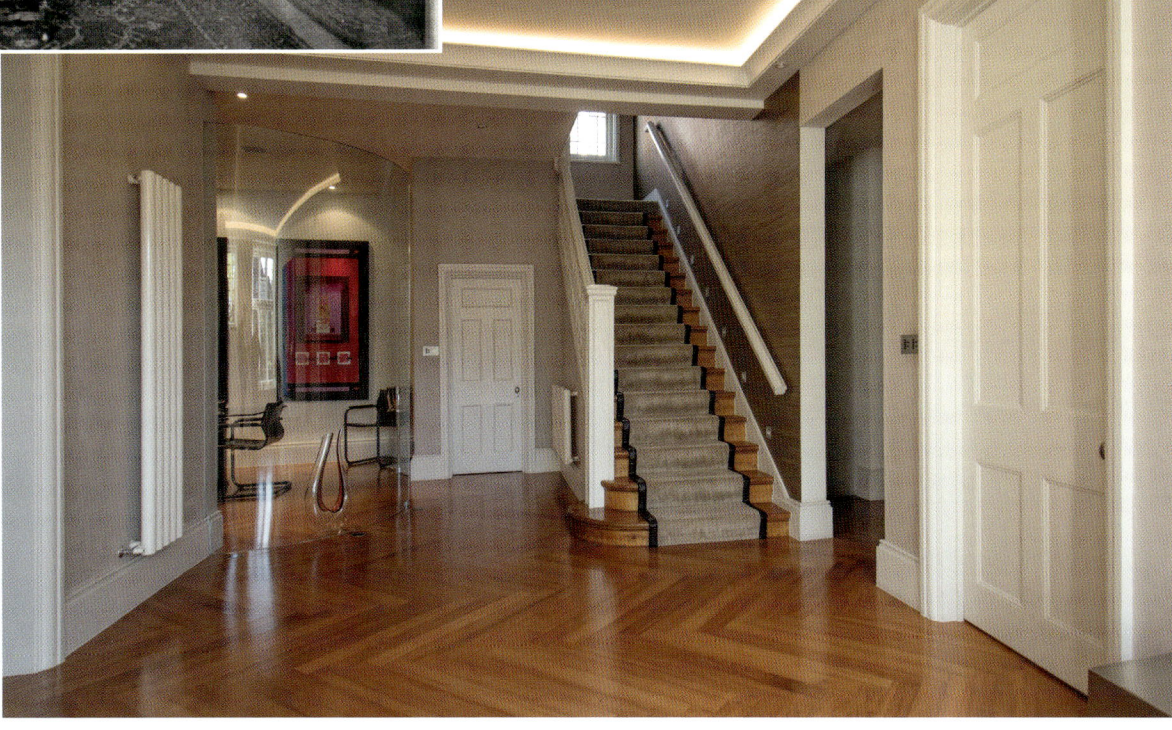

The hall today features the original staircase, a teak floor plus a modern curved plexiglass panel visually separating the dining room from the hallway.

The building works took about nine months, including dealing with all the permissions and restrictions from Camden council, by which time the couple had fully converted and refurbished the entire house.

During the rebuilding work, Ron and Linda managed to liberate the staircase. As was the fashion in the 1950s and '60s, the spindles below the handrail had been boxed in, but it's now fully restored to its original state. Unfortunately, however, they were unable to liberate a wonderful ceiling. Peggy Farebrother was a Dentist and Peter was a doctor. His surgery occupied the front room, which originally enjoyed an impressive Adam-style ceiling and decorative cornice. Unable to find a restorer during the rebuild, this ceiling is still in situ, hidden behind a protective false ceiling, silently waiting to be rescued one day. In the late C19 and early C20, the revival of the Adam style competed with the Arts and Crafts movement, so it is interesting that these two themes find themselves in the same house.

"We feel that this is a great old home!" Ron continues. "We love the six-angled bay windows even though they are energy inefficient.

When we did the refurb, we replaced 60 of these

207

The front living room, with its six-angled bay window and false ceiling hiding an architectural treasure.

Detail of original plasterwork on the cornice below the false ceiling.

individual windows as per the initial design, leaving the original frames. We also tried to bring it back to the original floor plans as far as possible. The kitchen is still the kitchen, for example. Nothing was touched on the front and side exterior of the house."

Ron recalls how he learned of the history of where he now lives. "Some thirty-odd years ago, when I was in my 40s, there were about ten people in their 70s and 80s residing locally, having moved in during their 20s and 30s, and in the evenings, they would tell me stories about the locality." Citing some examples, he

A marvellous seat emplacement in an upstairs bedroom provides fun while cleverly enhancing the architectural detail of the window behind it.

continues: "The other side of the street being developed five years before this side. And originally, the road wasn't called Heath Drive; it was West Hampstead Avenue. A resident renamed it after proposing to the borough council in 1906 that he would plant trees up and down the street if they agreed to change the name to Heath Drive. Which indeed is what happened."

Ron and Linda's love for this house shines through everything they have done to preserve this building as it was originally intended to be – a family home, albeit with seven bedrooms! And even if the thought of downsizing has occasionally crossed their minds, they remain firmly attached to their remarkable house as Peggy did before them.

It could be said this Quennell-designed house epitomises all that the Arts and Crafts movement intended: the creation through architecture of a functional home that would nurture its inhabitants, who in turn would nurture their environment. At No.33 Heath Drive, thanks to the patient and careful restoration by Ron and Linda, this significant symbiosis has been fully regained. ■

Continuing the colour scheme of the living room, the elegant dining room has doors opening to the front garden.

No.33 Heath Drive in 1906, seen from Bracknell Gardens, *photo, H W Bennett.*

Remarkable Homes of NW3

Heath Drive continued

No.28 Heath Drive in springtime.

Developed initially as West Hampstead Avenue (see previous page), the road was renamed in the early C20 to reflect its proximity to Hampstead Heath. Nos.28-29 are a semi-detached pair of brick-built houses featuring Quennell's trademark bay windows. This "pleasantly leafy road of 1890 onwards has some of Quennell's best work," records Pevsner. The imposing house at No.28 is another excellent example of the architect's designs of the period, built c.1907.

The current owners fully appreciate the unique features of their home. One aspect they particularly enjoy is the ceiling height, which, unlike some Victorian residences, strikes a perfect balance, creating an inviting and homely atmosphere in the well-proportioned rooms. And they delight in the larger-than-usual internal doors, contributing to a genuine sense of spaciousness. Another standout feature is the exceptionally-wide staircase.

Previously living in Camden Town, the owners have made No.28 their home for over two decades. The couple knew the previous owners, making the transition seamless, requiring only a few personal touches upon moving in. Unusually, there is a bomb shelter in the rear garden, an intriguing historical relic. And the garden itself deserves special mention as it's exceptionally long – surpassing nearly twice the average length for the area. Adding to the garden's natural beauty, a pair of magnificent mature oak trees stand majestically, likely remnants from the original West Heath estate. "A good tree will often sell a house," writes Quennell in his notes on modern suburban houses.

Viewed from the inside, dressed with heavy Jacquard drapes, the bay window looks spectacular.

"The accommodation generally required is the three usual reception rooms – [while] sometimes Drawing and Dining Rooms will suffice," says Quennell.

The dining room exhibits a fine example of Quennell's wonderful six-angled bays, a speciality of the architect, who notes that the "Morning sun streaming into the Dining Room at breakfast time ensures such a pleasant start to the day's work that it is worth the arranging."

Quennell also notes: "It is always worth the while to spend some money on the Hall and Staircase – they are first seen, and first impressions go a long way."

The front and rear gardens are very much a feature here. The rear garden (see next page) climbs as high as the roofline of the house. Designing and setting out the gardens took over 18 months and both are now well established. A small pond features at the upper end of the rear garden, fed with a calming trickle of water. ■

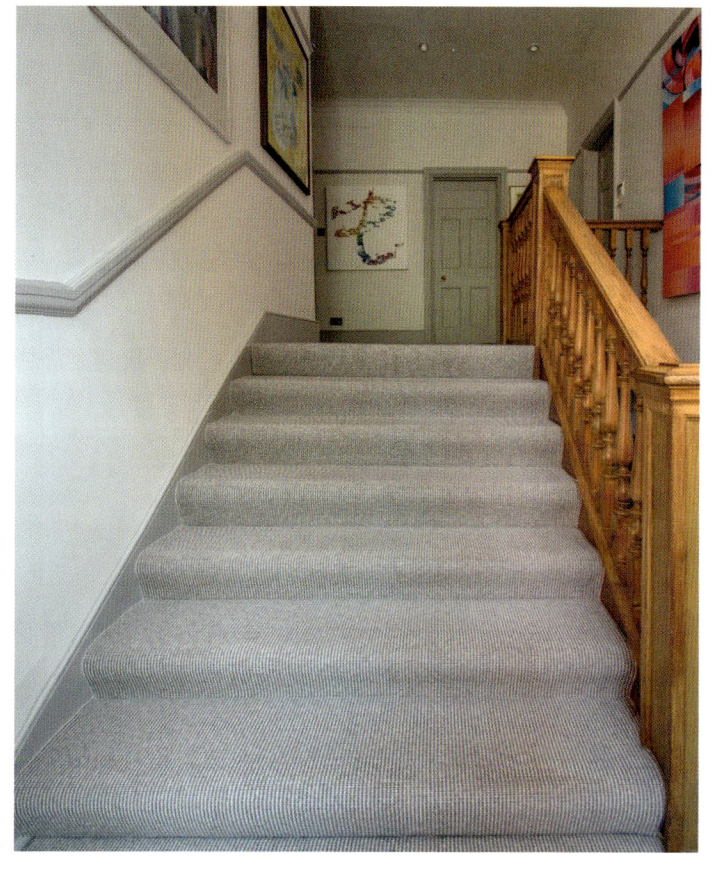

The exceptionally-wide staircase.

The large staircase window featuring stained glass panels overlooks Heath Drive.

Swings and Roundabouts

The current owners of No.5 Greenaway Gardens (see p196), lived next door at No.29 Heath Drive, moving out a couple of years after the owners of No.28 took occupation.

And just a few doors north of these lovely houses, another local resident of Heath Drive was Thomas J Wise, a well-respected bibliographer. He was also said to be a prolific and creative literary forger. "In 1910, when Wise came to live in No.25," says Christopher Wade, "His book collection was considered supreme, but in 1934 many were revealed as forgeries. After Wise died here in 1937, his Ashley Library, forgeries or no, was sold to the British Museum."

Kidderpore Hall, Kidderpore Avenue

Kidderpore Hall, West façade 1890, *Harold Lawes,* later recolour.

This stately Greek Revival-style white stucco building rises prominently at the brow of Kidderpore Avenue – leading off a road initially called West Hampstead Avenue, later renamed Heath Drive. *Kidderpore Hall* was designed by T Howard and constructed for John Teil in 1843, a wealthy leather magnate and East India merchant. Teil named his house after his extensive tanneries located in Kidderpore, a district on the outskirts of Kolkata (then known as Calcutta).

In 1891 the newly-named Westfield College moved here following its acquisition and conversion into a college for women. Having been founded as the London College for Ladies in October 1882, with only five students, by Constance Louisa Maynard, Ann Dudin Brown, Caroline Cavendish, and Mary Petrie, the College was previously based in two houses, Nos. 4 & 6 Maresfield Gardens, Belsize Park.

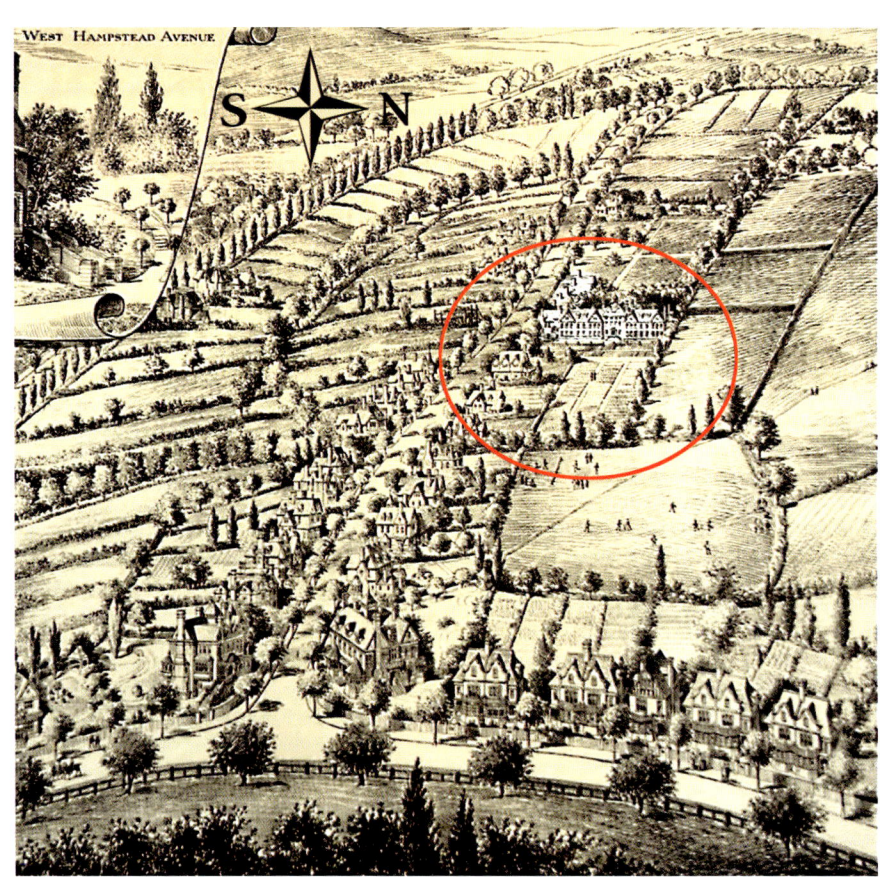

Looking west up Kidderpore Avenue, to *Kidderpore Hall* (ringed). West Hampstead Avenue (later Heath Drive) runs north-south in the foreground – from *The Building News,* July 1891.

Front of *Kidderpore Hall* with its stately, six Ionic-columned portico supporting an entablature with a dentil cornice, approached by wide steps.

The grand, semi-circular colonnade bay of *Kidderpore Hall*, west façade.

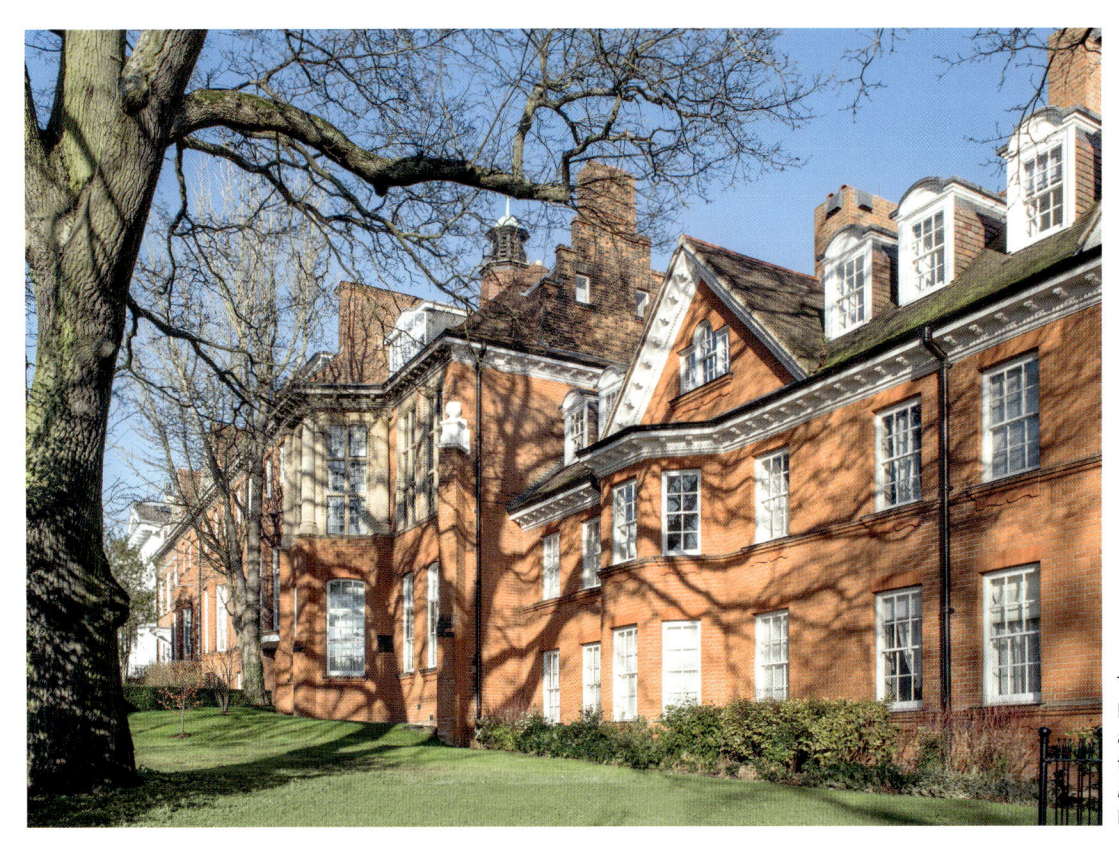

The Dubin Brown, Skeel Library, and Bay buildings are part of what is known today as *Hampstead Manor*, overlooking Kidderpore Avenue.

Pioneer of women's education, Constance Louisa Maynard (1849 1935) was the first woman to read philosophy at the University of Cambridge.

Westfield College opened with the specific aim of preparing women for degrees from the University of London. The College introduced the study of botany in 1905, which enabled female students to take part in research. With male students admitted for the first time in 1965, the campus later became home to King's College London students from 1989. It merged with Queen Mary College in the 1980s, becoming Queen Mary University of London in 2013 at another location.

Three years later in 2016, the entire complex was redeveloped and renamed *Hampstead Manor*. The original 5 Grade II-listed buildings have been variously converted – there are now 156 homes across 13 buildings, part sensitive conversions, and part new builds.

The Neo-Baroque 4-storey Skeel Library. This elegant, Grade II former library built in 1903-4 retains its well-preserved leaded windows.

Remarkable Homes of NW3

Frognal Grove in 1782, viewed from the north, etching and aquatint, *Maria Prestell*. The furthest building with just two storeys without a bay is today's No.105 Frognal.

Frognal Grove

Architect Henry Flitcroft designed Nos.103-111 Frognal. This splendid, characterful group of houses was originally one large property, with Flitcroft himself residing in what is now No.107. Extending either side of the central building were further wings, with the stabling at today's No.109 Frognal.

Henry Flitcroft (1697–1769).

Wisteria-covered entrance to Nos.105 & 107 Frognal.

The exposed brick section of No.105 Frognal. The yellow brickwork of the added 2nd floor is visible above the original 1st-floor windows. The white stucco of No.103 is to the left, with green-shuttered No.107 to the right.

Steps leading up to No.105 Frognal viewed from the south.

Henry Flitcroft specialised in the Palladian style of architecture. His works include a temple for Henry Hoare's magnificent Palladian gardens at Stourhead and the design for the rebuilt church of St Giles-in-the-Fields constructed between 1731 and 1733.

Acquiring Frognal Grove in 1741 from Thomas Watson-Wentworth, the Earl of Malton, Flitcroft replaced an old structure of around 1700 and built what is now Nos.103-111 Frognal. The principal block is No.107 where Flitcroft lived for the rest of his life. No.105 was his study wing – originally just 2 storeys in red brick, a traditional splayed bay and a further 3rd storey in yellow brick was added in the mid-C19 by architect George E Street (1824-1881), the designer of the Law Courts in the Strand.

The current owner Mr M, then living in Willow Road, bought No.105 Frognal in December 1989. Shortly after his aquisition, he had a house history prepared by Penelope Olsen who records:

> The rooms in the old part of the house [Nos.105 & 107] retain their original decoration, with wood panelling painted a biscuit colour throughout, simple moulded cornices and bookcases with pediments and carved friezes. The house has suffered rather in the matter of fireplaces, only two having survived, a plain wooden one in the entrance hall [No.107] and a marble one bearing a female mask of the kind often introduced in his houses by Flitcroft.

Remarkable Homes of NW3

Flitcroft's original buildings were very cleverly divided into four separate properties (Nos.103, 105, 107 & 109-11) in the 1950s. "This house was just the study for No.107, the main house next door," notes Mr M, who found this property one day in 1989 when reading an edition of the *Ham&High* while on a train travelling north. Mr M also owns a hill farm he is currently rewilding.

Having immediately booked a viewing, he knew the instant that he saw the place that he would buy it. Even though the whole house was rather tired and very 1960s in style. Mr M then made quite a few upgrades in keeping with the Grade II* listing and the age of the house.

"I put in the stone flooring with under-floor heating on the ground floor," he says. "At some point the wrong type of floor had been installed on the study floor so I replaced that flooring but otherwise the room is pretty well untouched. All the cornice work is original in the study library." Today, the study looks very similar to the way it appeared over 70 years ago.

"This house should be seen in context with next door. I don't think they've done much to the house at No.107, which is very

Section of the superb surviving cornice work in the study library.

The study window today.

The study of No.105 Frognal in 1949, *archive*.

Following in Flitcroft's footsteps, architects Norman & Wendy Foster of Foster Associates lived here at No.105 from 1977 to 1980.

Rear view of No.105 Frognal and part of the adjoining No.107.

good news from a preservation point of view."

Although a 2nd floor was added at some point in the distant past, Mr M had the staircase extended in 1990 to access a further additional floor created at the top of the house. This floor accommodates an attractive guest bedroom, a bathroom and – barely visible from below, a small terrace that offers wonderful views over London.

The glass-covered area over the basement extension (which is now the kitchen) was once the backyard with the garden accessed via stone steps beyond. The two supporting iron pillars in the kitchen extension come from a Sheffield railway station.

The rear of the house has a 'Venetian look' with a delightful garden that extends out well beyond the house. "This is very much like a secret garden. You wouldn't believe you were in London – Frognal Grove is a fabulous area, and I just love this place," says Mr M. ∎

Rear of No.105 with steps down to the glass-roofed kitchen.

Upper Frognal Lodge with its 1st floor windows in round-arched recesses, viewed from the front of No.105.

Upper Frognal Lodge in 1911, AR Quinton.

Upper Frognal Lodge, Frognal

This seven-bedroomed Georgian house as it stands today is Grade II-listed. Despite the alterations made early in C19 and late C20, it has retained many of its period features, which include the wooden panelling, door surrounds and fireplaces. The Frognal frontage has recessed sash and casement windows with early C19 Gothic and later glazing. The first floor features lovely round-arched windows, a central niche, and a marvellous full-width cast-iron balcony.

"We were rather taken with the house because it reminded us of somewhere we knew a while back," say the owners. Previously living on Denning Road, they moved to Christ Church Hill, "A wonderful place, beautifully done, very open and modern with a view of the Heath." But they wanted a change. As it has turned out it's been a big change from open-style living to something very traditional.

The couple acquired *Upper Frognal Lodge* during September 2016. "When we took it over it was very tired," they recall. "Soon after moving in we awoke one day to find the roof leaking, so we redid the lead roof." They say it's good they didn't get down to work on the other needed improvements immediately, wisely preferring to wait until they had lived here for a while. All the necessary restoration works and interior decorating projects are now complete.

A glorious overdoor panel.

These improvement works turned out to be a bigger undertaking than they imagined – to them, it still seems a never-ending project. But, as they emphasise, "We are very glad we went ahead, it's been fantastic for us." And with five to seven bedrooms various family members can come and stay. There is one further project they would love to undertake one day – reinstating the imperial staircase which, sadly, was removed some while back. In fact, there's a second staircase which might have been used by support staff for a previous owner.

Upper Frognal Lodge today, still looking wonderfully elegant with its white-painted stucco.

Ground floor front window.

Ground floor side window.

Part of the cosy and comfortable living room.

The adapted imperial staircase, sadly no longer with divided flights.

One of the original fireplaces.

A view from the garden. Its landscaping and planting have created a haven of tranquility.

Outside, featuring a magnificent tree, the *Upper Frognal Lodge* garden is absolutely beautiful. The conservatory, while very attractive, wasn't a particularly practical, functioning room so they have virtually rebuilt it. The couple consider living here to be like being in the country. There is a small river nearby and so they have lots of frogs visiting their garden! As for their own preferred watering holes, "Previously we would go to *The Wells Tavern*, now our local is *The Holly Bush*, and we particularly like 28 Church Row – it's a treat to go there."

Living in such lovely surroundings, this couple have everything to be thankful for. Full of Georgian charm, surely the delightfully elegant home they have created is equally content with its owners. "There's a wonderful feel to the house and garden that's certainly out of the ordinary – and maybe we are too," they say with big smiles.

Britain's first Labour Prime Minister, Ramsay MacDonald, took up residence here in 1925 after moving from his previous home in Howitt Road, Belsize Park which could no longer accommodate his extensive library. MacDonald continued to live at *Upper Frognal Lodge* until his death in 1937. A later resident was Donald Ogden Stewart (1894-1980), an American writer and screenwriter who is best known for his sophisticated golden age comedies and melodramas. Stewart was a casualty of the blacklisting by Hollywood in 1950, subsequently escaping McCarthyism when he and his wife emigrated to England in 1951.

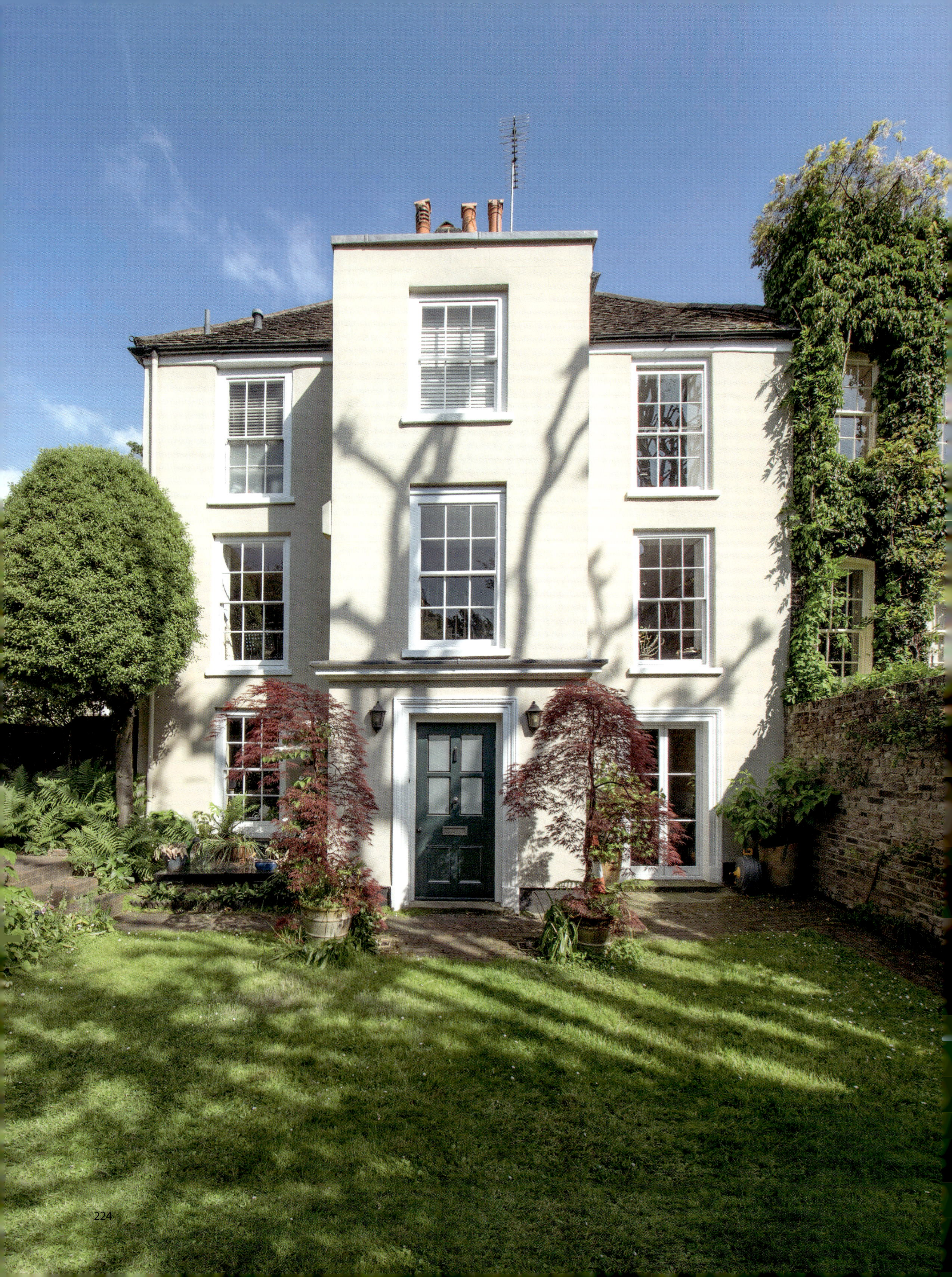

Grove Cottage, Frognal

Two buildings on the upper end of Frognal were joined together in C18 as an inn, variously known as *The Duke of Cumberland's Head, The Windmill, Ye Pilgrim,* and most recently, *The Three Pigeons.* Nos.108 & 110 Frognal date back to Queen Anne's reign (1702-14). Now separate dwellings, No.110, *Grove Cottage*, is an end-of-terrace 3-storey house faced in stucco. The hipped roof with its central chimney stack is perfectly balanced by the full-height central portico, with a cornice at 1st-floor level. The commemorative brown plaque on the side wall is for the poet and *Punch* editor EV Knox, who lived here from 1945 to 1971.

The present owners are Micheline and Robin Ellison. Micheline is a literary agent representing writers for stage, television and film. Robin is head of strategic development for pensions at an international law firm and visiting professor in pensions law at the Cass Business School. "Robin is from Manchester, and I've always lived in north west London," says Micheline. "So when this house was on the market in 1985 we came to take a look – and fortunately, we were able to buy it."

The original hallway and staircase.

Grove Cottage façade – the vine-covered No.108 can be seen next door.

Remarkable Homes of NW3

Part of the original chimney. Unusually, all the rooms are positioned around the chimney which is central to the building.

A corner of the living room.

Just before the couple moved in, Sting was living next door at No.108. "Then, when we first arrived we were fortunate to meet Mary Knox, the widow of E V Knox, who was living across the road." Daughter of artist and book illustrator E H Shepard, Mary Knox was a children's book illustrator best known for illustrating the *Mary Poppins* series of stories written by P L Travers (see p241). Her husband Evoe was the editor of *Punch* from 1932 to 1949. "Mary had many fond memories of the house, telling us how wonderful it was living in *The Three Pigeons*, as it was then called," notes Micheline.

"Just under 40 years ago the house decor was completely different," Micheline recalls. "The walls were covered in brown hessian with orange carpeting. But what we particularly liked were the windows." There are so many windows it's wonderfully light everywhere, although there's not a lot of wall storage space left for books. "In the 19th century, new windows were installed in Georgian style to make it look 'posh'," says Robin.

"When we first came to live here it still had a double front door," notes Robin. "As it was originally a tavern it had a traditional wooden front door that opened in two sections and it just leaked air. So we replaced it a couple of years ago with a new door which is totally draught proof." The couple have made quite a few improvements over the years. A studio building had been built in the rear garden many years ago. Initially a music room cum sound recording studio, today it is a completely self-contained apartment with a kitchenette and bathroom, plus its own entrance.

Georgian window and view from the kitchen.

We thoroughly enjoy every area of the house," says Micheline. "My office is partly here and partly in Highbury. Our two boys have now left home, so Robin has taken over one of their rooms, while I've got several little desks dotted around the house. It all works for us really well." *Grove Cottage* also has an extensive cellar with the traditional beer drop trap door. The cellar is pretty well intact, but as Micheline points out, "inevitably here in Hampstead there are problems with the water levels. The feeder streams to the Tyburn and Westbourne run nearby, and occasionally we have water ingress to the cellar, but we can deal with that."

"We think the classical walled cottage garden makes the house very welcoming," adds Micheline. "Unlike some of these larger Georgian and Neo-Georgian houses down the road, we feel we're truly part of old Hampstead – it's a privilege living here." Micheline has been clearing out and planting alongside the footpath leading to Mount Vernon that runs along the side of the house. "The footpath is being used more these days, especially since the Covid pandemic lockdown, which is lovely, and I continue maintaining it in my spare time," she says.

The Mount Vernon footpath just up from *Grove Cottage*, Frognal – visible on the left.

Once serving the community overtly as an inn, today lived in by people who also contribute to their community, albeit more discreetly, this remarkably old house has seen over three hundred years of service, while its attractive architecture continues to add to the beauty of Frognal. ∎

A peaceful corner of the *Grove Cottage* walled garden.

Romney's House, 1910, AR Quinton, built on the site of a coach house and stables.

Romney's House, Holly Bush Hill

Picturesque and weatherboarded – *Pevsner*

An end of terrace property, No.5 Holly Bush Hill was converted from the former stables and coach house belonging to a mansion called *Cloth Hill* (today, No.6 The Mount). George Romney acquired the timber-famed property in 1796. Samuel Bunce was then employed to redesign a house fit for Romney to use as a studio and display gallery. Romney, a renowned portraitist, is generally ranked third after Reynolds and Gainsborough. On numerous occasions, Romney painted Emma Hart, later Horatio Nelson's mistress, Lady Emma Hamilton.

George Romney "came to settle on Holly [Bush] Hill in search of the fulfillment of the nobler thoughts which he had long cherished," records Anna Maxwell. But, unfortunately, his quest was cut short. Three years later, due to his failing health, he had to sell the house and return home to his wife Mary in Kendal, South Cumbria.

After another eight years, in 1807 the building was enlarged "with tea room, upper ballroom, and new card room," says Pevsner, in order to create the Hampstead Assembly Rooms, where the first Heath Protection meeting was held in 1829. Over the following years it was host to lectures by John Constable and other famous speakers. Later, in the 1880s, the Hampstead Constitution Club used the premises when the Assembly Rooms lost out to the new

Emma Hart, later Lady Hamilton, 1785-6, George Romney
©National Maritime Museum, Greenwich, London.

228

Romney's House in the 1950s, the main entrance with the garage on the left and porch on the right, *archive*.

The Assembly Room, Romney's House in the 1930s, *Architects' Journal*.

Hampstead Vestry Hall on Haverstock Hill. Concerts and dances were held here until the opening of the Conservatoire on Eton Avenue. For ten years from 1929 it belonged to Sir Clough Williams-Ellis, who remodelled the property to use as his home and office for his architectural practice. The superb pilastered assembly room survived for many years. It is now divided into two bedrooms by a pair of curving full-height partitions preserving the pilasters and balcony.

The Grade I *Romney's House*, No.5 Holly Bush Hill, with its elegant and distinctive white-painted weatherboarding remains a private residence.

The Holly Bush tavern.

Just off Holly Bush Hill, around the corner from *Romney's House*, the attractive and welcoming Grade II *Holly Bush* tavern on Holly Mount has survived pretty much as it was, becoming a pub in 1928.

The Holly Bush was also converted from stables. The tavern was linked to the Assembly Rooms from 1807 to cater for the meetings. Fortunately, the hostelry has "miraculously resisted modernisation in recent years," records Christopher Wade, adding, "among its snug nooks and old wooden panels, are fine displays of etched glass."

Holly Mount itself dates back to 1643, with a number of C18 houses along the narrow street. ∎

The historic *Holly Bush* tavern with its stucco frontage and canopy hood.

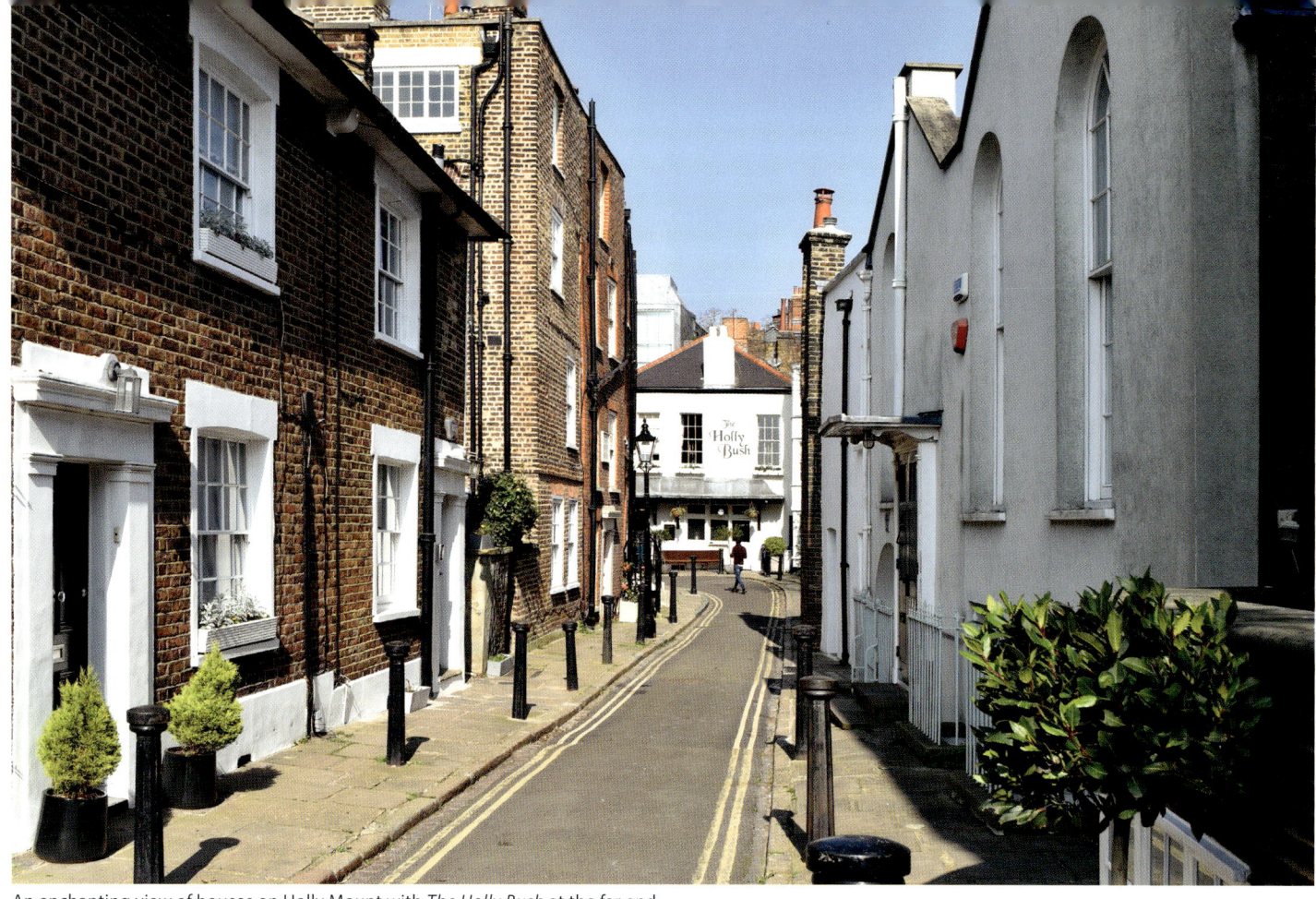

An enchanting view of houses on Holly Mount with *The Holly Bush* at the far end.

The Holly Mount steps lead down to Heath Street, *illustration A R Quinton* c.1910 – apart from the growth of the tree, little has changed to this day.

The *Grove Lodge* façade presents a tiled roof with dormer attic windows. The two storeys are faced in white painted stucco. *Admiral's House*, with its blue-framed windows, is set at right angles to *Grove Lodge*.

Grove Lodge, Admiral's Walk

Whenever Admiral's Walk is mentioned, it is likely that *Admiral's House* initially comes to mind. But the adjoining property *Grove Lodge*, fronting Admiral's Walk with its rear garden extending as far as Lower Terrace, is an equally important building, although its origins are less well understood. C18 mapping indicates that there was always an element of *Grove Lodge* that abutted *Admiral's House*, which has led some to conclude that it was constructed as a service wing for that house. However, this property is so very different in character and appearance that although it's said to have once been a rectory, its earliest 1700 origins are more likely to have been those of a country farmhouse.

As the *Ham&High* reported in April 2015, The Heath & Hampstead Society describes *Grove Lodge* as "an extraordinarily fine and largely complete survivor of its 1700 period," and "its importance cannot be overestimated." Whatever its origins, *Grove Lodge* has earned its own place in Hampstead's history. Although it would be easy to conclude that the house has always looked as it does now, images generated over the years show how it has evolved from the modest house painted by Constable into the substantial Grade II family home of today.

Grove Lodge rear garden view *c.*1905.

Rear garden view *c.*1913 *archive images.*

The garden view in 2022 – the 2020 side extension with its basement, finished in white painted stucco, is on the right.

Needless to say, the house has undergone many changes as the years have passed. Around 1913, the northern wing of the house was extended, and the lateral expansion included two large bays below a mansard roof.

Despite more than three centuries of occupation, the house has retained all its quirkiness and homely atmosphere. Writing of *Grove Lodge* at the end of the C19, Anna Maxwell records: "It was a curious rambling building, full of narrow passages and unexpected steps leading to small rooms stowed away in odd corners and it possesses several secret cupboards and strange recesses hidden behind panelling." Fortunately, these have largely been preserved by the current owners.

Caspar and Celia Berendsen are happily married and have lived in Hampstead together with their five children since 2007. "We were previously in No.6 Holly Place, which we restored and sold before moving here," says Caspar. However, when the couple purchased *Grove Lodge* in 2014, it was in terrible shape. "The property had been deprived of essential maintenance and had received precious little investment," Caspar recalls.

Caspar and Celia have revamped the entire building, extending its surface area to include a basement. "A great deal of work was required to rectify the seriously deteriorated state of the structure," continues Caspar.

A glorious C17 Flanders tapestry hangs above the consol table in the hall.

The formal sitting room enjoys windows on three sides.

A light-filled study in a child's bedroom.

Ancient times and modern lights.

"It's now fully refurbished with all the building work completed in 2020." The house has now taken on a modern version of its original early Georgian form, with very little remaining of the original C18 fabric. For example, the C20 entrance portico that faces Admiral's Walk opens onto a hallway associated with a staircase that appears to date from the Edwardian period.

"We could see the potential straight away, but it was my designer wife who led the project," says Caspar. "Celia spent a lot of time working on the interior restoration along with two other designers, one architectural and one interior furniture related." The result is clear to see. Wonderfully clean and fresh, with well-thought-through elements retaining the feel of the original house. Overall, the home has a most interesting layout. Light floods in everywhere, and the choice of wallpapers and their strategic placement is particularly noteworthy.

Grove Lodge is deceptive. It's impossible to appreciate how extensive the house is from the external views, either the front or the side. The different architectural phases of the house's history are still very apparent within its walls. Many of the smaller rooms are accessed through passageways with short runs of stairs set at odd angles, and these passageways can veer off in unexpected directions and lead to the discovery of some lovely little rooms and odd cubby holes.

The bay-windowed drawing room, with its mix of traditional and modern furniture, is tastefully decorated in pale grey and white.

Bespoke pomeganate wallpaper forms the backdrop to the dining room furniture.

An antique wardrobe and lamp are set against the hand-painted wallpaper.

Child's bedroom with hand-printed 'Clematis' wallpaper.

Door to the garden terrace from the dining room.

Steps up to a bedroom suite.

If the interior space of *Grove Lodge* is already formidable, then one must not forget the garden, which has been given the same lavish and professional attention to detail. It is large enough to include an orchard and an orangery. "Our garden designer John Hoyland is responsible for the gardens at Glyndebourne," notes Caspar.

Leading off Lower Terrace is a pretty gateway to a property that sits next door to *Grove Lodge*, the Grade II *Netley Cottage*. Little of it can be seen from the road, making it all the more intriguing. Dating from around 1779, it was also likely to have originally been a farmhouse. An extension was added to the southwest of the cottage in 1910, and the 2-storey property was rendered in stucco. This very private cottage adjoins *Grove Lodge* on its northern side. "Netley Cottage next door became available when the then owner decided she was going to sell it," explains Caspar. "We bought the cottage, and restoration is due to be completed in 2023."

Both properties have been home to remarkable men. The Oxford Don Charles Appleton (1841-1879) lived in *Netley Cottage* for several years, being visited by both Sidney Colvin and Robert Louis Stevenson while he did so. Of his time there, Appleton's biographer Archibald Henry Sayce wrote: "The pretty artistic home where it was his pride and pleasure to bring together gradually the goodly collection of books, engravings, china, old furniture..."

A corner of the garden and the orangery.

The delightful entrance to *Netley Cottage* in 2021.

Grove Lodge, with *Netley Cottage* to the left.

237

John Galsworthy, the novelist and playwright lived in *Grove Lodge* from 1918-1933, during which time he completed *The Forsyte Saga* and won the Nobel Prize for Literature. "The Galsworthys bought the lodge and moved as soon as they could, spending five nights in late September 1918 at the Kensington Palace Hotel while 'bag and baggage' were transported and painters and decorators set to work," records James Gindin in *John Galsworthy's Life and Art.* "Reached through a tiny courtyard, *Grove Lodge* had a number of smaller rooms opening out into a large L-shaped bay-windowed drawing-room with views of the garden and the heath beyond," continues Gindin. "It was, by all accounts, elegantly decorated by Ada. The deep bay window in the drawing room was set round with a blue-covered seat, there were low bookshelves and Ada's grand piano. Pale walls and off-white paint, Persian rugs, parquet, pictures, Chinese needlework … There would be one perfect pink Azalia or a blue Hydrangea in a pot."

Grove Lodge entrance – the blue plaque records author John Galsworthy's erstwhile residence.

Interestingly, *Grove Lodge* has Galsworthian links to another NW3 property: No.41 Belsize Park, where Gabrielle Coudron and Marion Ford Anderson lived. The Ford Andersons were cousins by marriage to John Galsworthy, and it has been said that he based *The Forsyte Saga* on them.

Gabrielle Coudron and Marion Ford Anderson outside No.41 Belsize Park c.1914. *Photo courtesy John Hibbert.*

Admiral's House, Admiral's Walk

Tall and imposing, the substantial *Admiral's House* on Admiral's Walk is extraordinary architecturally. Built in brick, rendered and painted, this semi-detached 3-storied 3-bay building, with an attic and basement, overlooks a walled garden on the south side. The hipped roof of the original section is slated. Enjoying splendid views in every direction, it has been known by several names in its long life.

Golden Spikes
Originating from 1700, and known at the time as *Golden Spikes*, it was built for a successful wine merchant, Charles Keys, who lived here until his death in 1753. Rebecca Mackworth, Key's daughter, inherited the house.

The Grove
From 1775 the house was renamed *The Grove* by the eccentric Naval Captain Fountain North (1749-1811). North was descended from a noble Norfolk family. He acquired the freehold in 1791, and buying up small pieces of land, he extended the boundaries of the property. A large extension was added in the 1790s (alterations and additions followed).

Admiral's House, or *The Grove* as it was known in 1911, *A R Quinton.*

Remarkable Homes of NW3

The Grove during Fountain North's residency, archive image from 1796.

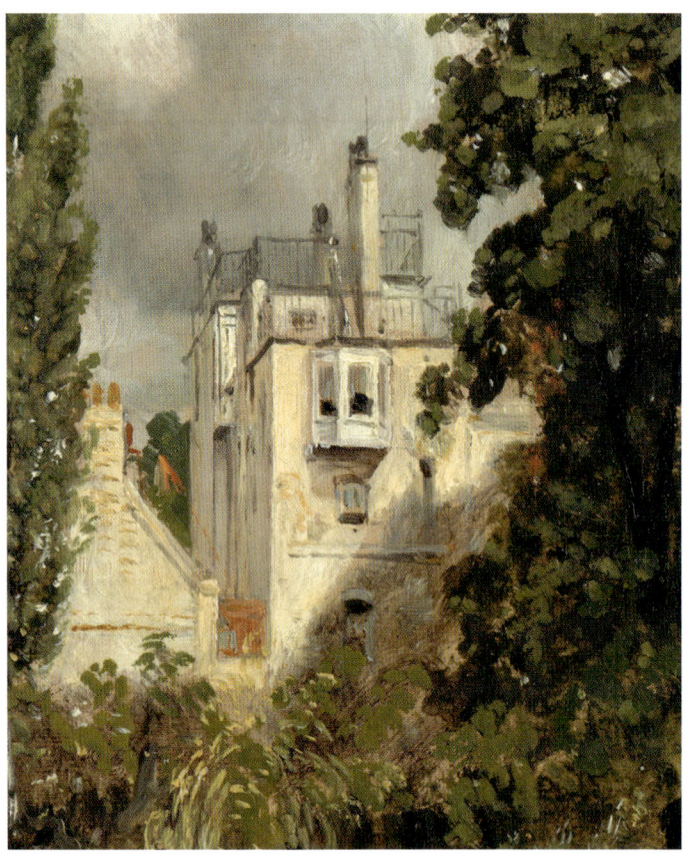

The Grove, Hampstead, detail, *John Constable c.*1821-22, *Tate images.*   Right, a similar view of the house as it is today. *The Grove* has been depicted in at least four paintings by John Constable, including one titled *A Romantic House in Hampstead.*

Researcher Felicity Marpole established that Fountain North almost certainly made the nautical alterations to the building, including the addition of the curiously distinctive quarterdeck on the roof. North made it his home until he died in 1811, leaving the property to his wife and son.

In the mid 1800s, *The Grove* became home to George Gilbert Scott RA (1811-1878), who was inspired to participate in the Gothic Revival by the architect Augustus Pugin. It was said that in 1856 that the Scotts were going up in the world. By 1861 the family had five living-in female servants at *The Grove* – a nurse and a cook, a housemaid, as well as a waiting maid and a parlour maid. The Scott family lived at the house until 1864. Scott was the architect of many memorials, churches, cathedrals, and major building projects in London and elsewhere. These include the Midland Grand Hotel at St Pancras Station, the Foreign and Commonwealth Office, and the Albert Memorial in Hyde Park. Scott was knighted for his work in 1872, taking the title Sir Gilbert Scott.

Admiral's House

Some one hundred years later the house became home to John Fortescue and his wife Winifred, who lived here from 1917 until 1926, when John retired and left Hampstead. It was the Fortescues who renamed their home *Admiral's House* and so it has remained. James Gindin, in *John Galsworthy's Life and Art: An Alien's Fortress*, writes: "Admiral's House, in Galsworthy's time, was owned by Sir John Fortescue, described by Galsworthy when he once invited Charles Scribner to dinner with him as 'the King's Librarian and author of the History of the British Army…' "

John & Winifred Fortescue arriving in New York in 1922, *archive*.

John Galsworthy and John Fortescue were not only neighbours but friends and would go for walks on Hampstead Heath together. The fifth of the nine novels in the Forsyte Saga, *The Silver Spoon* published in 1926, is dedicated to John Fortescue, who was knighted by the King in the Spring of 1926.

Having married John in 1914, Winifred Fortescue gave up her stage career and launched an interior decorating and dress designing business. Later writing articles for *Punch* and other newspapers, she started a Women's page for the *Morning Post*.

Mary Poppins

In 1933 P L Travers began writing her *Mary Poppins* series of books, of which there were eight published between 1934 and 1988 Illustrated by Mary Shepard (see p226). It is likely that the final name of this Grade II building and, indeed, the eccentric Fountain North inspired P L Travers in the creation of her Admiral Boom character, who enjoyed firing a cannon from his roof.

After twenty years of siege, Walt Disney finally obtained permission to make the 1964 *Mary Poppins* movie, but contrary to popular opinion, *Admiral's House* itself did not feature in the film. However, key features from its architecture were incorporated into the studio film set built for the scenes representing the home of Admiral Boom.

Admiral's House has been under the same ownership since the 1980s. ■

Admiral's House is accessed directly from Admiral's Walk. Originally added in the C19, along with the conservatory set above it, the entrance has been further modified over time.

P L Travers (1899-1996) as Titania in *A Midsummer Night's Dream*, c.1924, *archive image*. She worked briefly as a professional Shakespearean actor and was first published as a teenager.

Constable's House, Lower Terrace

Constable's House, No.2 Lower Terrace, Fred Adcock, 1909.

Continuing down to the western end of Admiral's Walk, a small green and the delightful No.2 Lower Terrace come into view. Often fleeing London in the summer months, generally to Suffolk, following his marriage to Maria Bicknell in 1816, John Constable RA (1776-1837) escaped instead to Hampstead in 1819. He took lodgings near the Whitestone Pond at *Albion Cottage*.

Around this time, Constable decided to paint his landscapes on a six-foot by four-foot-six canvas. It was also the year that Constable sold the first of these, *The White Horse,* the painting that saw Constable become elected to the Royal Academy. But, unfortunately, just as his success as an artist was beginning, so was the tragedy of his wife's illness. Maria Bicknell Constable started showing signs of tuberculosis, which took two of her brothers. Her condition prompted the Constable family to return to the clean air of Hampstead on a more permanent basis, and in 1821 they lodged at No.2 Lower Terrace, along with Mrs Elizabeth Roberts. Taken on as their nanny and governess/nurse, Nanny Bobs, as the children called her, would henceforth hold this artistic family together.

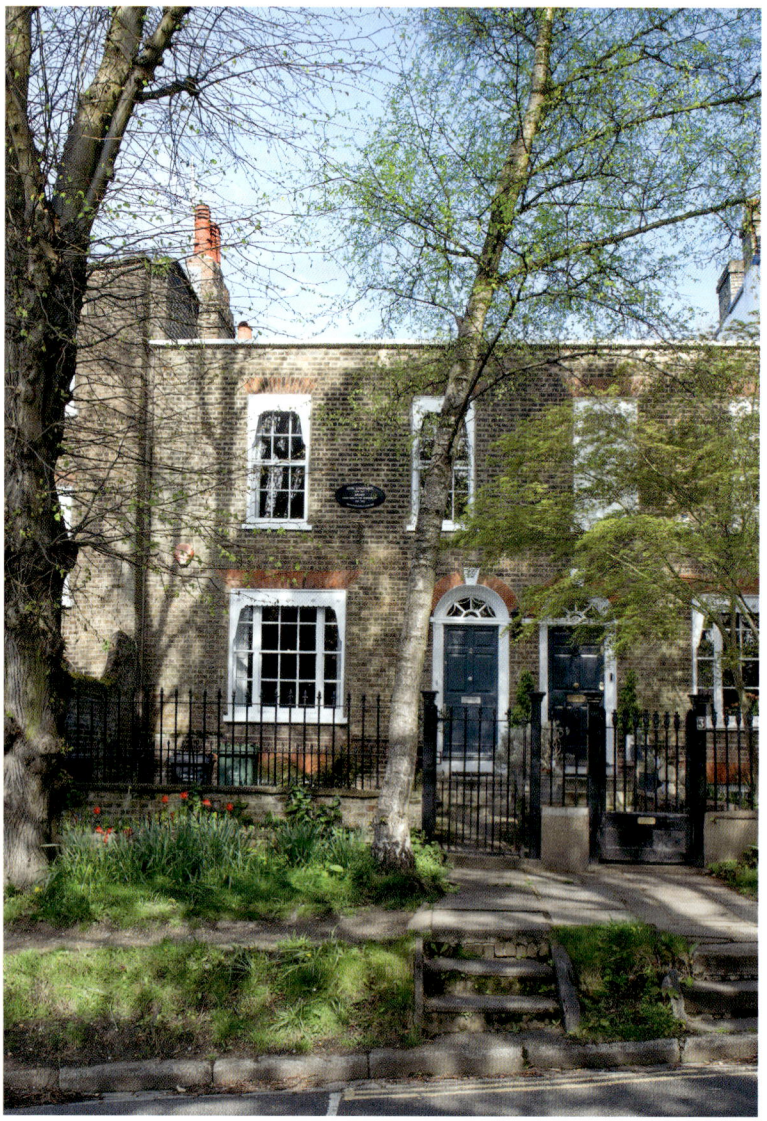

No.2 Lower Terrace today.

242

The Grade II Gatehouse of *Branch Hill Lodge*, the pillars marking the Lodge driveway.

This pretty house was one of four pleasing late-Georgian cottages, and the Constables stayed there from 1821 to 1823. A time that covered his paintings *The Hay Wain* and *View on the Stour near Dedham* was also a time when he worked on many paintings of his Hampstead neighbourhood, including views of *Admiral's House*.

After 1823 the Constables moved to *Stamford Lodge* on the eastern side of Heath Street. Then, with Maria's health ever worsening, in 1826, they removed to No.25 Downshire Hill, by which time John had completed his 'six footer series'. Another move in 1827 took them to No.40 Well Walk, the fashionable location near the Heath (see p160). From there, Constable had a commanding view of London centered on St Paul's Cathedral. Soon after moving in, he wrote to his friend John Fisher, "Our little drawing room commands a view unequalled in Europe – from Westminster Abbey to Gravesend." Sadly, in November of 1828, Maria died only ten months after giving birth to her seventh child. John Constable, profoundly bereft, dressed in black thereafter until his own death nine years later. John and Maria Constable are buried alongside each other in the churchyard of St John-at-Hampstead.

Further along the road from No.2, sitting at the junction of Lower Terrace and Frognal Rise, is a flamboyant Gothic-revival-style gatehouse linked to some fascinating history. The Gatehouse was added when a grand, early C18 mansion was remodelled c.1868 by Samuel Sanders Teulon, architect of St Stephen's, Rosslyn Hill. The original house was known as *Bleak Hall* and *Judges' Bench House*. The present house *Branch Hill Lodge* is partly by Teulon, although rebuilt in 1901. After that, it underwent various changes of regime until the building was bought by Camden Council in 1965, extended, and turned into a retirement home.

Interestingly, a large mansion once stood nearby on Birchwood Drive, off Templewood Avenue. It was owned in 1888 by the silk merchant John Spedan Lewis. He named it *Spedan Tower*, and the family lived there until his death in 1928. It would be his son, also named John Spedan Lewis, who would establish the constitution of the John Lewis Partnership in 1929. History has noted this in the naming of the southern driveway leading from the Gatehouse to *Branch Hill Lodge* and Branch Hill Estate – it's called Spedan Close.

Remarkable Homes of NW3

Squires Mount

Houses once home to Elizabeth Taylor and Richard Burton

View looking up East Heath Road towards Squires Mount, drawing *G Childs c.*1840.

Squires Mount, once home to a well-known wool merchant, is today the name of the relatively quiet road leading to a large house built by Joshua Squire. He was a Factor at Blackwell Hall, the centre for the London wool and cloth trade. This grand residence, built for himself in 1714, was surrounded by extensive grounds. The property was girdled by Cannon Lane and East Heath Road on its other two sides and dominated this hilly area. And thus did Squire's Mount become the name of the modest roadway leading to his house.

Joshua Squire's magnificent house glimpsed through its gates is discreetly hidden away on Squires Mount.

A terrace of five charming cottages was built in the mid-C19 on the same side as Joshua's house, and Squires Mount lost its apostrophe. The house itself was occupied by Edwin Field (1804-1871), the law reformer and artist during the late C19, and at one time in its history, its sheer size made it suitable to serve as Mrs Holt's School for Young Ladies. Today, its 1714 origins, together with Neo-Georgian additions by Edwin Field's brother Horace *c.*1900, and the separate *Chestnut Lodge* in its grounds, gives the estate Grade II* listed status.

On the opposite side of the road, facing the first cottages on Squires Mount, are what appear to be two Victorian era Neo-Georgian style houses. But surprisingly, Nos.11&12 Squires Mount only date from the 1950s. Over the decades, these two houses have seen life as both a single residence and as two separate houses.

"I am the Founder and Chair of the Turkish Acıbadem International Hospital in Istanbul, which is located on the waterfront of the Sea of Marmara," says Dr Said Haifawi, the current owner of both houses, who had made his initial purchase sight unseen.

As he explains: "One of the visiting doctors had been living on Squires Mount. One day, back in 1991, he called me and said, 'there is a very nice house [here] on the market'. It so happened I was looking for a property in Hampstead, so the next day I made an offer – without even seeing it! The offer was accepted, and we secured it." And in the nick of time, because immediately afterwards, offers to buy the house were flooding in from home and abroad.

The house that Dr Haifawi and his wife Gulsen bought in 1991 was No.12, which had earlier been inhabited by the composer and lyricist Sandy Wilson (1924-2014), best known for his musical *The Boy Friend*, and then, famously, by Elizabeth Taylor (1932-2011) and Richard Burton (1925-1984). They had owned both properties. In 1972 Taylor and Burton (on writing to a Mr and Mrs Crossley of Beech Hill Avenue, Hadley Wood) had referred to No.11 as 'The Cwtch', (a Welsh word for a cubbyhole).

Elizabeth Taylor (later Dame) was, of course, indigenous to Hampstead. She was born at *Heathwood*, No.8 Wildwood Road, Hampstead Garden Suburb. Richard Burton was a Hampstead resident, having lived at No.6 Lyndhurst Road, Belsize Park between

1949 and 1956. As one can imagine, back in the 1970s, the paparazzi were often camped outside their Squires Mount address when Taylor and Burton were in residence. "I understand that at that time it was all one house, but that when they divorced, they split it into two," continues Dr Haifawi. "Having bought No.12, we didn't change it much at all. It has an extensive open ground floor area and is in a wonderful location just by the Heath. Then, when it became available ten years or so later, we were able to acquire No.11 next door for my son Yaser. When he later moved away, we sold it to a

Squires Mount Cottages in 1911, *AR Quinton*.

Nos.11 (in the foreground) and 12 Squires Mount as seen from the terraced cottages and looking towards the junction with East Heath Road.

director of an American bank in the UK."

Dr Haifawi took the precaution of asking his neighbour to give him first refusal should he ever want to sell the house. A wise move, as Dr Haifawi adds, "He did move away after a few years, and so we bought it back again!" Today the Haifawi family members live in Hampstead most of the time. All agree that their Hampstead home is of great importance to them. "The beauty of living here is that we can walk on the Heath, and above all, we love the fresh air, and the oxygen!"

Which is more than can be said for the previous occupants of the old lock-up in Cannon Lane.

Façade and a corner of No.12 Squires Mount.

Remarkable Homes of NW3

This segment of the lane links Squires Mount to Well Road, and at No.11, set into the high wall surrounding the former magistrates court at *Cannon Hall*, there are the remaining doors and windows of the old 1730 lock-up where prisoners were kept while waiting to appear before the magistrates at No.14 Cannon Place. The lock-up was in use until 1832.

Today, this high wall imprisons quite another matter – an architectural gem originally designed by Edward Greenway in the 1970s. His house has been sensationally renovated at the turn of this century but still hides discreetly behind its C18 façade. Interestingly, this section of Cannon Lane also brings us full circle, as it displays a street sign which retains the apostrophe for Squire's Mount.

No.6 Lyndhurst Road – once home to Richard Burton. During his Old Vic season, he would rehearse his Shakespeare in the garden – his voice booming across the fences, much to the pleasure of his immediate neighbours.

The door to the old lock-up in Cannon Lane, and in the foreground, one of the cannons.

Cannon Hall, Cannon Place

Cannon Hall in 1911, A R Quinton.

Just around the corner at the end of Squires Mount, a remarkable building comes into view: *Cannon Hall*, No.14 Cannon Place, a detached residence of considerable historical significance. Its name is taken from old military cannon repurposed as bollards and placed all around the Hall in 1838 under the stewardship of its inhabitant, Sir James Cosmo Melvill (1792-1861). Sir James, a distinguished British administrator, held the notable distinction of serving as the final secretary of the East India Company.

Sir James Cosmo Melvill, by *Eton Upton Ellis, c.1853.*

Steeped in history and sitting in half an acre, this Grade II* residence with its five splendid reception rooms and six bedrooms has retained well-preserved examples of fine panelling in some of the rooms, including the rear staircase and some early-C19 fireplaces in the extension.

As one leafs through the pages of the historical annals chronicling the residents who preceded Sir James in calling *Cannon Hall* their home, the property's captivating narrative unfolds, stretching back to the early 1720s. Among these distinguished occupants in the early days, Sarah Holford leased the house from 1745. Her time of occupation is confirmed by an engraving after Chatelain dated that year, looking to the south, titled A Prospect of Hampstead from the corner of Mrs Holford's Garden.

View down Cannon Place with the *Cannon Hall* gates in the foreground.

Remarkable Homes of NW3

Moving on sixty years to 1780, the Hall was occupied by Sir Noah Thomas (1720-92), Physician-in-ordinary to George III, and Sir Noah's portrait was painted by the future Hampstead resident, George Romney (see p228).

Sir Noah Thomas, detail, painting by *George Romney*, 1781.

Cannon Hall today. Constructed in brown brick with red brick dressings, on 3 storeys, dating from around 1720 with later alterations and additions.

Leading from the grand entrance hall there is an outstanding feature in the form of a fine early-C20 staircase built in mid-C18 style with twisted balusters and carved brackets.

The record pages reveal that a magistrates' court was established in the stable block, and the various sitting magistrates judged prisoners from the Hampstead parish lock-up in Cannon Lane (see p246). Many of the magistrates lived in the house over the years. The court operated from about 1730 until soon after the formation of the Metropolitan Police Force in 1830.

Cannon Hall was later acquired by Gerald du Maurier, the highly regarded actor-manager in 1916.

Sir Gerald du Maurier (1873-1934).

The impressive mid-C18- style staircase, *photo Edward Hill*.

Cannon Hall seen from the grounds, photo Edward Hill.

Gerald was the son of George du Maurier, who lived at *New Grove House*, Hampstead Grove (see p258). To great acclaim, Gerald du Maurier played the dual role of George Darling and Captain Hook in *Peter Pan, or The Boy Who Wouldn't Grow Up*, at the Duke of York's Theatre, London, on 27 December 1904. Gerald du Maurier and the playwright and author J M Barrie were to become close friends. Gerald lived at *Cannon Hall* with his wife Muriel Beaumont and his three daughters until he died in 1934. The sister of Angela du Maurier (1904-2002) and Jeanne du Maurier (1911-1996) was the renowned author Daphne du Maurier (1907-1989), who grew up here from the age of nine.

After 1934 the du Maurier family sold the house to Mrs Muriel (Wilson) Warde who lived here until she died in 1964, leaving the house to her nephew Iain Graham Menzies (1895-1979), and following his death, the house was again sold. And that closes our record book of distinguished past residents of *Cannon Hall*.

On the big screen, *Cannon Hall* features in the film *Bunny Lake is Missing* (1965) starring Sir Laurence Olivier, directed and produced by Otto Preminger. It also features in the movie *Tenet* (2020), written and directed by Christopher Nolan.

Part of the former coachman's house and stable block with the weather-boarded clock and bell turret.

From right to left: No.10 New End, No.12 and No.14.

New End

By the C19 the hamlet of New End on the slopes immediately above the Wells was crowded with the cottages of the poor – *Pevsner*

On the road that runs eastward from Heath Street down towards Well Walk, there is a glorious survivor from c.1725-26. One of three elegant, terraced houses, No.10 New End is distinguished from Nos.12 &14 by its black painted window frames. Listed Grade II as a group; these houses consist of attics with dormers, 3 storeys of multi-coloured stock brick, offset by the gauged red brick segmental arches over all the sash windows, and stuccoed basements set behind iron railings. The three houses were refaced in the late C19 and while they originally had slate roofs, all the roofs are now tiled.

When the current owners bought No.10 in January 2013, only a few changes to the interior were needed because the previous owners had restored the house to an extremely high standard. The cornice detailing, doors and all the woodwork have

A column head in the hallway.

Window looking out onto New End with its working shutters folded back into their casings.

No.10 New End interior door and wall panelling.

been preserved or restored. The updated windows, changed about 20 years ago, are in the correct Georgian style. All the window shutters have been beautifully renovated and are fully functioning. At some point, the wall between the front and back rooms was opened up, producing a flow through ground-floor area. Unusually, as part of the rewiring, all the electrical outlets are installed beneath the floorboards so they're not visible above the skirting. A solution the current owners consider most appropriate for a building of this age.

The original kitchen was in the basement, as to be expected. Unfortunately, some while ago it has been completely gutted, so there is not a single period detail remaining. However, the current owners have preferred to relocate their kitchen to the ground floor (as have Nos.12 &14). The upper floors have been disturbed very little and are well preserved. Some original fireplaces remain, and the ground and first-floor fireplaces still function well, with even the bathroom also enjoying a small fireplace.

Having always lived in older properties, the owners were delighted to find this most suitable period house in Hampstead and in such close proximity to the Heath. Especially since they consider the Hampstead air to be far fresher than in town. As did the medical profession in the C19. No.10 New End adjoins the massive buildings that Henry Edward Kendall designed as the infirmary for the Hampstead Union workhouse, founded in 1869. The infirmary was renamed the New End Hospital in 1922 and it operated until 1986.

No.10 New End, the stuccoed basement glimpsed behind the railings, sits next door to the ornate red brick building that was the New End Hospital.

The previous New End Theatre building is now the Village Shul.

The *Duke Of Hamilton*.

Directly opposite the western end of the hospital on the north side of the road was the hospital's mortuary (where Karl Marx was laid out before his burial in Highgate cemetery). This building is said to have been connected to the hospital by a tunnel, enabling the discreet transfer of the deceased. The building was used as the New End Theatre from 1974 before being converted into a Jewish cultural centre in 2011.

And usefully sited next door to the mortuary at Nos.23-25 New End is the *Duke of Hamilton*. Little changed today; a small alley to the left of the pub leads up to Elm Row and No.12 Hampstead Square (see p255).

Further down the road on the same side as No.10, making the corner of New End and facing the *Old White Bear* pub, sits the splendid building that used to house the Hospital's Dispensary. Given all these early medical connections it is unsurprising to note that even No.10 was itself once occupied by a doctor.

Thankfully for the owners of the beautiful Georgian house at No.10, they are not only living in a remarkable architectural gem but also enjoy expansive views of the city from the rear of their lovely home. No longer "crowded with the cottages of the poor", New End is quite the opposite today.

The old Provident Dispensary (built 1853), *c.*1986
Wellcome Collection Gallery, CC-BY-4.0
This building has since been refaced and is looking very dapper.

Gang Moor and Whitestone House

The Grade II-listed *Gang Moor*.

Opposite Whitestone Pond at the upper end of East Heath Road, amidst trees and greenery, is the private thoroughfare known as Whitestone Lane. And here, we find two large houses mostly hidden from view. The first one, *Gang Moor* is located at the upper end and seen here through the attractive iron gates. Built in yellow stock brick on 3 storeys, the property dates from the early C18 and was re-fronted in the early C19 with later alterations. This was the home of the engraver W J Linton and his wife Eliza Lynn from 1862 and to George du Maurier and his family from 1869 (see also p125). They had moved here from No.4 Holly Mount. Then in 1872, the du Maurier family moved on to 27 Church Row. In the biography of her father written in 1934, and titled *Gerald: A Portrait*, Daphne du Maurier describes *Gang Moor* as "standing on the very summit of Hampstead Hill facing Whitestone Pond with a clear, uninterrupted view towards every point of the compass."

View across Whitestone Pond looking north.

Remarkable Homes of NW3

Next door to *Gang Moor,* just down Whitestone Lane, and called successively *Heath House, The Lawn* and then *Whitestone House,* this significant mansion dates from the Regency era. Since that time it was considerably redesigned and enlarged in the 1930s by Sir Clough Williams-Ellis (see p229), best known as the creator of the village of Portmeirion in Wales. The property has recently undergone further updates and improvements, with everything finished to the highest standards of design and workmanship.

Uniquely positioned with extensive views over the Heath, *Whitestone House* was also home to the Victorian writer and suffragette Beatrice Harraden (1864-1936) as well as the landscape artist Henry Mark Anthony (1817-1886). He was often favourably compared to John Constable and praised by William Rossetti for his fine landscapes. It has been suggested that Constable, when renting the adjoining *Albion Cottage* in 1819, used the garden studio of *Whitestone House*. Christopher Wade says foundations of a studio were found under the lawn; these were presumably also used by Anthony during his residency from 1858-1886. Somewhat later, from 1912, the manipulative therapist Sir Herbert Atkinson Barker (1869-1950) occupied the house. He was an advocate of the avoidance of surgery and developed a highly successful technique. ■

Whitestone House, Whitestone Lane.

The Italianate village of Portmeirion, designed by Clough Williams-Ellis, *photo, oatsy 40,* CC BY 2.0.

Whitestone House garden view, *archive photo, Jeremy Wight.*

Lawn House, on the southwest side of Hampstead Square. Note the two brick, in-filled 'blind' windows: one at the top left and the other on the first at the right.

Lawn House, Hampstead Square

The present owners of *Lawn House*, No.12 Hampstead Square, acquired the property in 2008. The building was in serious need of restoration. Prior to undertaking the project, the highly-respected conservation architect Jonathan Lawlor was asked to research the house and its history. He concluded that *Lawn House*, comprising 3 storeys in brown brick, plus a basement opening onto the rear garden, was built in 1709, at the start of Queen Anne's reign (1709-1714). The structure of the house was subjected to several further alterations, notably in the Georgian period of the late C18, after which a 3-storey Victorian extension to the rear of the building was added, plus another rear extension in the late 1930s.

The early-C19 portico with modified, fluted Doric columns and pilasters. Gauged red brick flat arches to flush-framed sashes with C20 glazing.

The house likely derived its name from the large lawn it once possessed, but that terrain, along with its entrance drive from Hampstead Square, was sold off in Edwardian times (1901-1910). At some later date pivot windows were installed, remaining in situ until the present owners purchased the property. The centre section opened while the upper and lower sections were fixed; the windows were considered ugly and totally inappropriate for this historic building and had to be replaced.

The totally inappropriate pivot windows of *Lawn House* in 2007-8, photo, Jonathan Lawlor.

255

The restored Georgian windows have gauged red brick flat arches to flush-framed sashes with C20 glazing and aprons.

Rear elevation with the 1938 Crittall window extension, *drawing, Jonathan Lawlor*.

Rear elevation in 2008 showing the Crittall window extension.

On informing the planners that the owners wished to exchange these pivot windows for Georgian-style replacements, Camden officers duly visited the site to measure up. They were subsequently rigorous in ensuring that the couple followed all the correct procedures for the restoration of the building, listed Grade II in August 1950. The owners were extremely careful in restoring the many Georgian features both inside and out.

A 1930s extension on the first floor at the rear was another architectural travesty. The owners applied for permission to take it down and replace it with something more in keeping and as near as possible to what may have been there before. The replacement of the front windows and the restoration work at the back required a house history, so architect Jonathan Lawlor was duly appointed, and he spent months preparing the planning application.

Lawlor discovered that plans to adapt the house dated 1938 featured the addition of the steel Crittall window glazed extension, raised from the ground on stilts up to the first floor. He noted that it sat uncomfortably across the Victorian additions and the Queen Anne wing. As part of the ongoing research into the house's history, it was discovered that the poet and mystic Evelyn Underhill had lived here in the late 1930s. In fact, it was Evelyn Underhill who fitted the Crittall windows.

Christopher Wade notes of Underhill that she "was a disciple of Baron von Hugel, a collaborator of Tagore and revered by T S Eliot. She has been called a 'very human, very English saint'." Even so, the owners got rid of the extension and its Crittall windows. Interestingly, as so many people are digging basements and building extensions, this project is probably the only one in NW3 where the house has been made smaller!

Lawlor also discovered how the south-facing rear elevation might have looked before and after the 1880s. "The house was originally 1 room deep to the west and 2 rooms deep to the east," he writes. "The ground and first floor contained the important rooms, and the basement and garden were given over to utility for servants and a working garden." He also noted that the L-shaped building "remained largely unaltered for about 150 years.

It was probably in the late 1880s when a 4-storey rear extension, dumb waiter, and bay window were built to fill in the gap at the back."

Once Underhill's extension was removed, the couple were unsure as to what should replace it. Lawlor proposed that they balance the large Victorian extension and gain some interior volume by adding another oriel window to the one already existing. (An oriel window is a bay that protrudes from the main wall but does not reach the ground). So it was decided to extend it down and duplicate it on the floor below.

Even though the front is Georgian and the side and back are Victorian, it's still rather odd on entering the living room to discover the Victorian extension with its bay windows, making the room unexpectedly deeper than it would have been originally. The bedrooms are also Georgian rooms extended with Victorian rear windows.

The owners were fortunate to be able to install an original Georgian fireplace – even though it was not original to this house. It came from a Georgian home in Sussex. The Sussex owner had ripped out their original fireplace together with its swan's nest grate, wanting to replace it with a Chesneys fireplace. So following a straight swop, *Lawn House* now has an authentic Georgian fireplace.

The present owner's love for this old house is evident in every detail of their commendable restoration, thanks to the skills of Jonathan Lawlor. ∎

Rear view of *Lawn House* today – the darker brickwork on the left is the Victorian extension, and the new oriel window is on the right.

Interior view of one of the oriel windows.

The Georgian fireplace with its swan's nest hob grate.

The rear Victorian extension of *Lawn House* towers over three charming C18 cottages built on land formerly occupied by the *Duke of Hamilton* public house stables. The steps beside the end cottage lead down to the pub on New End.

257

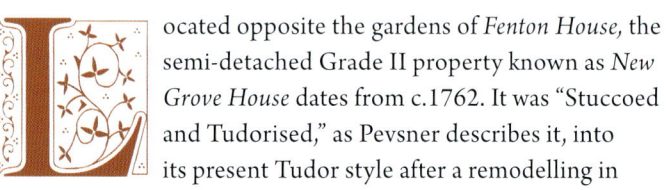

Hampstead Grove

Located opposite the gardens of *Fenton House*, the semi-detached Grade II property known as *New Grove House* dates from c.1762. It was "Stuccoed and Tudorised," as Pevsner describes it, into its present Tudor style after a remodelling in the mid-C19. When first built, *New Grove House* was appended to the side of *Old Grove House* (seen behind the haycart). Constructed of yellow stock brick with stone and red brick dressings, its full-height entrance bay is within the white-painted stucco section.

Today *New Grove House* is divided into three dwellings. Looking towards the building from the buttressed garden wall of *Fenton House*, seen above in the foreground, we are considering two houses: the stuccoed tower and the chimney-stacked tower belongs to *New Grove House* (now No.28); the single-windowed tower and the remainder of the visible building is now No.28a, more generally known as *Du Maurier House*.

New Grove House in 1911, AR Quinton.

Hampstead Grove with *Du Maurier House* in the foreground. The blue gate in the wall leads to the front door of *Du Maurier House*.

Du Maurier House

Du Maurier House is so named because it was once the studio of the distinguished artist and writer George du Maurier who lived here for 21 years until his death in 1896. For years, du Maurier and his St Bernard dog were regularly seen walking on the Heath. Father to Gerald du Maurier and Grandfather of Angela, Daphne and Jeanne (see *Cannon Hall* p242), he is buried in the parish churchyard of St John-at-Hampstead.

Corinne van Oudtshoorn, who now owns No.28a, invited her neighbour Alberto Toffoletto, Professor of Law at Milan University, now residing in No.28, to discuss their two homes. When George du Maurier was in residence here in Hampstead Grove, this property was undivided. "*New Grove House* was only converted into three properties in 1986," explains Alberto. It now comprises *New Grove House* where I live, *Du Maurier House*, where Corinne lives, plus what is now No.9 The Mount Square, located at the rear. No 26, *Old Grove House*, seen in all the photos and engravings, has nothing to do with this property."

"Several descriptions are scathing," says Corinne. "Pevsner's 'Tudorised' comment is not at all appreciated – Gothicised would be kinder. Nor is the less than flattering claim that it was 'tacked onto the side' of *Old Grove House*." This 'Tudorisation' took place around 1840, followed by a number of alterations. *New Grove House* had 23 rooms, and as it was built on a steep hill, the back of the house has four floors, and a cellar – while the front has three. The wing of the house has two floors with garages below. The two garages are accessed from The Mount Square.

"I previously lived on the raised ground and first floor of James D Linton's studio house at No.35 Steele's Road," says Corinne, "a unique Queen Anne-style house," (see p31). At that time, Corinne was getting together with her husband, an organisational psychologist, who often worked from home. "So we were looking for somewhere suitable, and in 1994 the estate agent who found my Steele's Road flat came up with this unique house in Hampstead Grove.

"As it was possible to access the study without entering the main part of the house, it was perfect for my husband's work. When I first saw *Du Maurier House*, I fell in love with the beauty of its architecture," recalls Corinne, "The rather romantic Gothic style of its bath stone mullioned windows, and its 3-story tower protected by bird-like gargoyles peering out from above. Sadly, hard frosts over the years have taken their toll and a number of stone features have been lost."

The five-paned gothic style bay window of George Du Maurier's studio.

The ground floor sandstone-framed mullioned bay window.

A delightful fireplace in *Du Maurier House*.

The gallery bedroom in the former studio of *Du Maurier House*.

George du Maurier's study/studio, 1876, *The Building News* archive. Note the roof beams were not revealed at that time.

Exterior view of George du Maurier's studio windows.

The sitting room of *Du Maurier House* is a wonderfully comfortable place with a delightful courtyard view. "The garden is not overlooked, apart from Alberto next door!" adds Corinne with a laugh. "It's unbelievably peaceful on a summer's evening with the courtyard drenched in sunlight until the last moments."

George's studio in *Du Maurier House* "has a north-facing window and is now a bedroom," says Corinne. The archive illustration of the studio with George at work looks very similar to how it is now, except that the roof space has been opened up and a gallery now runs along the right side of the room.

Daphne du Maurier once said that George du Maurier's studio was "the best room in the house … with its many windows."

New Grove House

The adjoining *New Grove House*, now the home of Alberto Toffoletto and his wife, was love at first sight. Alberto, who studied law at the LSE in the 1980s and now teaches law at the University of Milan explains: "When we first saw the property, we were impressed overall. I was especially taken with what is probably one of the highest roof terraces in Hampstead. It was a lovely day, marvellous blue sky and I found the large terrace so truly incredible I immediately made an offer."

This acquisition occurred when the market collapsed in 2009 – an excellent time to buy. "The vendor Ramsay Homa encouraged me to up the first offer, we did the deal, and I bought it," recalls Alberto.

While the couple also realised that the house needed a lot of work to bring it up to standard, they made minimum changes except in the kitchen, which underwent a serious updating. The doors and door frames are original, as are their rose features that match the roses on the corners of the plasterwork cornices. "We did all the wall decorations and carpeted the house in white throughout," says Alberto.

At the time, Alberto was opening a London office for his firm to provide Italian legal services to UK companies. And *New Grove House* was ideally situated for the commute to New Bond Street. "I find this a place to relax, as if I'm on holiday, even though we're in a big city – unbelievable!" says Alberto. "I love the windows, the greenery, the trees, and we can see right into the fabulous garden of *Fenton House*. All the views are fantastic, especially the sunsets."

Looking west from the roof terrace of *New Grove House*. *Admiral's House and Grove Lodge* can be seen on the right.

View to the east with Christ Church and the London skyline beyond.

New Grove House on Hampstead Grove.

Living in a building formerly inhabited by famous people, whether writers, artists or actors, has its fun side too. "One day," recalls Alberto, "a tourist saw me outside and the tourist said, 'You're the famous film director Ridley Scott'," I said, "No, he lives next door!" [true at the time] The tourist replied, 'I don't believe you, I want a picture' – and insisted on taking a photo of us together!" And Corinne adds, "And I have even heard tour guides come by and state that Steven Spielberg lived here! [not true].

George du Maurier

Born in Paris, George du Maurier (1834-1896) spent most of his life creating illustrations for *Punch*. His novel writing followed when in his mid-fifties.

Anna Maxwell recalls in her book *Hampstead:* "His neighbour, Canon Alfred Ainger, himself of French descent, delighted in du Maurier's wit and in all his graceful fun; he speaks of him as

261

New Grove House dual-aspect living room windows with marvellous views.

A *New Grove House* staircase and landing.

The door frame rose features match the corner roses of the plasterwork cornicing.

262

New Grove House front entrance.

Part of the plaster cornicing with corner roses.

Indeed, Canon Ainger (1837-1904) particularly enjoyed *Punch* magazine, but the two Frenchmen had much else in common. Close friends since the 1870s, they met daily for some fifteen years, and were often seen deep in conversation during their walks on the Heath.

Later in life, du Maurier wrote three novels, *Peter Ibbetson,* Harper & Brothers (1891), a humorous illustrated work, initially published in parts in *Harper's New Monthly Magazine.* His second work was the Gothic horror novel *Trilby,* Harper & Brothers (1894), and his third, *The Martian,* Harper & Brothers (1898), was an autobiographical work published posthumously. ∎

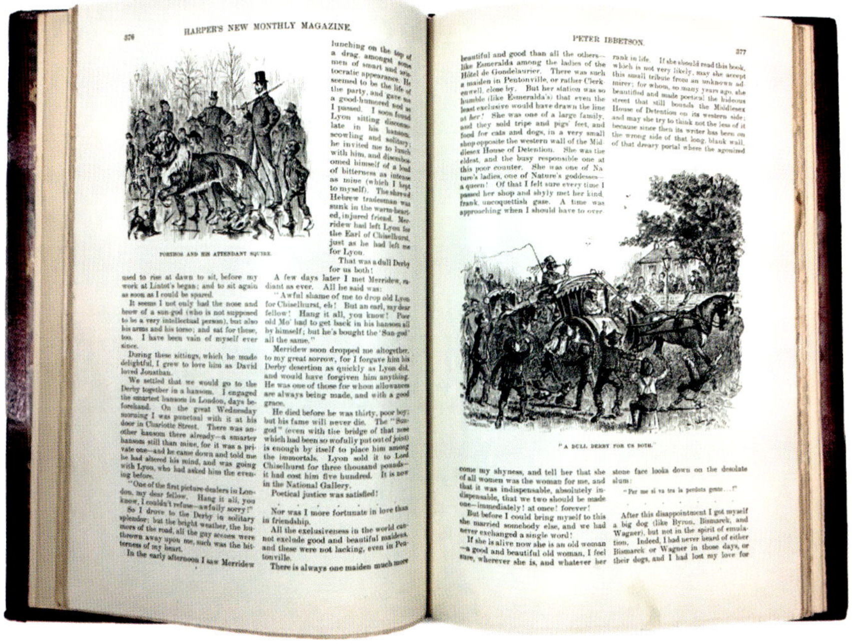

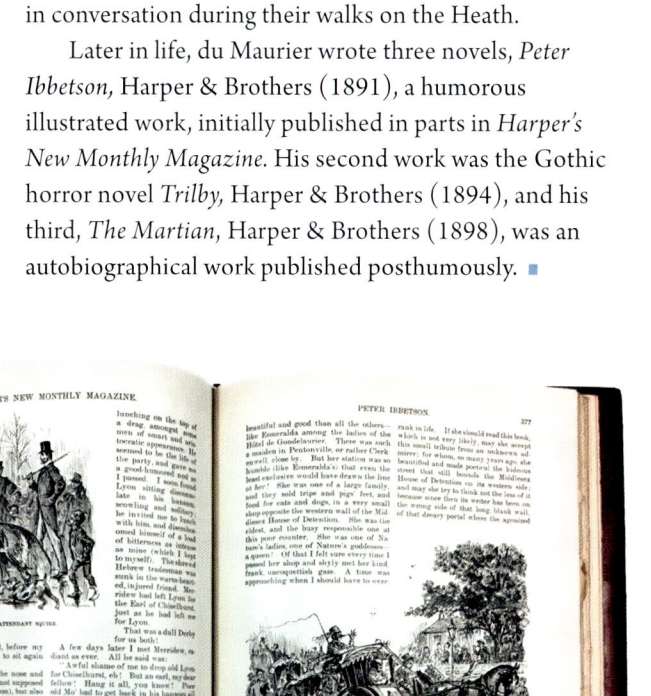

the most generous and genial host, 'the tenderest of husbands and fathers'." But, Maxwell continues, "The artist's health, despite the appearance of such high spirits, was never of the best, and we may thank the bracing air of the Heath for the stimulation of his physical strength." As well as producing illustrations for *Punch* magazine, du Maurier created illustrations for other periodicals, including *Harper's, The Graphic, The Illustrated Times,* and *The Cornhill Magazine.*

Pages from *Peter Ibbetson* in *Harper's New Monthly Magazine.*

263

Remarkable Homes of NW3

Hampstead Grove continued

As is frequent in the C18 development of villages, here are bigger individual houses, behind the terraces of the main street –
Pevsner

Today, a row of semi-detached houses can be glimpsed behind a wall on the opposite side of Heath Street to where the old *Upper Flask Tavern* once stood. Originally known as 'The Grove', its name was changed to Hampstead Grove in 1937 to avoid confusion with The Grove in Highgate. Six Neo-Georgian semi-detached houses were built at the upper end of Hampstead Grove in 1936. This grove, with its fine old trees, runs parallel to Heath Street, from where the rear elevations of these houses are visible.

The *Upper Flask Tavern* on Heath Street sold flasks of water from the Hampstead Spa, *engraving, C J Smith,* 1837.

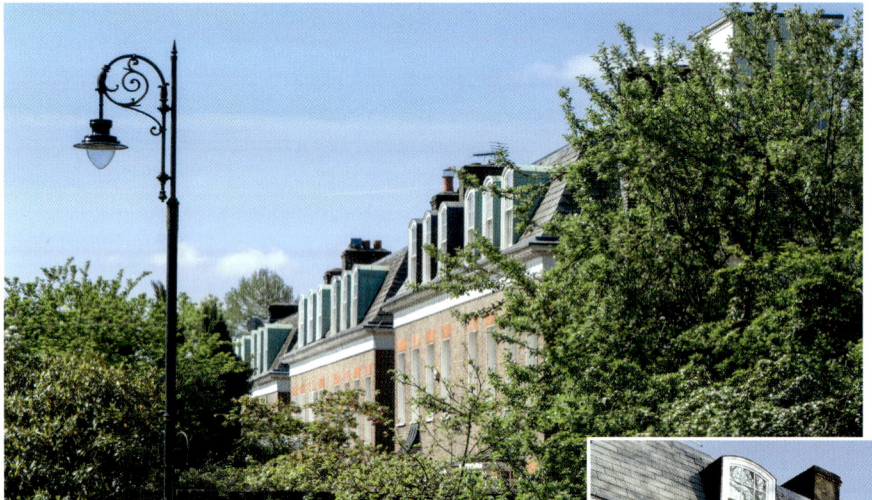

Houses on Hampstead Grove viewed from the upper end of Heath Street.

These semi-detached houses are particularly unusual because their front doors face one another onto a courtyard. Here we are visiting No.36, the home of Robert Perlman, company chairman, and his wife Roberta, a movement teacher of the Feldenkrais Method.

"I used to live in Belsize Park Gardens in the 1980s but have lived here since Robert and I were married over 30 years ago," says Roberta. "We particularly like the side-facing front entrance and think it's nice to open your front door to that unusual aspect across a courtyard. But it's a choice and, over the years, three out of the six houses have made the change to a forward-facing front door." Two pairs of houses share glass canopies – most convenient when it's raining. These canopies were probably added in the 1960s.

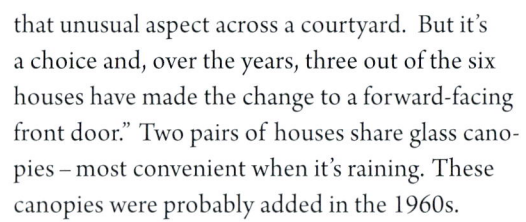

"Robert's family bought No.36 in the 1970s," notes Roberta. "They refurbished and modernised the pre-war house, most notably converting the original garage into a new kitchen."

Neo-Georgian houses on the northern part of Hampstead Grove.

No.36 Hampstead Grove frontage.

The front door of No.36 facing its neighbour just across the courtyard. Note the vertical window on the left.

French doors access the garden terrace from the kitchen.

"Robert and I moved here in 1991. We were fortunate to find an excellent architect named Victoria Manser, and we carried out a huge amount of work to the property, including laying oak flooring and installing underfloor heating throughout most of the ground floor."

The kitchen had already been extended to the rear of the house but now features the double doors with the fanlight above, that had initially been used to access the garden from the living room. Architect Victoria designed an extension to the living room in line with the kitchen, resulting in a well-proportioned room and a lovely run of French doors facing the garden.

No.36 Hampstead Grove rear garden view.

The living room with windows and French doors, the kitchen is to the left.

"We matched the cornicing everywhere to the 1930s originals. We very much wanted to respect the character of the original house while drawing in more light and creating a practical family living space."

To bring light from the rear of the house into the entrance hall, the original doorway to the reception room was dramatically widened to achieve a semi open-plan effect. "We had intended to keep that space open," Roberta continues. "So when our interior designer suggested putting a floor-to-ceiling wrought iron gate there, I was initially rather dubious. But she convinced me – and she was absolutely right. It looks wonderful! She cleverly designed the gate's ironwork to echo the ironwork of the original staircase."

To introduce more light into the hallway, Victoria replaced the tiny window under the staircase with a longer, vertical one.

In 2014, some further adjustments were made to the ground floor layout, and while retaining its original arched red brick profile, the garage door originally located on the right of the front door, finally ceded place to a window. "The house continues to be a work in progress," says Roberta. "We have been really happy here over the years and feel so lucky to live close to the Heath and be just a few minutes walk into the bustle of Hampstead Village. Shops and businesses come and go, but there is a constancy about Hampstead, something timeless and serene."

No.32 Hampstead Grove was once home to Lord Cottesloe, who was chairman of the South Bank board that oversaw the building of the National Theatre.

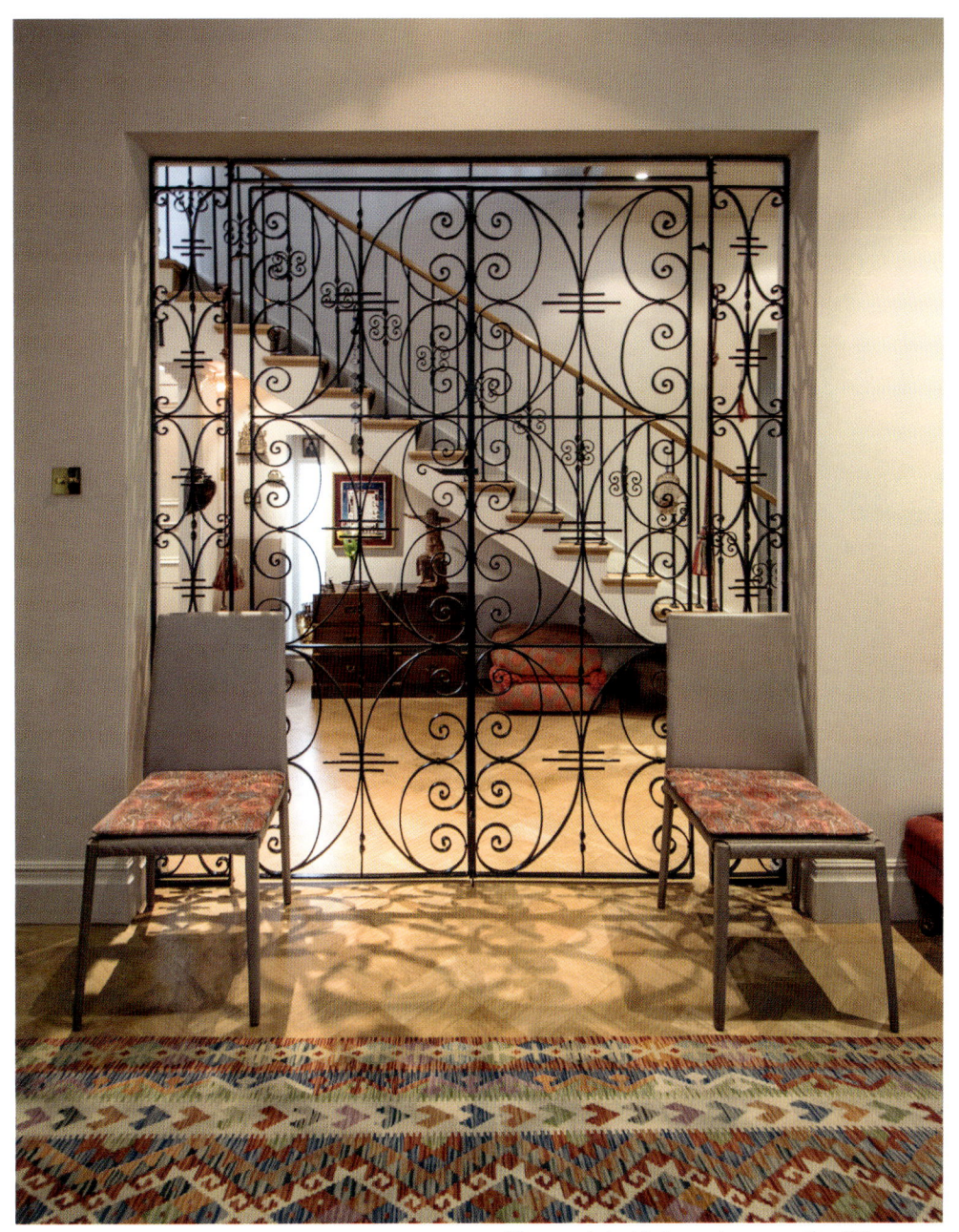

The grand, double iron gates access the sitting room.

No.32 Hampstead Grove with its repositioned front door facing the road.

Capo Di Monte

It's rare to come across a delightful Georgian cottage, especially when you least expect to find one. Nestling in a corner right on the edge of the Heath just off Judges Walk is such a cottage, dating back at least as far as 1762. Originally two or more smaller cottages, it is now combined into one to produce this exquisite detached 2-storey, six-bedroom cottage orné. The Grade II property is rendered in white-painted stucco with weatherboard extensions at the rear, plus a basement.

Although the building has been altered over time, some features have survived and are now restored. *Capo di Monte* was already over a hundred years old when it became home to actress Sarah Siddons (1755-1831), moving to Hampstead for her health and to be near her doctor in 1804-05. A leading actress of her day, she found great success as Lady Macbeth, her most famous role, which she first performed on 2 February 1785. *Capo di Monte* subsequently became known as 'Siddon's Cottage', and an S-shaped black wall plate is visible on the front of the house.

"Here Mrs Siddons enjoyed a long visit to her favourite Hampstead, in the quiet of her life's evening," recalls Anna Maxwell in her book *Hampstead,* "when the sounds of public applause were beginning to fade away, for she had at that time retired two years from the stage."

In the following century, other notables lived in this lovely house. Firstly, Samuel Woodburn. As Constable, living nearby in 1821 recalled: "Samuel Woodburn was the well-known picture and print seller of St. Martin's Lane, who then occupied the cottage now known as Capo di Monte, the same house in which Mrs. Siddons had previously lodged." Then there was Edward Magrath

(1790-1861). Magrath was a founder member of the Athenaeum Club, and in short order became its first secretary when the nominated member, Michael Faraday, finding himself overstretched, relinquished the role to his good friend Magrath. It was also Magrath who would later recommend his relative Spencer Hall for the vitally important role of librarian at the club. Spencer was the brother of the William Hall of Chapman and Hall, the publishers of (among other notables) Charles Dickens.

In C20, the architectural and art historian Sir Kenneth Clark (1903-1983) and his family lived in the cottage during the 1940s. Later, from 1966 through to 1969, he wrote and filmed the material for the BBC TV series *Civilisation: A Personal View*. The series, and the book published in the same year, made Kenneth Clark world famous. From 1949 the cottage became home to the journalist, novelist and broadcaster Marghanita Laski (1915-1988). As Christopher Wade recalls, Laski was hailed as "the undisputed queen of the English language".

Christopher Wade notes that Judges Walk has over time been called many other names, among them Upper Terrace Avenue. He is however, of the opinion that Judges Walk is more likely to have taken its name from a nearby house, today known as Judges Walk House. Initially created in 1745 for the Master of the Rolls, Sir Thomas Clarke, and later occupied by several other senior justices, it was originally known as the Judges' Bench House. This is most likely a contraction of the descriptive, 'the House of the Judges of the Bench'.

Sarah Siddons as the Tragic Muse, *Sir Joshua Reynolds* Google Art Project.

Judges Walk, after a drawing by Clarkson Stanfield, c.1850. Said to be so named because during the great plague it was used as a meeting place for the judiciary when they were sitting at Hampstead. As Thomas Barratt has concluded, "The story is perhaps not altogether improbable; but we should prefer documentary or historic proof."

Capo di Monte in 1910, *A R Quinton*. "From under the elms of Judges' Walk Sarah Siddons could look straight forward to the place of the Flagstaff and the Pond." – Anna Maxwell.

Remarkable Homes of NW3

Ferncroft Avenue

Architect CHB Quennell (1872–1935).

Ferncroft Avenue is the work of the well-established architect CHB Quennell designing hand-in-hand with builder George W Hart. The avenue dates from 1899-1900 and was developed over the fields and meadows of Platt's Farm. Ferncroft is a long, straight, gently undulating avenue linking Platt's Lane with Heath Drive.

Here we are visiting a typical house, No.36 Ferncroft Avenue, that is something of a tardis, looking much larger inside than it appears from the outside. A colourful and attractive interior awaits. The current owners, Liese and Stephan, came to London from Cape Town in 2007. Liese van der Watt is an African art historian and curator while her husband Stephan works in advertising. "We rented for years before moving to the first house we bought, which was on Canfield Gardens in South Hampstead," says Liese. "After a few years, we started looking around in Hampstead. Stephan found a house that was not selling during the Covid period."

The house underwent a tasteful but modern makeover in 2010-12 that, unfortunately, removed much of its original Quennell interior.

Front door with stained glass in four shades of green.

View from the dining room. The white structure beyond is the upper part of the light well that extends down to the lower ground floor.

The kitchen and seating area opens onto the garden terrace.

"The previous owners had installed a large glass light well extending down to the lower ground floor at the rear. And the pre-existing basement was made slightly deeper," explains Liese.

"When I first walked into the house, I thought, 'Mm, this is interesting; the light well makes a tremendous difference to the ground and the lower ground floors," Liese recalls. "The remainder of the house was very nicely done and well presented, but not to my taste; it was modern, too modern. I'm far more of a traditional, homely person."

Nevertheless, the couple decided to go ahead and buy the property, realising that it would have to undergo major changes to make it their own. Things like the staircase. It had been replaced with a modern variant, boxed-in with a stainless steel handrail. "It was nicely done but inappropriate for this house," continues Liese. "It cost quite a bit to install an appropriate replacement."

The couple changed the kitchen and family area flooring, installing a beautiful stone floor specially imported from France. "We like panelling on the walls, so we've installed quite a lot of that around the house. I wanted to make it older and more traditional," adds Liese. The kitchen extension was already in place, but it had one large sliding door to the garden that has now been replaced with more traditional opening glass doors. "Our architect, Thomas Griem, proposed adding a lantern that allows light into the area from above that's double glazed and opens for ventilation – it's just wonderful." All the doors can be opened to the garden terrace.

Seating area in the garden room.

The colourful and inviting garden terrace.

"We installed a new kitchen – Peter Huberman of Kitchens Kitchens in Belsize Park did a wonderful job for us," continues Liese. "I wanted a little pantry and Peter managed to get the proportions just right. I'm an antique hunter and found the large kitchen table on the website of a place in Belgium." The couple had brought a set of tall double doors from their previous house which were adapted to make them fit. They feel that these doors help bring an element of grandeur.

Quennell's original location of the door leading to the front room was set at an angle. The architect changed that and introduced a new set of metal and glass doors. Sadly, all the original fireplaces were removed previously. "I wanted stone fireplaces," says Liese, "I found a couple in Norfolk – something with a French feel – old, but not English. I love Louis XIV furniture – I find it all works visually." Tastefully decorated with new cornicing, the ground floor, including the front room, is now totally transformed into a truly comfortable home.

I love my garden, and gardening gives me so much pleasure," says Liese enthusiastically. "Beaufort and Rampton Landscapes helped to design the courtyard garden. This location is quiet and peaceful; we feel so fortunate to live here. The house is so close to the Heath it's wonderful for walking our dog – we use a little shortcut at the end of Heath Drive."

No shortcuts have been taken by this couple in their quest for the perfect fusion of ancient and modern, creating a beautiful home with a remarkable garden for the enjoyment of their family and friends. ■

The kitchen pantry with one of the pair of tall doors.

Part of the delightful courtyard garden of No.36 Ferncroft Avenue.

Hollycroft Avenue

Hollycroft Avenue dates mainly from *c.*1905-6 and was developed over the fields of Platt's Farm. George W Hart constructed some houses on the road. The architect of No.24 Hollycroft Avenue was C H Saunders, and according to Alastair Service it was built by William J King. Interestingly, the initial conveyance for this property is dated 15 August 1905 and was made between the Hampstead West Heath Land Co Ltd and Lily Spencer-Churchill, Duchess of Marlborough (née Lillian Warren Price).

Lily Spencer-Churchill (1854-1909).

The current owners of this lovely home on Hollycroft Avenue are Kristien Carbonez, from Leuven, Belgium, and Simon Pritchard, from Adelaide, South Australia. They met while Masters students

Dining room and double-height atrium on the garden level.

Natural light illuminates the house through its numerous windows.

at the University of Heidelberg, Germany in 1996 and married in Brussels in 1997. After spending three years in Belgium practising law, and following two years in Washington DC, the couple moved to London in 2003. "We rented for many years and bought our first apartment on Broadhurst Gardens in West Hampstead, living there from 2009 to 2016," says Simon. "But when our third child was born it was just too small for us," recalls Kristien. "Aside from space, we didn't have easy access from the kitchen to the garden, which was communal. "We moved to Hollycroft Avenue in December 2016, so we've been here just over seven years."

The previous owners undertook the fundamental redesign of this house and are responsible for the double-height conversion at the rear of the property. "This five- to six-bedroom house acquisition was a splurge option; it's a little on the large side, but it's a good problem to have, with each of the three children enjoying their own bedroom," says Simon.

"The exterior is very much the same as when we moved in," says Kristien. "We've opened up a few walls, but otherwise the interior is the same apart from the decor – previously, it had a completely different feel. We repainted everything and installed wooden floors throughout the house, and we furnished it." Interestingly, the couple are still in touch with the previous owners. When they returned to revisit the house,

The atrium from the upper level.

they commented on how it feels so very different now.

"We spend a lot of time in the kitchen on the garden level," says Kristien. "We added the decking outside, but the BBQ isn't used as often as my Australian stereotype would suggest!" says Simon. "We very much like the front living room in the winter where it's nice and cosy. And the front room is ideal for entertaining." Kristien heads up the London office of a Belgian law firm while Simon is also a lawyer, both spending some of the week in offices in the City and some days working from home; and during the Covid period, the couple added a pleasant garden office.

"You're in a big city, but you are also in a country village and so we feel very privileged to live here," Simon emphasises. "We're very near to Hampstead Heath Extension, and Golders Hill Park is only about five minutes walk away," adds Kristien. "And the neighbours are very nice too." The couple have come to know many of the neighbours on their side of the road especially well. "It helps to make you feel part of a community. We often bump into friends in Hampstead and people we know from Belsize Park," says Kristien. "Now, of course, we really appreciate the space which comes into its own when we have family and friends round."

The couple have made their home a delightful space, art abounds everywhere and the house is absolutely beautiful. Some of the artwork is British and some is Aboriginal art, brought back from Australia where they visit kinsfolk and friends quite regularly.

Kristien and Simon have created an extremely stylish home for their family, incorporating excellent design and great décor. ■

The stylish front living room of No. 24 Hollycroft Avenue.

Views across the garden towards the garden room.

HOVSE FOR THE R^{EVD} C VOYSEY·B·A· AT PLATT'S·LANE HAMPSTEAD

Voysey's original design for *Annesley Lodge,* image *RIBA Collection.*

Annesley Lodge, Platt's Lane

Thrillingly, this short stretch of road was once known as Duval's Lane, after the notorious C17 'gentleman highwayman', Claude Duval. Over time the name became verbally corrupted into Devil's Lane. Although the word 'Platt' of itself derives from the word for a small plot of land, the name of this road was changed to Platt's Lane in recognition of the reputed oriental scholar and Bible specialist Thomas Pell Platt (1798-1852), who had lived nearby in Child's Hill House for many years.

An Arts and Crafts house of exceptional quality, No.8 Platt's Lane is a long, low building designed by CFA Voysey (1857-1941), a pioneer of the Modern Movement (see p34). Voysey's architectural practice at the time was in Melina Place, St John's Wood.

The British Architect of 28 February 1896 states: "The house [is] built in stock brick with Monk's Park stone dressings and iron casements, and roughcast on all external brickwork, finished over with lime white. The roof [is] covered with Broseley tiles, and all the external wood and iron painted pale Brunswick green."

Having built the house for his father, the Rev Charles Voysey, in 1896, Voysey used one of his middle names when calling it *Annesley Lodge*. Pevsner describes this L-shaped building as "Roughcast, with stone dressings to a remarkable long band of low first-floor windows just below the eaves. The mullions have no mouldings at all, and the whole house is astonishingly ahead of its date."

The Grade II *Annesley Lodge* sets Voysey's 'classic style' marking the appearance of elements such as the roughcast chimney stacks, the horizontal bands of sandstone connecting with the sills of the upstairs

Voysey's detail of the quoined yellow sandstone window dressings, the groupings of vertical window modules and the horizontal banding. Note the sloping buttress and the red window drapes.

windows, interposing them with the wall buttresses.

Although the house is now divided into four flats, its external appearance has been preserved. The main entrance was through the central doorway, beyond which was a large entrance hall. It was Voysey's opinion that all these features, which included porches and doors that were unusually wide in relation to their height, created a sense of shelter and welcome.

Remarkable Homes of NW3

Looking out through a typical window with leaded panes. Note the large tree in the garden.

Section of the Victoria Regina wallpaper designed by Voysey as originally hung in the entrance hall in 1901. This is a reproduction by David Berman of Trustworth Studios, Massachusetts.

The only surviving image of the original entrance hall as published in *Studio*, 1901.

Originally, the ground floor was entirely paved with red quarry tiles, although there is a suggestion that the dining room was the exception to this, and it would have had wooden flooring. Blues and greens pertained in the hall, where the walls were papered with the very distinctive 'Victoria Regina' wallpaper while the woodwork, including picture rails and other detailing was picked out in deep green.

Today, this wonderful building is well screened from the road by trees and hedging. And the tree by the gate, once pretty insignificant, now stands majestically and provides welcome shade. The right-end gable seen from Kidderpore Avenue sits

Annesley Lodge today. This view shows how the main entrance (beyond which was the large entrance hall) is set back into the far corner of its plot.

adjacent to another extraordinary building. The left-end gable can be glimpsed from Platt's Lane. Even though it is now divided internally, the building still conveys its original sense of well-being, peacefulness and sheer homeliness. One of the present owners settled here in 2001 and is well aware of the good fortune of living in such a remarkably nurturing house.

In the 1950s, *Annesley Lodge* was home to a psychiatrist and his family, and the house continued to be a private family residence until it was sold, becoming a nursing home around 1970. This change of use occurred during the decade of less awareness of the need to preserve the fabric of buildings like *Annesley Lodge*. Inevitably, the building's conversion into a nursing home resulted in internal changes and even damage to the structure. Many of the original fitments and woodwork were removed and disposed of – some of the original windows were taken out and exchanged for modern versions. As a result, the building went into a steady decline leading up to the 1980s; suffering greatly, it had become derelict by the time it was converted into flats in 1983.

But then, about ten years ago, one of the flat owners received a visit from the daughter of the psychiatrist family who had grown up in the house. No doubt she was pleased to see the building still looking good. Thankfully, the developers were able to install replicas of the original windows, and despite everything, some of the fireplaces managed to survive the decades, as had the door frames – although this house is not so ideal for tall people, as the ceilings and door heights, somewhat lower than is usual today, are another Voysey signature.

As can be seen from his original design, Voysey had focused principally on red, yellow, white and green when creating his exterior. The original colour of the internal woodwork was Brunswick green, while the external wood and ironwork was a pale Brunswick or Leaf green. One of the owners recently managed to track down the correct shade, and there's always the possibility that restoration of the correct green could be reinstated in the future. Voysey believed a home "should have all the qualities of peace and rest and protection and family pride." By great good fortune, this jewel of a house is still standing, and now that its listed status protects it, this building should never be neglected again. ▪

Remarkable Homes of NW3

West Heath Road

Maps in 1936 depict a striking disparity in the development of West Heath Road. While the western portion featured a cluster of established residences, the eastern side remained conspicuously bereft of any housing. The following year, in 1937, formal approval was granted for the construction of eight detached private dwellings along this particular stretch of West Heath Road, each with a minimum frontage of 50 feet. Here we are focussing on No.93, one of the later houses built post-1950.

The current owners of No.93 are Rudy Metta, a finance director and his wife, Nathalie, formerly a PR and marketing professional who now dedicates herself to running the home, motherhood and voluntary work, raising money for Camp Simcha and Chai Cancer Care.

The couple have called this house home for sixteen years. Nathalie's journey to the UK began in her mid-teens when she initially settled in Hampstead Garden Suburb. Rudy on the other hand, was residing in the Knightsbridge area when their paths intertwined. Nathalie reminisces, "We both agreed that we should purchase a house in Hampstead and embarked on the quest to find the perfect property." Then, Rudy recalls, "While I was at my desk in the bank, I received an email alert from the Hampstead estate agent marketing the property. So I asked Nathalie if she would like to go

The comfortable living room.

The dining room with French window to the garden.

and view the place." Which she did, and she loved it. That was sufficient for Rudy, and the couple decided to go ahead and purchase the property.

"When I first visited the house, it was evident that there had been extensive renovations," says Nathalie. "There was a new kitchen extension and a converted loft, creating an extra floor," she explains. Rudy adds, "Yet, the work was somewhat rudimentary and required a touch of refinement to align with our tastes. Numerous interior upgrades were in order, including installing air conditioning throughout the property. Originally, the house had a garage, which we later transformed into a playroom for our children." The couple decided to rent out their Knightsbridge apartment for three years before ultimately selling it.

When it came to their choice of furnishings, "We chose colours that reflect our style," says Natahlie. "Each room has its own colour scheme from the décor to the furniture and cushions and our taste in art. Rudy loves a masculine feel and I bring in the colour to blend and bring warmth to each room. We feel out home compliments our combined taste."

Nathalie and Rudy embarked on this new chapter in their mid to late twenties. Coupled with the birth of their children (a son four years later and a daughter two years after that), memories of vibrant gatherings and parties fill their recollections.

When they moved in, the garden comprised two levels, with the second one heavily overgrown. "It was akin to a fox's den," Nathalie recalls. "Given that the kitchen opens directly onto the garden, we view it as an extension of our home, ideal for hosting barbecues on the first level." The couple resolved to reconfigure the second garden level, creating an additional terrace. The former fox's den is now transformed into a dedicated relaxation space, nestled beneath a canopy of trees, while a third-level, a tree-lined play area, is large enough for football practice.

Remarkable Homes of NW3

The primary bedroom with the dressing room to the right.

The kitchen extension with its skylight enjoys direct access to the tiered garden.

Nathalie and Rudy's time here in this comfortable post-war home continues to be a marvellous experience for their whole family. "We find it a truly nurturing environment for our children," Nathalie affirms. "Every season graces us with its unique beauty; snowfall in winter transforms the landscape into a captivating wonderland. And it's absolutely gorgeous in springtime with blossoms everywhere."

The couple consider this to be a beautiful neighbourhood, "We are blessed with lovely neighbours, every street has its individual charm and the area is remarkably free from pollution. The stillness of the air up here is truly wonderful." ∎

The second terrace is dedicated to relaxation, while the steps lead up to the third-level play area.

Highview House as it is today. For years it was one of the few properties on this section of West Heath Road. The original funicular is on the left.

Highview House, West Heath Road

Positioned high, really high, and accessed via a flight of winding steps, this rectangular house is softened by its attractively flowing, elegant curves, its finely-detailed brickwork beautifully executed. Graced with terraced gardens front and back, No. 97 West Heath Road is no ordinary home.

The house makes its first appearance on the Ordnance Survey map of 1950. "I understand that the house was built shortly after WWII in 1948, and at that time much of the area on the eastern side of the road was still undeveloped." says its current owner, Nunzio Quacquarelli. "When first built, the house would have enjoyed uninterrupted views of farmland across Cricklewood towards Wembley and the stadium at a time when it held the 1948 Summer Olympics. It must have been spectacular in those days." Nunzio is an information data specialist who founded QS Quacquarelli Symonds Ltd in 1990, best known for the QS World University Rankings. His offices are in South End Green, but a couple of days a week Nunzio is able to work from home. "I have a dedicated study and it's remarkably peaceful, despite the relative proximity to the Finchley Road," he says.

"I had been looking for a house in this locality for two years, and it came on the market when the previous lady owner passed away. So I requested an immediate viewing." Nunzio continues:

The view from the front terrace in springtime.

"From the moment my wife and I had stepped across the threshold, we knew we wanted to live here. I acquired the house in 2005, and over 17 years it's been fascinating to see how the view across to the west of London is constantly changing."

Nunzio learned from the mother of Gerard Ronson (the business tycoon and philanthropist) that their family owned the property shortly after it was built. "I believe that the Ronson family did very well financially after introducing Formica laminate

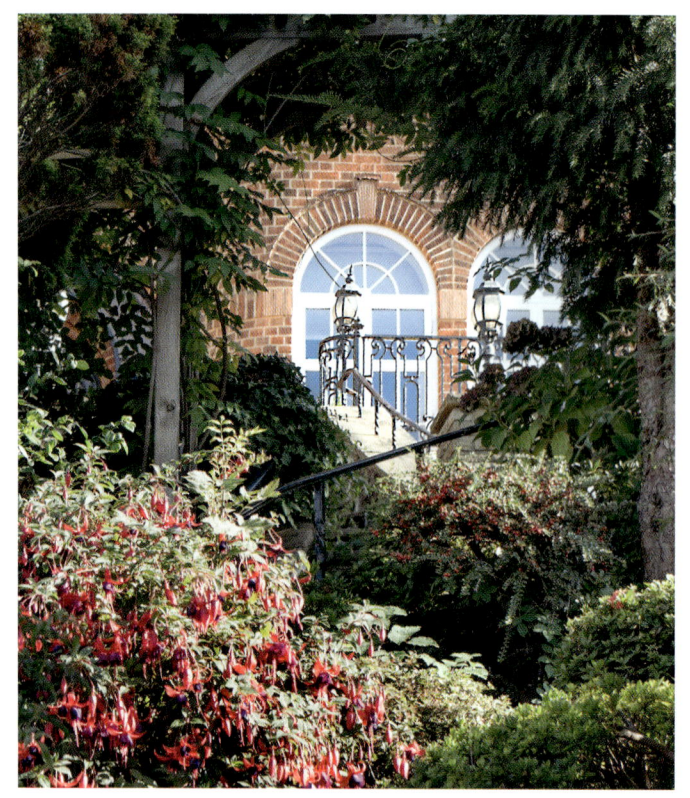

Today, fuchsias soften the approach to the front of the house, while trees and trellis supporting the taller greenery partially mask the property from the road.

> into the UK," adds Nunzio. Indeed, in 2005, the kitchen still had all its original fittings, complete with an early version of Formica work surfaces. Due to its elevated setting above the road, the property originally had a funicular lift. "We used it to get from street level up to the front door until a few years ago when we finally had to take it out of service," says Nunzio.

Originally the front garden was tiered with a Japanese planting scheme. "We have maintained that theme although we have taken out some of the tiers," says Daniela, a practicing Reflexologist. "When we first arrived, there was no tall greenery – the front terraces were totally exposed, it was all stone. As all the windows were post-war metal, 92 principal windows had to be replaced during the renovation work. The present conservatory in the rear garden was designed to allow an uninterrupted view of the trees and sky. "Having a sunroom as part of the house can cause a bit of a heat problem – cold in winter, hot in summer," says Nunzio. "We went through many iterations with our architect, and he suggested these gas-filled glass panels which regulate the temperature really well." This excellent solution removes the need for blinds, so the tops of the trees are visible all year round. "Looking up on a sunny day with a blue sky is fabulous," says Daniela. "And Nunzio can see all of the rear garden from where he likes to sit," she adds. "Among the planting, there's a wonderful Japanese Acer that changes its colour spectacularly in the autumn. But the best time for this rear garden is in April," notes Daniela.

Daniela and Nunzio.

"I have to confess that when we first arrived the furniture everywhere was very grand, far more luxurious then than it is now," explains Nunzio. "The dining room was furnished in the style of Louis XIV with incredibly elegant chairs. It was just too much for us."

There are many quirky elements around the house, and the couple have tried to retain them. Virtually all the original woodwork has been maintained, including the solid doors. Cornices and other superb original details abound. Beautiful wood carvings are everywhere, with delicate plasterwork and even miniature Corinthian columns.

In addition to the panelling, as well as the little nooks and crannies, there is a fabulously snug bar – also as it was originally. Every home should have one. "Maintaining the house is a continuing

Corner of the original living room as it was in the house brochure.

responsibility though, and it's all hard work," adds Nunzio.

"I adore the house. Children used to enjoy running right around the upstairs gallery. It's a very happy home," Daniela says with a big smile. "I look after it, clean it, and give our home tender love and care. I also do all the gardening, which gives us so much pleasure." And the whole atmosphere of this remarkable and happy home leads one to conclude that the house appreciates its loving owners as much as they relish living within it. ■

Every room is tastefully finished in a variety of styles.

The double-height hallway, staircase and gallery.

Remarkable Homes of NW3

The original, elaborate bathroom, little changed.

This plot on the eastern side of West Heath Road has its own remarkable history. On 21 April 1887, the Ecclesiastical Commissioners completed a conveyance of this land to Henry Gaisford Gotto. Was Henry intending to perpetuate a family tradition? His Uncle, Edward Gotto, had begun building *The Logs* on his East Heath Road land (see p176). But Henry worked in the family stationery business established by William Parkins and his father, Henry Jenkin Gotto, in 1845 – and time was not on his side. The year after Parkins & Gotto won a Royal Warrant of Appointment, when walking on Fitzjohn's Avenue on a cold winter day, Henry slipped and fell, dying from his injuries on 3 January 1894 at the age of 51. His plot would remain untouched for another 54 years.

One of the *Highview House* living room Corinthian columns and an alcove.

This snug-cum bar has remained as it was originally conceived. These days it serves as a consulting room for Daniela.

286

West Heath Road Golders Hill

A house called *Fernside* once occupied a plot between Finchley Road and the northern section of West Heath Road. The property, located opposite the western edge of Golders Hill Park, included a large garden with a small pond, as can be seen on the map of 1880. The mid 1920s saw three sister houses built on Church Commissioner's land by two brothers. These had large gardens and were located virtually opposite today's Golders Hill Swan Pond. We are visiting the most northerly of these sister houses, No.229 West Heath Road, built in 1926.

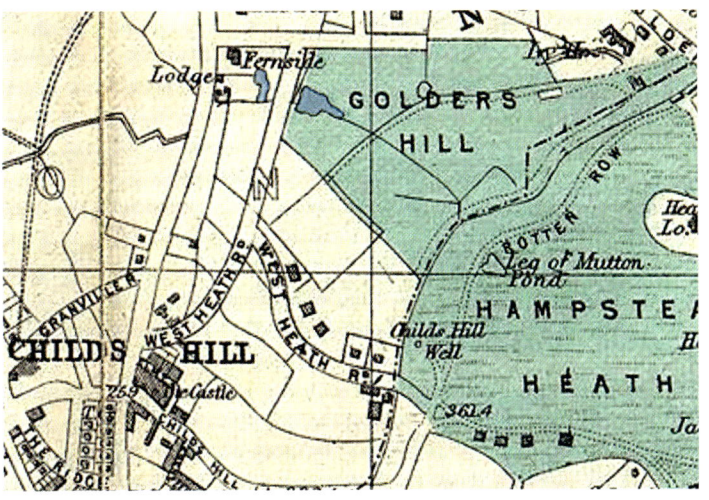

"A cabbie once told me there are just three T-shaped roads in London, and West Heath Road is one of them," says Tim, the owner. "I was a student at Imperial College in the early 1980s. I recall visiting Golders Hill Park and the pond and looking at some large houses beyond in their semi-rural setting. I didn't think anything more of it at the time. That was in 1983." For most of the 1990s, the owner lived in New York but towards the end of that decade he decided to return to the UK and began looking at houses in North London.

Fernside on West Heath Road with a pond in the garden opposite Golders Hill, 1880 map.

Golders Hill Swan Pond.

No.229 West Heath Road.

287

Remarkable Homes of NW3

The library leading through to the living room with the new extension beyond.

A corner of the homely living room.

"I was looking at properties reaching from Hadley Wood down to Belsize Park, and No.229 was the 50th house that I saw," recalls Tim. "I remember it was raining heavily, and, trying not to get too wet, I didn't pay much attention to the house's immediate surroundings except for the unusually large rear garden. So the next day, the estate agent arranged for me to view the house again and I realised that this was the house I saw as a student. So I decided to buy it there and then. That was 1997."

For another 10 years Tim spent half his time in London and the other half in the USA. "I didn't do much with the house at first. I let go of my apartment in Manhattan in 2003 and focused everything in London," Tim recalls. "Susan came over, we got married and had a child who is now 17. The local environment here is attractively leafy and yet six miles from the centre of the capital. I love London and know enough cities around the world to appreciate it and not take it for granted. The garden is half an acre – the feel of the place is absolutely beautiful. I can't see us ever selling the house."

The couple wanted the front part of the property to remain as it was. "I have tried to keep the original features with Crittall windows and anaglypta panelling," says Tim. The house has been enlarged considerably since the early days. What was once the dining room is now a library and there were five bedrooms – now there are six. They have extended the rear of the house but have retained within the build, the original rear wall and classic bay window of the ground floor that originally looked out onto the garden and a pond.

"One of the nice aspects of this house is the 1920s ceiling height. This is a lovely cosy room, especially in the winter with the fire. On a summer's day, it's bright because I have these large ceiling apertures in the extension with floor-to-ceiling windows to the garden." They added rear extensions in 2011 and 2019. "We decided to retain the original rear outside wall to create an 'outside-inside' effect," explains Tim. "The architects designed a large sunroof so the light shines through and into the rear of the house." They created a lower level to the new extension which has a very modern feeling contrasting with the traditional theme of the original dwelling. ■

An Anaglypta door surround in the hallway.

The extensions, the Art Deco turret and chimney, with the two sister houses to the right.
There is now a feeling of depth and space on the upper level, and the garden still has a little pond
– a nod to *Fernside's* original pond.

Upper level of the rear extension with the original rear bay window on the right, above the stairs leading to the lower level. A glass bridge links the two living spaces.

Wyldes Farm in 1857, oil painting by John Wood, Camden Local Studies and Archives Centre.

Old Wyldes, North End

Undoubtedly the oldest house in Hampstead, *Old Wyldes* was once the farmhouse of a medieval estate called *Weildes* granted to Eton College by Henry VI. Many of the estate's fields make up today's Hampstead Heath Extension. This historic house is an extremely rare surviving example of a timber-framed building in the London area. Dating back to around 1593; the 2-storey farmhouse, timber framed, weatherboarded, with no foundations, built on packed earth, still stands. According to David Sullivan an adjoining large brick and weatherboarded barn, dating from at least 1740, albeit now much altered, was later linked to the farmhouse by an extension built *c.*1820.

John Collins, the tenant farmer in about 1783-85, was followed by his son, John Collins Jr. In the early 1800s, he rented out four of the farmhouse rooms, accessed via a separate entrance. Charles Dickens stayed here with his wife Catherine following the tragic death of his sister-in-law Mary Hogarth. Bernard Roseborne, who had purchased *Old Wyldes* in the 1980s, knows the history of the house well. "At that time, in 1837, there was an open doorway from the room Charles Dickens rented into the barn next door, and in all, there were nine or ten bedrooms," he says. "Then the barn was converted by Charlotte Wilson around 1890-1900. An early Fabian, Charlotte Wilson (1854-1944) was an active campaigner for the preservation of Hampstead Heath, and she occupied the house from 1884," notes Bernard. "I also learned that architect Raymond Unwin's widow used to let out *Old Wyldes* and the barn to architectural students. Some of those tenant students used to come back and visit us from far and wide, which we welcomed."

Bernard and his family lived at *Old Wyldes* for thirty years. "Towards the end of 1980, we were living in a cottage nearby when we learned that the then owner had put *Old Wyldes* on the market," recalls Bernard.

Sydney Lloyd had previously bought the entire place at auction in the early 1960s, and in 1964-65, Lloyd converted it back again into two properties. "So, there was now *Old Wyldes*, the original farmhouse, and *Wyldes*, the barn. Then, in 1968, David Sullivan bought *Wyldes* for his growing family, and Philip Venning OBE acquired *Old Wyldes*, the farmhouse, in 1969. "I paid £205,000 for the farmhouse in 1981," says Bernard. "I was also going to buy the barn at the same time, but the vendor wanted too much money as the asking price was £235,000."

Having bought *Old Wyldes,* the Roseborne family was living in *Beach Cottage* nearby while work was underway on the farmhouse. "One day, a neighbour knocked on the cottage door

The adjoining weatherboarded barn today.

The Grade II* *Old Wyldes* as it is today.

and said, 'your house is on fire!'. Flames were licking 50-60 feet into the air from the house. I rushed over immediately. Fire engines were there. I sat in the garden crying," recalls an emotional Bernard. "The fire had virtually destroyed the roof. Fortunately, there wasn't too much damage to the house itself." It then took Bernard two years to rebuild the old place. "We put it back into a better state than when we bought it," says Bernard.

"We restored the farmhouse to its former glory – all the massive oak beams were replaced. Everything was pinned. No nails or screws. New drains were installed, and nearly everything was new. "We restored it to its original four bedrooms. It has wonderful old ship floorboards from the 1700s in the bedrooms. The main bedroom, the room Dickens had rented, has a vaulted wooden ceiling."

"Living there was an absolute dream for us – it's where we brought up our four children, plus our dogs and cats." Unfortunately, in 2011 the family had to move away to West Hampstead for practical reasons. "The place was very high maintenance, the weatherboarding requires painting every 3-4 years, plus we needed to downsize," recalls Bernard. "We were really sad to leave because all the neighbours are very interesting people. The William Blake society members used to visit to perform in the garden. And the house was in the American guidebook of London. Forget *Fenton House*, *Admiral's House*, and *Burgh House* – this is the oldest one."

Bernard has a further recollection. "In the mid-2000s, *The Sunday Times* had a pull-out section of the most desirable houses of the world – not London, not the UK, but the entire world – and *Old Wyldes* was in the listing for its literary associations. It has been said that of all the houses that Dickens lived in, *Old Wyldes* is probably the most 'Dickensian' house of all." Indeed, the literary and artistic associations are considerable. As well as Charles Dickens and Charlotte Wilson, the landscape painter John Linnell (1792-1882) stayed here, and it was visited by Samuel Palmer and William Blake in the 1820s. John Constable knew the farmhouse. It also became a meeting place for George Bernard Shaw, Sidney Webb, Edith Nesbit, and many others. ∎

Canon Samuel Barnett (social reformer) and Dame Henrietta Barnett (founder of Hampstead Garden Suburb), *painting by Hubert Herkomer.*

The Wyldes estate was acquired by Dame Henrietta Barnett, who formed a committee to raise money by public subscription, and in 1907 bought 80 acres of land from Eton College 'for use as a public open space for perpetuity'. This is now known as the Hampstead Heath Extension.

Dame Henrietta also bought more land to build a new kind of suburb, and heading another committee, raised enough money to buy a further 243 acres. Two distinguished architects, (Sir) Edwin Lutyens and (Sir) Raymond Unwin, designed Hampstead Garden Suburb with building work commencing in 1907. As the project's master planner, Raymond Unwin lived in *Wyldes* in 1906, and he used the barn as the estate office until 1914. After Unwin died in 1940 his daughter-in-law continued to occupy the barn for a further 20 years.

Henrietta Barnett's home, *Evergreen Hill*, archive image (next door to *Erskine House* p297).

Northstead, North End Avenue

Set in a fabulous location not far from *Old Wyldes* (see previous pages), a sweeping driveway leads to this substantial 4-storey spectacular period house called *Northstead*.

Internally, beyond the splendid hall and fine staircase are grand reception, dining and entertaining rooms, all gracefully proportioned, plus a wonderfully spacious dual-aspect orangery with full-height windows. The property is actually semi-detached and dates from 1867. At one time, it was home to actress Anne Crawford (1920-1956), a contemporary of Margaret Lockwood and Phyllis Calvert. Anne Crawford's movie and TV career spans the years 1938-1956. Her Hampstead house was selected to feature in *Homes and Gardens* in the August 1956 issue of the magazine. Regrettably, she died two months later of leukaemia, aged just 35.

Sissel Godfrey, a retired restaurateur originally from Norway is the owner now. "We bought the house on the 18th of November 1983, and we moved in on the 22nd of May the

Northstead as it was in 1956.

The dining area is at one end of the beautifully proportioned room with a handsome marble fireplace and the kitchen area beyond to the left.

The living room on the first floor running the whole length of the house leads to the orangery beyond. An Adam fireplace is in the left foreground.

A majestic living room window.

Part of the orangery with its floor-to-ceiling windows.

The spacious kitchen and dining area with a lovely Norwegian cupboard on the right.

following year," says Sissel. "So I have lived here for 39 years." Sissel has three grown-up children, a boy and two girls, but sadly, her husband Peter passed away four years ago. "My husband was English, he owned Oracle Advertising, and when he retired he left the company to his staff," she recounts. Sissel was in the hospitality business and ran a large, successful restaurant in Great Castle Street near Oxford Circus for over ten years. First opened in 1945, it operated seven days a week with 24 staff and could serve 140 covers. Some customers had been dining there for over 40 years.

The house originally had six bedrooms, but two have been converted into larger bedrooms. "The house has a newer extension with an orangery on the first floor," explains Sissel. "But virtually everything else has been retained as it was originally." Although Sissel did have mahogany windows installed

Sissel's four-poster bed (which dictated the house they would buy) in the grand main bedroom located on the second floor above the drawing room.

throughout and she also replaced the skirtings. "Many of the original skirting boards were shallow, so I had much deeper versions specially made," she adds. All the doors and frames were replaced as well. The flooring is Swedish oak. "I particularly appreciate the generous ceiling heights, especially upstairs, as it creates a wonderful feeling of spaciousness."

The interior furnishings do full justice to this grand property with its gloriously large rooms. "All the furnishing ideas are mine, I feel you can't really have anything modern in a house like this. In my view everything has to be in keeping – and everything I have is old!" says Sissel laughing. "From the outset, we were looking for a house with a large enough bedroom for my generously-sized four-poster bed!"

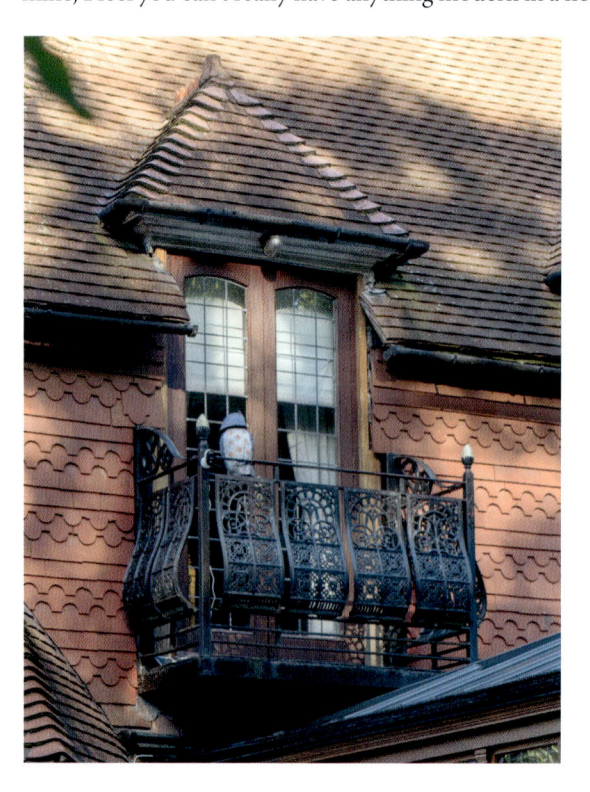

People tend to stay put in this area for a long time. "There is very little turnover of property owners in the surrounding area," explains Sissel. "People very rarely move away. There's one house in North End where the family has lived continuously for over 150 years. It is a wonderfully peaceful place to live."

Indeed it is, nestling as it does in a quiet corner at the far end of an enclave leading to Hampstead Heath. "The house feels as though one is living somewhere in the country, even though it's in NW3. I try to make the most of the Heath, often walking there with the dogs for up to two and a half hours daily. And although my walks are wide-ranging, I generally only meet two or three other people because I get up early." ∎

Hampstead's North End has an intriguing but little-known history. At one time, there was to be a station on the Northern underground line between Hampstead and Golders Green (under Hampstead Way). It was mostly completed but never opened. However, some 40 years later, during the 1950s, a spiral staircase was installed to provide access to a floodgate control room that was connected to the abandoned station below it. In the event of a nuclear attack during the Cold War, this standby control room was intended to facilitate the prevention of flooding in central London's underground network.

Erskine House, Spaniard's Road

Sitting at the very top of Hampstead Heath is *Erskine House*. Today's building is, in fact, adapted from the wing of a larger C18 house of that name which was pulled down in 1923. The original house was occupied by John Sanderson in the 1760s, architect of the parish church of St John-at-Hampstead.

From around 1783, this was home to Thomas Erskine, 1st Baron Erskine (1750-1823), and briefly Lord High Chancellor during the reign of George III. Erskine was an acclaimed jury lawyer and reputed to possess an excellent wit. While at his Hampstead home, he much enjoyed gardening as a change and a distraction from his activities in the Chamber and the Law Courts. "It is to Erskine's credit that even at the height of his prosperity he contented himself with so unpretentious an abode and lived here an unostentatious life when men of lesser wealth and inferior ability gave themselves up to display and extravagance," records Thomas Barratt in his *Annals of Hampstead*.

Erskine's House, engraving O Jewitt, c.1869.

Thomas Erskine, 1st Baron Erskine (1750–1823), *Circle of George Romney*.

Erskine House, Spaniard's Road, dating from C18. The white door accesses the house now known as *Evergreen Hill*.

"The house next to the Spaniards, and close by the entrance of Hampstead Heath, is called Erskine House," states Edward Walford (1823-1897) in his *Old and New London*. "The building is a plain white house, with a long portico opening upon the roadway. Of the house itself but little is seen from the road, excepting one end; a high wall shuts in what little garden it has on that side, and another high wall shuts out from observation the spacious gardens and grounds formerly belonging to it on the opposite side of the road."

Thomas Erskine lived here for over 30 years – he called it *Evergreen Hill* (a name now taken by the house next door. During that time, he enlarged the property and created a tunnel under the road that connected his garden to the extra land that he acquired from the Ken Wood Estate. Interestingly, as that particular house grew in size, so did its name contract: earlier known as Ken Wood House, after an interlude as Caen Wood House, it became Kenwood Place before arriving at the name by which it is known today, Kenwood.

Remarkable Homes of NW3

Anna Maxwell provides further details concerning *Erskine House*, writing in 1912:

> It is quite possible to visit the interior of Erskine House, observing the coloured-glass window on the stairs, which bears Lord Erskine's arms, with the baron's coronet and the motto which he assumed: 'Trial by Jury'. The lofty room upstairs, with its five tall windows, which, with other improvements, he added to the previous small house, saw very many distinguished dinner-parties, including one at which King William IV and the Duke of Wellington were present. Standing at the south windows in this room, we face the whole length of the Spaniard's Road.
> – Anna Maxwell, *Hampstead: Its Historic Houses, Its Literary and Artistic Associations*

Spaniard's Road in 1906, archive.

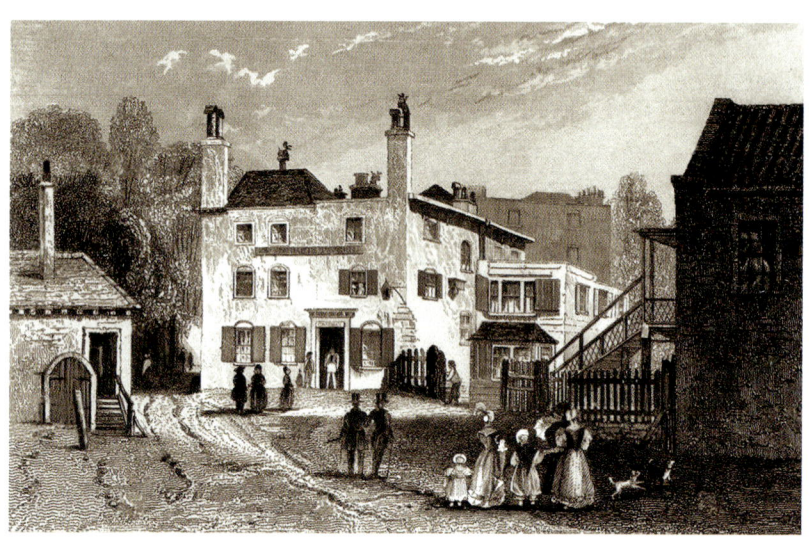

Next door to *Erskine House* is the Grade II C17 *Spaniards Inn*, brick built with timber framing and weatherboarding. Although the building has been altered over the years, the majority of its internal wood panelling is likely to be original – all of which results in an atmosphere steeped in history much appreciated by visitors.

The Spaniards Inn with Erskine House behind in 1845, archive.

The origin of the name given to this famous inn has become the subject of much speculation. However, the word 'Spaniard' is from the old French, whereupon the suffix 'ard' attached to the name of the country described its countrymen. That bears out the inn's purported association with the Spanish Ambassador to the court of King James, while the preference of highwaymen frequenting the roads just off the Heath itself has added Dick Turpin to the legends circulating around this remarkable location (see Duval's Lane p277). ■

The distinctive weatherboarding is clearly visible – an original 1755 boundary stone remains within the garden.

Selected Bibliography

Aitken, G. A., (Introduction and notes) *Richard Steele* (London, T. Fisher Unwin, Paternoster Square, 1894)

Baines, F. E., *Records of the Manor, Parish and Borough of Hampstead* (Whitaker & Co; J Hewetson, 1890)

Barratt, Thomas J., *The Annals of Hampstead* in three volumes, (London, Adam and Charles Black Ltd., 1912)

Belsize Conservation Area Advisory Committee, *Belsize Park: A Living Suburb* (London, 1986 and 2000)

British Listed Buildings, The National Heritage List for England, Historic England

Camden History Society, various editions of *Camden History Review* and Newsletters

Chappelow, A. C., *The Old Home in England*, (Mayfair, London, 1953)

Cherry, Bridget and Pevsner, Nikolaus, *The Buildings of England – London 4: North*, (Penguin Books, 1998)

Dixon, Roger and Muthesius, Stefan, *Victorian Architecture*, (World of Art, Thames & Hudson Ltd., 1978)

Environs of London: The County of Middlesex, A History of the County of Middlesex, Originally published by T Cadell and W Davies, London, 1795

Eton College Archives, Collections Administrator, Eton College Collections, Windsor

Gray, A. Stuart, *Edwardian Architecture: A biographical dictionary* (London, Gerald Duckworth & Co., 1985-6)

Howitt, William, *The Northern Heights of London* (London, Longman, Green & Co., 1869)

Jenkins, Simon and Ditchbum, Jonathan, *Images of Hampstead,* (Ackermann Publishing, 1982)

Kennedy, J., *The Manor and Parish Church of Hampstead, and its Vicars* (London, Mayle, 1906)

Land Registry, The, Registered old deeds, titles and records

Maxwell, Anna, *Hampstead: Its Historic Houses, Its literary and Artistic Associations*, (James Clarke & Co., 1912)

Mountfield, David, *The Coaching Age*, (London, Robert Hale & Co., 1976)

Norris, Mavis and Ian (ed.), *The Book of Hampstead*, High Hill Press, (London, 1968)

Park, John James, *The Topography and Natural History of Hampstead in the County of Middlesex* (London, printed for White, Cochrane, and Co., Fleet Street; and Nichols, Son and Bentley, Red Lion Passage, 1814, 1818)

Potter, George W., *Hampstead Wells, A Short History of their Rise and Decline*, (Bell, 1907; Carlile House, 1978)

Quennell, CHB, *Modern Suburban Houses: a series of examples erected at Hampstead and elsewhere*, B. T. Batsford (London, 1906)

Preston, J. R., *The Story of Hampstead*, (Staples Press, London, 1948)

Richardson, John, *Hampstead One Thousand,* (London, Historical Publications, 1985)

Service, Alistair, *Edwardian Architecture: A Handbook to Building Design in Britain*, 1890-1914 (London, Thames and Hudson Ltd., 1977)

Service, Alistair, *Victorian and Edwardian Hampstead*, Historical Publications (London, 1989)

Sharp, Dennis & Rendel, Sally, *Connell Ward and Lucas*, (London, Frances Lincoln Ltd., 2008)

Summerson John, *Georgian London*, (London, Barrie & Jenkins Ltd., 1962, 1988)

Thompson, F.M.L., *Hampstead: Building a Borough*, 1650-1964 (London, Routledge & Kegan Paul, 1974)

Victoria County History, *A History of the County of Middlesex: Volume 9, Hampstead, Paddington* (Originally published London, 1989)

Wade, Christopher (Author), Woodford, F. Peter (Ed.) *The Streets of Hampstead,* first published 1972 (London, Camden History Society, second edition, 1984)

Wade, Christopher (Author), Woodford, F. Peter (Ed.) *The Streets of Belsize,* originally published as *More Streets of Hampstead* 1973, (London, Camden History Society, revised, 1991)

Wade, Christopher, *For the Poor of Hampstead, for ever,* (Camden History Society, 1998)

Walford, Edward, *Old and New London: A Narrative of its History, its People, and its Places*, The Western and Northern Suburbs, Vol V, originally published by Cassell, Petter, Galpin & Co., London, 1873-8)

White, Caroline A., *Sweet Hampstead and its Associations* (London, Elliot Stock, 1900)

William Willett Ltd. Archive, The Paul Mellon Centre, Bedford Square, London

Wrigley, E. A., Schofield, Roger S., *The Population History of England, 1541-1871* (London, Edward Arnold Publishers Ltd., 1981)

Index

A

Aberdare Gardens 95
Aboriginal art 276
Adelaide ward 19
Admiral's House 232, 239, 243, 292
Admiral's Walk 232, 239, 242
Ainger, Arthur Campbell 15
Ainger, Canon Alfred 261, 263
Ainger, Rev Thomas 15
Ainger Road 15
Air Studios Lyndhurst 79, 81
Albert Memorial, the 240
Albion Cottage 242, 254
Albion Grove 110
Alice's Adventures in Wonderland 34
All3Media 157
Allan, John 138
Allen, Roy 79
Allingham, Helen 98
Allison & Foskett 133
Amesbury 134
Amesbury House 134
Amsdon, Lloyd 117
Anderson, Marion Ford 238
Andrea Benedettini Int 183
Annals of Hampstead 297
Annesley Lodge 277-279
Annigoni, Pietro 18
Anthony, Henry Mark 254
Antrobus House 134
Appleton, Charles 237
Arkwright Road 89
Arrobus, Montague 11
Arrobus, Sydney 11
Ashcroft, Dame Peggy 126, 153
Ashwell, John 117, 121
Athenaeum Club 269
Aumonier family, the 39
Avanti Architects 138, 141

B

Balance Designs 90
Bananarama 22, 24, 26
Barbauld, Laetitia 127
Barby Avenue 195
Barclay, Jane 22, 26
Barker, Richard Pierce 54
Barnett, Dame Henrietta 292
Barratt, Thomas J 124, 159, 269, 297
Barrie, J M 249
Barry, Edward 22
Batterbury & Huxley 31, 87
Bauhaus 151-152
Bax, Alfred Ridley 54
BBC, The 18
Beaton, Cecil 94, 194
Beaufort and Rampton Landscapes 273
Beaulieu Avenue 57
Beaumont, Muriel 249
Beevor, Catrina 41
Bell, Alfred 71
Bellingham, John 57
Belsize Architects 160
Belsize Conservation Area Advisory Committee ix
Belsize Crescent 76, 150
Belsize House xii, 57
Belsize Lane 54, 57, 59-60, 63
Belsize Park Gardens 45
Belsize Society, The ix
Belsize Story, The 79
Belsize Village 56, 81
Belsize Village Streatery 81
Belsize Walk, the 100
Berendsen, Caspar and Celia 233
Besant, Annie 133
Besant, Sir Walter 133
Bicknell, Maria 242
Bier, Elizabeth and Julian 110
Birchwood Drive 243
Bird-in-Hand, The xiii
Bird, S G 37
Bliss, Sir Arthur 172
Blood on the Page 101
Blue Tiles 149
Bogarde, Dirk 76
Bolton, Arthur 164
Boschetto, Linda and Ronald 206
Bowie, David 192
Boy Friend, The 244
Boy George 177
Bracknell Cottage 198
Bracknell Gardens 92-93, 202, 206
Bracknell House 202
Branch Hill Lodge, Gatehouse 243
British Architect, The 277
British Museum, The 212
Brown, Ann Dudin 213
Brydon, J M 33
Buckeridge, Charles 72
Builder, The 176
Building News, The 87, 260
Bull and Esdaile 184
Bull, Walter William 184
Burgh House 169, 292
Burlison & Grylls 72
Burlison, John 71
Burns, Cheryl and Jules 156
Burton, Richard 244
Burton, Tim 192
Bustin, Nicola 95

C

Calkin, Margaret and Harry 206
Cannon Hall 246-247, 259
Cannon Lane 244, 246
Capo di Monte 268
Carbonez, Kristien 274
Carroll, Lewis 190
Carswell, Catherine and Donald 112
Cass Business School 225
Cavalcanti, Olivia Barata 92
Cave, E H & H T 93
Cavendish, Caroline 213
Central Public Library 91
Chadwick, Brian 89
Chalcot Estate 19
Chalcot Gardens 34
Chalcot Square 15
Champneys, Basil 153, 155
Chantal and Neil 76
Chapel of St Mary & St John 125
Chappelow, Allan 101
Chappelow, Archibald 101
Chater, George 155
Chesneys 91, 257
Chesterford Gardens 156
Chester House 92
Chestnut Lodge 244
Chinese Guzheng 205
Christ Church, Hampstead 261, 181
Christian, Ewan 159
Christmas Carol, A 128
Churchill, Winston 1, 126
Church Row 123, 128, 131, 149, 168, 253
Claridge's Hotel 147
Clarke, Sir Thomas 269
Clark, Sir Kenneth 269
Clayton and Bell 71
Clifton Interiors 133
Coleman, William 99
Coleridge, Samuel Taylor 159
Collier, Ethel 41
Collier, John Maler 40, 43
Collins, John 290
Colvin, Sidney 237
Conduit Lodge 74
Connell, Ward & Lucas 137-138
Constable, John 99, 107, 125, 162, 228, 232, 240-242, 254, 268, 292
Constable's House 242
Conti, Tom x, 192
Cook, Peter 127
Cooper, Dame Gladys 4
Corten-clad steel 105
Cornwell, David 165

Cottage on the Heath 170
Cottesloe, Lord 70, 267
Coudron, Gabrielle 238
Crapper, Thomas 176
Crawford, Anne 293
Crispin, George 86
Cuming, Samuel 22, 27
Curtis, Jamie Lee 192
Czech Republic 104

D

Daleham Mews 77
Daylight Saving 10
DCS Universal 19
Debbie 37
Delius, George 27
Devil's Lane 277
Dickens, Charles 97, 269, 290
Dimsdale, Baron 84
Disney, Walt 241
Dolmans, Maurits 124
Dowling, James 118
Downshire Hill 99, 104, 107, 243
Duffield, John 160, 163
Duke of Hamilton 252, 257
du Maurier, Daphne 253, 260
du Maurier family 249
du Maurier, George 127, 253, 259, 261
Du Maurier House 258-259, 260
du Maurier, Sir Gerald 248
Duncan, Isadora 191
Durrington Walls 134
Dutch culture 56
Duval, Claude 277
Duval's Lane 277

E

Earl of Rosslyn 66, 79
East Heath Lodge 172
East Heath Road 172, 176, 253
East India Company 247
Eek, Piet Hein 56
Elizabeth, Joan 125
Ellis, Edward 97
Ellis, Harold 191
Ellison, Micheline and Robin 225
Elsworthy Road 1-4
Elsworthy Village 4
England's Lane 34, 48
English Heritage 138, 141
Erskine House 297
Erskine, Thomas 297
Eton and Middlesex Cricket Ground 10
Eton Avenue 40

Eton College 22, 34, 290, 292
Eton College Estate 22, 25, 45
Eton Court 50
Eton Road 17, 22, 26
Eton Villas 17, 160
Evergreen Hill 297

F

F3 Architecture & Interiors 177
Fahey, Siobhan 23
Faraday, Michael 269
Farebrother, Peggy and Peter 206
Faulkner, Amos 6, 8
Fawcett, Farrah 192
Feldman, Marty 177
Fellows Road 18, 23, 25
Fenton House 258, 260, 292
Ferncroft Avenue 270
Fernside 287, 289
Field, Edwin 244
Field, Horace 66-67, 163, 244
Field Lane Industrial School for Girls 129
Fields, Dame Gracie 149
Financial Times, The 80
Findlay, Françoise 5
Findlay, Professor John 39
Finkernagel Ross Architects 50
Fire Over England 107
First 999 call 3
Fitzjohn's Avenue 49, 72, 91, 97
Flask Walk 166
Flitcroft, Henry 216
Foley, Captain 178
Foley House 177
Formica laminate 283
Formisano, Fabrizio 92
Forsyte Saga, The 238
Fortescue, Win and John 241
Foster, Norman & Wendy 218
France Musique 129
Fraser, Angus (Gus) 134
Freemasons Arms, The 106
Freud, Ernst L 150
Frognal 91, 134, 138, 179, 198, 216, 220, 225
Frognal Close 150
Frognal End 133
Frognal Gardens 133
Frognal Grove 216
Frognal Hall 134, 142, 198
Frognal Lane 92, 142, 153, 158, 198
Frognal Lane Gardens 94
Frognal Priory 151
Frognal Way 127, 137, 142, 145, 148
Fry, Maxwell 137
Fulleylove, John 125

G

Gainsborough Gardens 160-165
Gallagher, Noel 33
Galloway, John 37
Galsworthy, John 238
Gamble, Will, architects 27
Gang Moor 253
Ganguly, Nupur 63
Garner, Thomas 133
Garnett, Dr William 190
Gartry, Lily 203
Gartry, Professor David 203
George, Prince of Denmark 60
George Tavern, The xiii
Georgina and Bernard 1
Georgian 124, 128, 130, 251, 268
Gindin, James 238
Gladstone, William 171
Glasgow Caledonian University 203
Glebe land 195
Glyndebourne 237
Glynn, Lisa and Richard 172
Godfrey, Sissel 293
Gold Dagger prize 101
Golden Spikes 239
Golders Hill Park 276, 287
Golders Hill Swan Pond 287
Goldschmidt, Berthold 76
Goodwin, Dr Thomas 84
Goodwin, Ernest 72
Gotto, Edward 176, 178
Gotto, Henry Gaisford 286
Granada Media 157
Greenaway Gardens 198
Greenaway, Kate 198
Greenhill 95
Greenhill Estate 91
Greenhill, house 97-98
Green, T K 95
Greenway, Edward 246
Griem Thomas, archirect 272
Grove Cottage 225
Grove Lodge 232
Grove, The 239, 240
Grylls, Thomas 72
Guinness, Alec 76
Guiterman, H M 136

H

Haifawi, Dr Said 244
Haifawi, Gulsen 244
Hall Oak 155
Hall School 34
Hall, Spencer 269
Ham&High 218, 232
Hamilton, Lady Emma 228
Hampstead Assembly Rooms 228
Hampstead Constitution Club 228
Hampstead Garden Suburb 20, 111, 132, 244, 280, 292
Hampstead Grove 259, 264
Hampstead Heath Extension 290, 292
Hampstead Heath Station 121
Hampstead High Street 95, 97-98
Hampstead Hill Gardens 83, 86
Hampstead Manor 215
Hampstead Parish Church 181
  see also St John-at-Hampstead
Hampstead Square 252, 255
Hampstead Subscription Library 97
Hampstead Union workhouse 251
Hampstead Way 296
Hampstead Wells 84, 124
Hampstead Wells and Campden Trust 18
Hampstead West Heath Land Co Ltd 274
Harben, Sir Henry 25, 91
Hardanger 11
Harding, Thomas 101
Hardisty family 125
Harley Street 84
Harper's New Monthly Magazine 49, 263
Harraden, Beatrice 254
Hart, Emma 228
Hart, George Washington 179, 193-194, 206, 270, 274
Haverstock Hill 31
Hawk Tavern 169
Hayes, Francine 134
Heath &Hampstead Society, The ix, 201, 232
Heath Drive 182, 206, 209-212,
Heathside, Heath Lodge 171
Heath Street 123, 250, 264
Heritage Architecture Ltd 103
Highview House 286
Hill, Arthur 99
Hill, Wills 99
Hill-Wood, Peter 153
Historical Society, the 80
Holford, Sarah 247
Holiday, Henry 158
Holl, Frank 66
Holly Bush Hill 228
Holly Bush, The 230
Hollycroft Avenue 274
Holly Mount 230
Holly Mount steps 231
Holly Place 133
Holly Walk 131
Hoo, The 67
Hope, Vida 76
Howard, Erika 124
Hoyland, John 237
Hubbard, Mina Benson 191
Huberman, Peter 273
Hughes, Richard 124, 128
Hunters Lodge 59-60, 62- 63
Hunt, Leigh 159
Hutchinson, Leslie 33
Huxley, Aldous and Maria 87
Huxley, Thomas Henry 40

I

Inglis, Brian 39
Invigorate Homes 90
Isaacson, Lesley 19
Ivy Bank 54, 57

J

Jabberwocky 190
Jacobi, Sir Derek 33
Japan 58
Johnson, Samuel 142
John Street 110
Judges' Bench House 243
Judges Walk 268-269

K

Kain, Fritzi and Raphael 181
Kanji, Aliya 50
Kate 31
Keats Grove 103, 110
Keats House 111, 113
Keats, John 159
Kendall, Henry Edward 22, 251
Kendall, Kay 75
Kenwood 297
Kerrison, William 107
Keys, Charles 239
Kidderpore Avenue 213, 278
Kidderpore Hall 213, 214
King, Charles B 163
King Henry's Road 16
King, William J 202, 274
Kipling, Rudyard 191
Kitchens Kitchens 273
Klippan House 159
Knox, E V 225
Knox, Mary 226

L

Lady Macbeth 268
Laing, R D 22
Lambolle Road 37
Langham Place 99, 107
Langland Gardens 92
Langland, William 92
Laski, Marghanita 269
Lassco 185
Lauren Nicholas Kitchen Design 58
Lawlor, Jonathan 255, 257
Lawn House 255, 257
Lawrence, D H 115
le Carré, John 165
Le Corbusier 137
Leeming, Frances and Robert 22
Legge, Walter 197
Legg, Henry S 163-164, 170
Leigh, Vivien 107
Levrant, Stephen 103
Lewis, John Spedan 243
Linton, Sir James D, Studio House 31, 259
Linton, W J 253

Little Library 75
Lloyd, Sydney 290
Load of Hay, The xii, 31
Lock-up, Cannon Lane 245-246
Lockwood, Margaret 293
Logs, The 176
Lonnqvist, Päivi and Markku 57
Louis XIV 284
Lower Merton Rise 5
Lower Terrace 232, 237, 242
Lucas, Colin 137
Lutyens, Sir Edwin 143, 147, 292
Lyndhurst Gardens 67
Lyndhurst Hall Congregational Church 79
Lyndhurst Road 67, 71, 244
Lyndhurst Terrace 71

M

Mabledon House 60
MacDonald, Ramsay 223
Mackmurdo, A H 169
Madani, Dr Gitta 89
Magdala Tavern 118, 121
Magnolia tree 94
Magrath, Edward 268
Mahler, Gustav 76
Malka, Sam 90
Man in the White Suit, The 76
Manor Farm 153, 155
Manor House, the 99
Manor Lodge 153
Manser, Victoria 266
Marianne and Alain 128
Maples & Company 194
Marcus, Helen 201
Maresfield Gardens 213
Marpole, Felicity 240
Marx, Karl 252
Maryon-Wilson 158, 179, 202, 206
Maryon-Wilson, Sir Spencer 49, 153
Maryon-Wilson, Sir Thomas 15
Mary Poppins 226, 241
Mason, Nick 178
Maxwell, Anna 142, 228, 233, 261, 268, 298, 304
Maxwell, James Clerk 190
May, E J 163
Maynard, Constance L 213
McCormick, Matthew 90
McGregor, Scott 185
McLaren Excel 105
Melvill, Sir James Cosmo 247
Memory Thompson 153
Menzies, Iain Graham 249
Mercier, Stephanie 34
Metta, Nathalie and Rudy 280
Michael, Edward 158
Midland Grand Hotel at St Pancras Station 240
Miles, Gary 31
Miller, Andrew 87

Miller, Arthur 192
Milne, Oswald 145, 147
Minghella, Anthony 118
Minter, A G 137
Miro, Victoria 95
Mixed Bathing Pond 122
Mizrahi, Paulette 201
Modernist 28, 105, 136, 138
Moller, Karsten & Barbara 156
Monroe House 97
Moorfields Eye Hospital 203
Moreton 131
Morley, Roger 114
Morley, Sophie 114
Morning Post, The 241
Mortgage Corporation, the 25
Mosley, Nicholas 129
Mount Square, The 259
Mount Vernon 131, 227
Mr M 217
Mrs Holt's School for Young Ladies 244
Mummary, John 76
My Fair Lady 94

N

Nairne, Edward 125
Nairn, Ian 137
Nash, John 27
National Theatre, the 70, 267
National Trust 138
Natural History Museum 175
Neo-Georgian 135, 193, 202, 205
Netley Cottage 237
New End 250
New End Hospital 251, 252
New End Square 169
New End Theatre 252
New Grove House 249, 258, 261
Nightingale, J S 176
Nolan, Christopher 249
North, Captain Fountain 239
North End Avenue 293
North House 40
Northstead 293
Novoa, Maria and Mario 15
Nunn, Thomas Hancock 79

O

Oakhill Avenue 184, 195, 198
Ode to a Nightingale 159
Old and New London 127, 297
Old Conduit House 71-72, 74
Old Conduit Lodge 72, 74
Old Grove House 258
Old Home in England, The 101
Old Mother Red Cap xii
Old White Bear 252
Old Wyldes 290
Olivier, Sir Laurence 107, 249
Olsen, Penelope 217
Oracle Advertising 295

Ora, Rita 34
Ornan Road 54, 57-58, 60
Orwell, George 115

P

Palladian Gdns, Stourhead 217
Palmer, Samuel 292
Pankhurst, Emmeline 6, 191
Parkinson, Joseph architect 60
Park, John James 127, 160
Parliament Hill 114
Pawson, John 95, 175
Peires, Susan 131
Perceval Avenue 57
Perceval, Spencer 57
Perlman, Roberta and Robert 264
Perrin's Walk 125
Peter Pan, or The Boy Who Wouldn't Grow Up 34, 249
Petrie, Mary 213
Pevsner, Nikolaus 17, 27, 45, 60, 76, 123-124, 137, 148, 161, 190, 193, 210, 228, 250, 258, 264
Phillips, Peter architect 147
Pickett, Joseph 114, 117, 121
piloti 138-140
Pitman Tozer Architects 89
Platt's Farm 274
Platt's Lane 277
Plowright, Dr Oliver 126
Plowright, Piers 125
Plunkett, Caroline 25
Pond, Hampstead No.1 121
Pond, Hampstead No.2 117
Pond Street 83, 86
Portmeirion 254
Pownall, George 15
Prance, Reginald Herber 181
Preminger, Otto 249
Prettysac 201
Primrose Hill 15, 114
Primrose Hill Road 19
Prince Arthur 97
Prince Arthur Road 95-97
Prince Consort Road 76
Priory Lodge 142, 145, 148
Pritchard, Simon 274
Provident Dispensary 252
Provost Road 27
Punch magazine 225, 261, 263

Q

QS World University Rankings 283
Quacquarelli, Daniela and Nunzio 283
Queen Anne 6, 8, 60, 123, 225, 255
Queen Anne-style 87
Queen Mary University of London 215
Quennell, CHB vi, 158,179, 193-194, 206, 210-211, 270

R

Rackham, Arthur 34
Radio France 129
Randall and Pile 202
Rantzen, Esther 173
Rea, Russell 70
Redfrog Residents Association 184
Redington Road 110, 156, 158, 179, 181, 184, 190, 193, 195
Redington, Sir Thomas 179
Regency 99, 106, 110, 167, 254
Regency architecture 104
Regents Park 27
Retrouvius 15, 175
Reynolds, Sir Joshua 269
Rhodes, Thomas 117, 121
RIBA Award 141
Richardson, Sir Ralph 91
Richard Steele's Cottage xii
River Tyburn 72
Roberts, Elizabeth 242
Roberts, Thomas 79
Robson, Dame Flora 107
Roebuck, The 84
Romantic House in Hampstead, A 240
Romney, George 228, 248
Romney's House 228
Ronson, Gerard 283
Roseborne, Bernard 290
Rosecroft Avenue 198
Rosemount 167
Rossetti, William 254
Rosslyn Estate 79
Rosslyn Gardens 63
Rosslyn Grove 79
Rosslyn Hill 86
Rosslyn House xiii, 66- 68
Rowlatt, Penelope 86
Royal Academy 72
Royal Opera House 22
Rylands Memorial Library 155

S

Saint, Professor Andrew 11, 31, 148
Sanderson, John 297
Saunders, C H 274
Schoenaich, Brita von 44
Schubert, Brandon 80
Schwartz, Lea and Peter 104
Schwarzkopf, Elisabeth 197
Scott, Adrian Gilbert 143
Scott RA, George Gilbert 71, 240
Scott, Sir Ridley 261
Scribner, Charles 241
Seaford Lodge 25
Service, Alastair 67, 155, 160, 169, 179-180, 184, 190, 193, 274
Service, Douglas William 169
Service, Luisa, 4

Sharp, Charles S 117, 121
Shaw, George Bernard 191, 292
Shaw, John 15, 17, 22, 27
Shaw, Richard Norman 159, 198
Shelford Lodge 67
Shepard, E H 226
Shepard, Mary 241
　see also Knox, Mary
Shepherd's Path 72
Shepherd's Well 72-74, 143, 145
Shirlock Road 89
Sibertswold 5
Siddons, Sarah 268
Sikka, Neil 95
Silver Spoon, The 241
Silvestrin, Claudio 95
Singer, Isabel 69
Singer, Simeon 69
Sitwell, Dame Edith 115
Skeel Library 215
Smith, David T 26
Smouha, Sabine and Jeremy 198
Sotheby's 185
South End Farm 114, 121
South End Green 84, 110, 114-115, 283
South Hampstead High School 18
South Hill Park 117, 121
South Hill Park Gardens 22
Spalding, Henry architect 63
Spaniards Inn, The 298
Spectator, The 31
Spedan Close 243
Spencer-Churchill, Lily 274
Spielberg, Steven 261
Squire, Joshua 244
Squires Mount 244, 246
Stamford Lodge 243
Stanfield, Clarkson 97, 269
Stanfield House 97-98
Steele's Cottage 31
Steele's Road 31, 259
Steiger, Rod 192
Steinfeld, Josi 8
Steinfeld, Alan 8
Stephen Levrant Heritage Architecture 103
Stevens, Alfred 17
Stevenson, J J 1
Stevenson, Robert Louis 237
Stewart, Donald Ogden 223
St Giles-in-the-Fields 217
Sting 226
St John-at-Hampstead 145, 243, 259, 297
St John's, Downshire Hill 99
St John's Wood 49
St Mary's, Oxford 72
Stokes, John 79
St Paul's Cathedral 17
Streatery, the Belsize 56
Street, George E 217
St Saviour's Church 22, 27, 30, 34

St Stephen's Church 72, 85, 181, 241
St Thomas' Hospital 203
Studio M R 133
Sturges, William 136
Sullivan, David 290
Summerson, Sir John 17, 22, 27, 87
Sunday Times, The 292
Sun House 137, 145
Swierkosz, Krysia 147

T

Tatchell, Sydney 127
Tate, The 25
Tate, William 60
Taylor, Dame Elizabeth 75, 244
Taylor, Sir Andrew 70
Teil, John, merchant 213
Templewood Avenue 94, 193
Tennyson, Alfred, Lord 169
Teulon, Samuel Sanders 67, 243
The Holly Bush 223
Thelen, Chris 27
Thomas, Dylan 115
Thomas, Sir Noah 248
Thompson, FML 8, 22
Thompson, Ian D 99
Three Gables, The 66
Three Pigeons, The 225, 226
Tidey, Daniel 45
Till, Charles 176
Tim 287
Tobin Close 18-19
Tobin, Jocelyne 18
Tobin, Julian 18-19
Todd, George 60
Toffoletto, Professor Alberto 259-260
Tottenham Court Turnpike xi
Travers, P L 226, 241
Turpin, Dick 298
Twiggy 76, 150

U

Underhill, Evelyn 256
University of Milan 260
Unwin, Sir Raymond 290, 292
Upper Flask Tavern 264
Upper Frognal Lodge 220
Uziyel, Freda and Izak 184

V

van der Watt, Liese 270
Vane House xiii
Vanity of Human Wishes, The 142
van Oudtshoorn, Corinne 259
Venning, Philip 290
Victorian Gothic Revival Style 114
Vietnamese Embassy 45
Village Shul, the 252
Voysey, CFA 34, 277, 279

W

Wabe, The 6, 190, 192, 194
Wade, Christopher 63, 79, 107, 115, 149, 160, 179, 212, 230, 254, 256, 269
Wadham Gardens 6-13
Wagenfeld, Philip 133
Walford, Edward 127, 159, 297
Walford, Geoffrey 136, 138
Waller, Frederick 40
Walliams, David 33
Walton, Sir William 133
Washington, The 48
Watch House, the 133
Waterhouse, Alfred 79
Watson-Wentworth, Thomas 217
Wedderburn, Lord 66
Wedderburn Road 66
Well Road 176, 246
Wells and Campden Trust 178
Wells, H G 127
Wellside, Well Walk 160
Wells, Rudyard 191
Wells Tavern, The 159, 223
Well Walk 84, 99, 159, 162, 243, 250
Wenning, Peter 156
Westfield College 213, 215
West Hampstead Ave 209-210
West Heath Road 179, 193, 280, 283, 287
Whitestone House 254
Whitestone Lane 253
Whitestone Pond 253
Whitfield, Kasia architect 37
Wickham, Anna 115
Willars, Dean, architect 19
Willett, William 4-6, 8, 10-11, 13, 34, 45
William Blake society 292
Williams-Ellis, Sir Clough 229, 254
Williams, John, guitarist 118
Williams, Mike 181
William Willett Ltd 136, 145
Wilson, Charlotte 290
Wilson, Kara 192
Wilson, General Sir Thomas Spencer 57
Windsor Castle 72
Winston, Rosie 133
Wise, Thomas J 212
Woodburn, Samuel 268
Woodd, Charles 67
Woods, William 99, 107
WWII air raid shelter 87
Wyldes 292
　see also Old Wyldes

Y

Yam, Wang 101
Y J Lovell and Son 137-138

Acknowledgements

Working on this project has been a profound privilege, made possible through the generous sponsorship and dedicated support of Michael McHale and Samuel Patterson of KIRE. Foremost, I wish to express my deep gratitude to my understanding and supportive wife, Frances Pinter. She has stood as a stalwart pillar of encouragement, displaying extraordinary patience and understanding, enduring my countless hours dedicated to this project – even when we were on vacation. My heartfelt appreciation extends to my friend and writing colleague, Mary Bennett, whose meticulous editing prowess and insightful contributions and ideas have significantly enriched and shaped the text. Any errors that remain are my sole responsibility.

I also extend my gratitude to Charles Hind, Chief Curator and H J Heinz Curator of Drawings at RIBA Collections, for his invaluable assistance. My grateful thanks go to Barbara Fisher for her valued help when researching Antrobus House. I offer a sincere thank you to Charlie Smith for graciously providing the photographs of *The Wabe*, and to Jonathan Lawlor for his generous help with the history of *Lawn House*. My thanks also extend to Tudor Allen and the dedicated staff at the Camden Local History and Archives Centre.

I was elated when Tom Conti graciously accepted the invitation to pen the Foreword, and my sincere appreciation extends to everyone involved in bringing this book to fruition. Above all, I offer my profound thanks and gratitude to each of the contributors who so generously shared their time and stories, allowing me to capture photographs of their remarkable homes.

Lastly, I reiterate my sincere gratitude to Michael McHale and Samuel Patterson, whose enthusiastic encouragement has accompanied this project since its inception and remained steadfast until its completion.

Letters on the map correspond to those at the head of each entry.

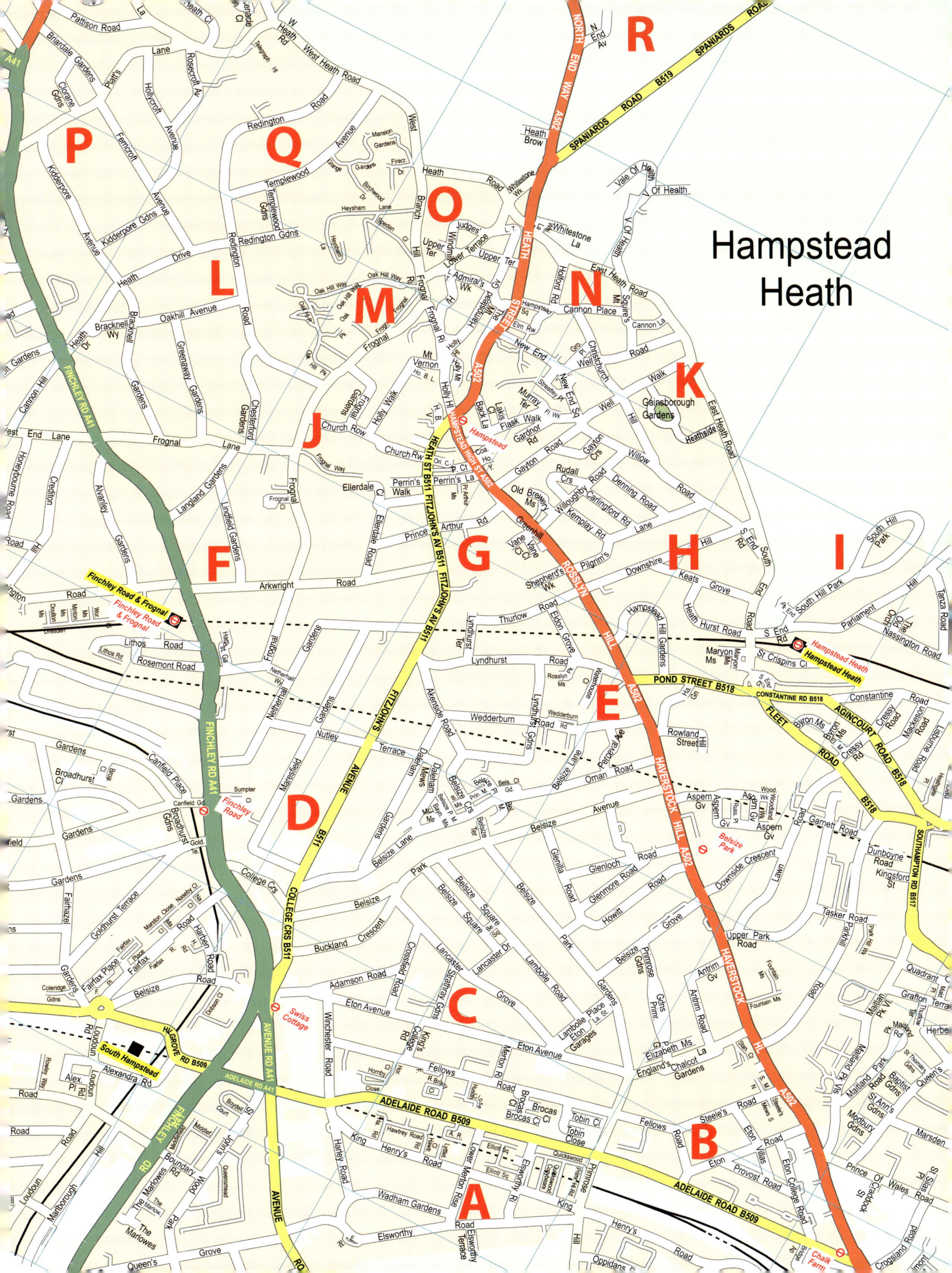

Hampstead Heath

About the Author

David S Percy was born and educated in London and is a long-standing resident of Belsize Park. He is happily married with one wife, two children and three grandchildren. Travelling the world researching ancient sites and making documentaries, Percy has filmed in Nagaland at the foothills of the Himalayas, from open-sided helicopters, out of the rear door of Hercules Aircraft flying at 10,000 feet and from camera-adapted ambulances in the Middle East.

An internationally award-winning filmmaker, his first local history documentary film was *Hampstead Garden Suburb* (1975). His theatrical movie *The Anna Contract* ran continuously in London's West End for three months in the 1970s. Percy created the missile tracking visual effects sequences for Ira Curtis-Coleman (video supervisor) in the John Landis movie *Spies Like Us* (1985). Further cinema credits include Director of Photography for *DiscoMania* (1979) and *Knights Electric* (1980), which is often referred to as an early precursor to the music video or pop promo. He also photographed a major theatrical movie featuring the Tornado aircraft for the British Ministry of Defence, *The Third Dimension* (1985).

Percy directed and photographed *The Belsize Story* in 2012, a feature-length film documentary of the history, architecture and people of Belsize Park. He also directed *Kohima: An Exploration of War, Memory and Gratitude,* Official Selection 8th Monaco Charity Film Festival (2013).

Percy has authored and co-authored many articles, publications and books co-compiling *Belsize Remembered,* a fully illustrated book with over 200 of his photographs. Featuring a collection of memoirs, it's a local best seller with a Foreword by Sir Derek Jacobi, published in 2017. His most recent local history title is *The Harlots of Haverstock Hill,* (2020). Percy also runs the Belsize Village website, belsizevillage.co.uk, and is Consultant Editor of *In the Square* magazine.

David S Percy, FRSA, ARPS

…Soft waves of loose hay lay around, the hill toward the north rose higher and higher, until there appeared at length a mass of tall trees which half hid the quaint copper steeple of the old parish church. But higher still rose the hill, up and up to the glorious Heath, where the gale burst round the corner, and nearly blew us, shrieking with joy, into the Whitestone Pond.

– Anna Maxwell (1865-1927)